With the Sun on Our Right

By Tim Moss

Next Challenge Books

First published in Great Britain 2018

Copyright © 2018 Tim Moss

Cover and map design by Anne-Sophie Rodet

Photos by Laura Moss or Tim Moss

Next Challenge Books

www.thenextchallenge.org

For our grandparents

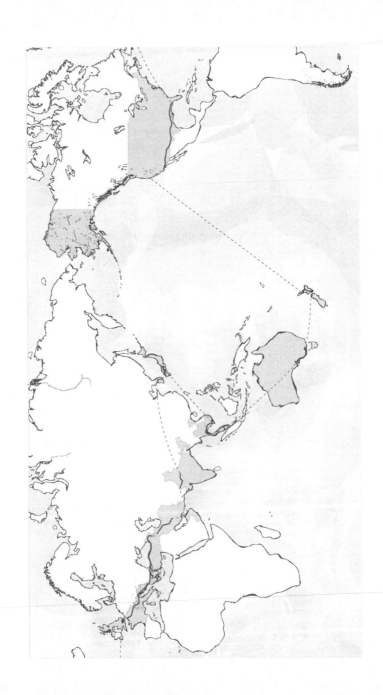

Prologue

When Laura and I arrived home after cycling around the world, we had spent almost half of our married lives on bikes.

We have always liked cycling. When we lived in London, we cycled everywhere: to work, to the shops, to the pub and to friends. Weekends and holidays often involved riding our bikes too. We even cycled from the church to the reception on our wedding day: me in shirt and tie, Laura combining her veil with lycra shorts. We had strings of tin cans and streamers dangling off the back of our bikes as thirty guests joined us for the ride. Our bikes also came with us on honeymoon, as we cycled across the Outer Hebrides.

So, when we told friends and family that we were planning to cycle around the world, it came as no great surprise. The truth is, we had been planning the trip since the day we first got together. On our first date, we had jokingly agreed that we would cycle to Australia, one day.

It may have been discussed in jest, but whenever we came back to the idea we would each insist we were serious. The idea fitted with our relationship: we already spent a lot of our time outside, exercising and exploring the world. Our second date, for example, was spent swimming across an icy cold lake in November.

A few weeks after we got together, Laura came up with a plan to run the length of every train line on the London Underground. Our weekends were soon spent running from one Tube station to the next, eventually covering up to 45 miles in a single day. That was twice as far as either of us had ever run before.

When Christmas came, I gave Laura a map of the world and we shaded all of the countries we wanted to cycle through. She then used it as a bookmark, to remind her of our plan every time she opened her book.

As well as being active people, we were both curious about the world. We had both lived abroad: Laura in Australia and me in New Zealand. Laura was also interested in international development and had spent time in East Africa. I had worked in expeditions and had been on climbing trips all over the world. Coincidentally, we discovered that we had each received the same bursary to study overseas: the Commonwealth Scholarship. It only goes to one person each year, and long before we knew each other, we had won it on consecutive years.

With this love of travel, Laura jumped at an opportunity to move to Oman for six months with her work and, being self-employed at the time, I was able to go with her. The two of us shared a flat in a country where we did not know another soul and we treated each weekend as an opportunity to explore. The highlight of our stay was crossing the small Wahiba Sands desert alone on foot, carrying all the water we needed to survive.

Technically, it was not legal for unmarried couples to live together in Oman so we had to pretend that we were married for the duration of our stay. By the time we got back however, Laura's fake wedding ring was replaced by a real engagement ring and, five months later, we were married.

The idea of going on a big cycling trip continued to be in the back of our minds and, by this point, we had shown each other that we were determined to 'do', not just to talk. As we pored over maps and read the blogs of other round-the-world cyclists, it became clear that the joke from our first date had become serious business. Our plan was to cycle from London to Australia, then back home across the United States.

The difficulty was deciding how and when to go. We needed to save up money and think about our careers. I worked freelance, organising expeditions for a living so I was flexible could leave at short notice but saving money was not easy. In contrast, Laura was working full time as a solicitor so, for her, saving money was less of

2

an issue but disappearing from her office for a year or more was not easy. It would mean leaving the job for which she had worked so hard for so long. She needed to figure out when she could reasonably take a career break and we both had to find enough cash to fund what could be a very long trip.

Although our friends and family had not been surprised by our plans, the idea still met with some resistance. Some colleagues at Laura's law firm thought it would be career suicide to quit her job and go off on a bike. Laura's mum was also concerned for our safety and initially suggested that she should follow us around the world in her car, just to check that we were safe. Once we convinced her that might be impractical, she compromised by insisting, only half-joking, that we not visit any countries whose name ended in 'stan'.

We had no intention of cycling through anywhere with obvious dangers like, say, Afghanistan or Pakistan, but our experience of living in the Middle East had shown us that the reality was often different from the headlines. Oman was just about the friendliest, safest place we could have imagined, but we would never have found that out if we had stayed at home. We needed to explore the world for ourselves.

Laura's mum and work colleagues turned out to be passing problems. Many of her colleagues understood her motivation, and her mum soon realised that there was no talking us out of it and eventually became one of the trip's biggest advocates.

The bigger problem was me.

As part of our preparation, we decided to cycle from Land's End to John O'Groats. We had done several cycle tours before but thought that we should see how it felt to go away, knowing that the experience might be extended for a year or more. On the second day, however, Laura looked over her shoulder to see me pushing my bike uphill. She was perplexed. I had never needed to get off and push before.

'You alright, love?' she asked.

'I just don't seem to have the energy.'

This was odd because I rode my bike all the time and had recently set the Guinness World Record for the longest distance cycled on a rickshaw. That had involved pedalling a huge, iron tricycle 1,000 miles from Scotland to London. As such, cycling up a hill, even a Cornish one, should have been fine.

When evening came, for some unknown reason, I could not face camping. Normally, I viewed camping as an opportunity, not a hardship. I loved nothing more than sleeping on top of a hill, beneath the stars, but that night, I could not bring myself to do it. I was almost scared of it and Laura eventually had to find us a hotel.

We started on our bikes again the following day, but when we reached a town, I told Laura that I could not cycle any further and needed to sit down. She went off to get me some food (knowing that hunger was often the source of my problems), and by the time she got back, I was sitting on the floor with my head in my hands, crying.

I prided myself on never giving up. I was constantly looking for challenges and always driving myself harder. In Oman, for example, I used to ride a loop of the local oil compound every morning before breakfast and cycled so hard that when I slumped over my bike after achieving a personal best, passers-by would stop and ask if I was OK.

But that had started to feel futile. What was the point of riding my bike in circles, just to beat my own time? And what was the point of riding a bike across Cornwall? Why bother riding a bike at all?

Those feelings had been building for several months. Years of working at home, on my own, had been taking a toll. I often had no human interaction for days at a time and I had not been making a lot of money either, which, combined with the recent loss of a key client, ate away at my self-esteem.

4

These issues all came to a head in Cornwall, and the only response I could muster was to sit on the floor, crying.

'What's wrong, love?' Laura asked when she came back from the shop.

'I don't know,' I replied, 'but I need to go home.'

The doctor told me that I had depression. I was expecting that but pressed him on what was physically wrong with me.

'OK, but why am I so tired all the time? Why can't I run or cycle anymore?'

'You don't understand,' he said. 'That's the depression too.'

I tried to pretend that this would not affect our plan to cycle around the world.

'I'll be alright once we get going,' I said.

For years, I had been looking forward to this trip. I was not willing to accept that this was an illness that would prohibit me from disappearing on my bike for a year. I just convinced myself that everything was still on track for our departure.

But the evidence was in front of me. As well as having no will to exercise, I became scared of social interactions. I would dwell on the slightest negative comments for days and, eventually, just avoided talking to people. It got to the point where I felt the need to physically hide. Laura came into our bedroom one day to find me curled up in a ball behind our bed, with my eyes clamped shut and my fingers rammed into my ears. I felt completely overwhelmed and needed to shut the world away.

This odd defence mechanism grew into a habit. It became so normal that I even hid behind the bed when my parents came to visit, and sometimes Laura would have to bring my dinner to eat on the floor, curled up in the corner of our bedroom.

As well as the hiding, I would break down during routine activities, like going to a supermarket, where the abundance of

5

choice overwhelmed me. On one occasion, I became so stressed-out during a train journey that I buried my head into my chair and put my fingers in my ears until Laura told me we had reached our destination. A doctor prescribed me a sedative after that, which Laura then carried with us for emergencies. A year earlier, I had crossed a desert, run an ultramarathon and broken a world record. Now I was reduced to hiding under beds and crying in supermarkets.

Still, I could not let myself believe that anything would get in the way of our big trip. It was the one thing that I was holding on to and I was not yet ready to let it go. I insisted that I would be fine, and we pressed ahead with planning our ride around the world. But when Laura tried to hand in her notice at work, she was crying so much that her boss suggested she take a little longer to think about it. She knew that I was not in a fit state to go travelling and, slowly, she helped me realise that myself.

So, we shelved our plans while I got help: drugs, group therapy, self-help books, mindfulness training, counselling, more drugs and, finally, CBT. As my health improved, I started applying for jobs and was accepted onto a teacher-training programme. The routine and regular human contact helped dragged me back to my normal self again. A year after our ill-fated first attempt, we returned to Cornwall on our bikes and aimed for Scotland. There were no breakdowns this time. And, crucially, we were disappointed when the trip came to an end because we wanted to carry on. I was back on track and so were our plans.

Laura's boss still thought she was mad, but accepted her resignation the second time around. I told my school that I would be leaving at the end of the year, then we terminated the contract on our flat and moved our stuff into the accommodating attics of our parents. We spent the summer catching up with friends and family, and timed our departure for the day after our friends' wedding.

The morning of our departure arrived and we were nowhere near ready. Piles of kit were sprawled across the living room of my parents' house, and we had no idea how to fit it all in. We were still packing our bags when my parents got in their car to drive to Hampton Court Palace, where we were soon due for our send-off. We hauled our heavy bags into the garage, clipped them onto our bikes and hurried after them. My younger brother locked up behind us then caught up on his own bike.

We had cycled with panniers before but only ever two on the back, never the full set of four with which we left home. We had also never bothered to try cycling with the new clip-in shoes we had been sent, so those first hundred yards were some of the wobbliest of our entire trip. We had to keep going, though, because we were running late. Besides, we were terrified that if we stopped then we wouldn't be able to unclip our feet before our bikes hit the tarmac, ending our trip before it had even begun.

We were greeted at the gates of Hampton Court by a sea of familiar faces, all beaming at us. They let out a cheer as we pulled in on our shiny steeds, fully laden and ready to take on the world. There were hugs and small talk and an overriding sense of dread: what were we about to do? We posed for photos then lined up with all the cyclists who would be joining us for the first part of our journey. Amidst cheering and a chorus of bicycle bells, we took our first pedal strokes towards Australia.

PART I

Europe

Chapter 1

'Good morning world! Looks like a fine day to cycle around you.' –
Tim

*'Home is now behind me, the rest of the world ahead. Head in a bit
of a turmoil.' – Laura**

We got all of eight hundred yards into our journey around the world
when we made our first stop.

A lonely figure had appeared at the side of the road. An older
gentleman, sitting in a wheelchair with a blanket over his knees, was
waving at us. It was my grandpa, John. He had not wanted to deal
with the crowd at Hampton Court but knew that our route would go
right past the end of his road.

Our group pulled up next to him. Laura dismounted to give him a
hug goodbye and I did the same. We would be away for at least a year,
but although we did not know it at the time, we would see my
grandpa far sooner than that.

Our destination for that first night was a picturesque spot in the
South Downs. I used to go there as a child on family picnics and,
latterly, my friends and I had used it for overnight bivouacs. It was
the perfect place to escape London and spend a night under the stars.
Unfortunately, I had no idea how to get there on a bike and neither
of us had thought to look at a map before setting off. My local
knowledge took us as far as the next town but our peloton soon
ground to a halt so we could look at our phones to find out where we
were going.

---

* During our ride around the world, Laura and I sent regular updates to our
Twitter accounts. Some of our messages are quoted at the start of each
chapter.

We were lucky enough to be joined by a group of friends for the start of our ride. Some were joining us for a day or two down to the coast and others were accompanying us all the way to Paris. Their lightly-laden bikes meant that they could power up the hills, while we puffed and panted behind, lugging everything we needed for life on the road.

Hills aside, my abiding memory is one of elation: cycling with a big group of friends in the warm, summer sunshine; laughing, joking and getting lost together. We had left our worldly worries behind and not yet been burdened by the weight of what we were about to undertake.

When we arrived at our designated spot for the evening, it felt like a tiny festival. My parents, and our extended family and friends, had driven ahead of us to set up tents, a bonfire and a barbecue. The next morning, we had to say our goodbyes to all those who had driven to join us or had only been out for a day's ride. Our shrinking peloton set off for the south coast beneath a double rainbow.

We had a ferry passage booked from Newhaven that evening but had not really considered how long it might take to get there until now. Apparently, we had set ourselves a rather tight timeframe. We ended up in a bit of a panic over the final miles, frantically trying to get to the terminal in time. We arrived with just enough time for one final fish and chip supper before boarding our boat to adventure.

Six of us cycled onto the ferry. We unfurled our camping mats in a quiet corner and caught a few hours' sleep. When we rolled down the ferry ramp on our bikes (always a thrill), it was into Dieppe and the middle of the night. We rode for a mile out of town before pitching our tents conspicuously at the side of a cycle path, too tired to worry about subtlety.

The following few days were spent following the well-trodden 'Avenue Verte' cycle route that runs from London to Paris. It was bliss. We cycled traffic-free, chatting side by side with friends and enjoying the French summer. Being part of a group whose only aim was to get to Paris also meant that we could just focus on the present: a nice cycling holiday with our friends, nothing more. We did not have to process the fact that we had just quit our jobs, moved out of our house and left our lives behind. We just had to follow whoever had generously taken on navigational duties that day and stop occasionally to gorge on bread and cheese.

But the honeymoon had to end at some point. We reached our destination – a friend's house outside Paris – and rested there for a couple of days until we plucked up the courage to bite the bullet and venture out alone. We said one last set of goodbyes and set off to cycle across France, to Australia and around the world.

That day also happened to be our second anniversary. Nothing could have been more fitting than to mark the occasion with the excitement and trepidation of embarking on a great journey together. That evening, we pitched our tent on a canal-side village green and treated ourselves to a cheap bottle of bubbly. We had cause to celebrate but needed to be frugal. If everything went to plan, we would still be cycling when our next anniversary came around.

We woke the following morning to gentle sunshine and packed away our tent, shaking off the morning dew in the process. It was a strange feeling to suddenly find ourselves alone. We had happily taken a back seat during the first week's riding to Paris but now there was no one else to suggest a target for the day or plan the route. It was just us. As if to emphasise our solitude, we had just left friends in Paris and the next people that we wanted to visit were my older brother and his wife, who lived in Australia. Getting there would take many months of cycling through two dozen countries, not to mention boats and planes at some point. We were sitting on a picnic bench in France, planning a cycling route to Australia with a world map, and it felt absurd. What on earth were we doing?

That was too big a question for us to process. All we could think about was the next few days. Route-planning before we left home had not extended much beyond a finger drawn across an atlas. We figured we would pedal across France, head for the Croatian coast, stay south until Greece, cross Turkey into Iran then keep heading east towards Southeast Asia. That morning, we just chose the country that we wanted to head for next (Switzerland), picked a town that was in the right direction (Dijon), and then worked out which roads would get us there. We could deal with the existential questions once we had a few more miles under our belts.

After winding our way through a web of quiet lanes, quaint villages and cobbled streets that day, we pitched our tent on the banks of the Seine when evening fell. With the sun setting behind us, we climbed into the river, combining the practical need for a wash with the illicit pleasure of a wild swim.

We set an alarm for the following morning then repeated the routine: ride until we were hungry and find somewhere nice for lunch, then ride again until we were hungry and find somewhere nice to sleep. It was the same as any other cycling trip we had done: ride, eat, sleep, repeat.

It was not until our fifth day alone on the bikes, that we realised we did not need to set an alarm. There was no need to get up at any particular time, just as there was no need to cover any particular distance each day. So, if we wanted to have a lie-in or spend the afternoon reading a book, then we could. However, as two motivated people who always have a goal in mind and half an eye on the next project – be it crossing a desert, running the Tube or cycling around the world – this revelation took a bit of getting used to.

We were both tired from the weeks of excitement that had preceded our departure and both wanted a break from being on the go all of the time. But just five days in, it felt a bit early for a rest day

12

so, as we pedalled along we spent several hours discussing whether we could justify an afternoon off. Should we be slacking off, so early in our trip? Did we need a rest or were we just being lazy? We had been waiting to go on this trip for such a long time that taking a break so soon was hard to justify.

It was a ridiculous conversation – if we were tired then, of course, we should just rest – but it exemplifies the strange world we had entered. Normally, our cycling trips only lasted a few days, so we could just wait until they were over to get some rest. But this trip was different. We were playing the long game. A few hours off the bike would have no impact on the journey as a whole, nor would a few days or perhaps even a few weeks.

So, that afternoon, feeling terribly indulgent, we pulled into a 'place des loisirs' park. We swam in a warm lake then whiled away the afternoon, reading books in the sunshine. When evening came, we cycled a leisurely few miles up the road and pitched our tent in a cornfield. We would take on the world tomorrow.

An afternoon off the bikes probably did more for our minds than our bodies, but either way we awoke refreshed. The local slugs appeared similarly energised however, and had besieged our tent overnight. The floor, roof and side walls were covered in them. We picked them off and loaded our bikes for another day's riding.

That morning, we joined the 'EuroVelo 6' cycle route, part of a network of bike paths that stretch across Europe. They vary in quality, but in France they are excellent and EuroVelo 6 offered several days of quiet roads and riverside cycling. At the end of the route, we stopped in Basel for the night, where Laura got scalded by a pan of boiling water.

There are two different versions of the water story. According to Laura, I knocked the pan off the stove and covered her leg in boiling water. In my telling, the pan was about to fall off and I attempted, unsuccessfully, to catch it. Either way, Laura had to spend an hour with her leg under cold, running water to stem the pain. After a trip to the pharmacy, we cycled into Switzerland with Laura's leg in bandages.

Stopping to check our map at the outskirts of town an hour later, a well-dressed, middle-aged lady approached us and introduced herself in fluent English. Apparently, some years before she had met a young woman on a bicycle at this same junction who was also at the start of an around-the-world cycling trip. The lady invited the cyclist to her house, fed her dinner and gave her a bed for the night. Following that experience, she now took it upon herself to help any other passing cyclists and wanted to extend the same courtesy to us. We were sorely tempted by the offer – a bed for the night, a shower and the promise of good food and wine – but we had only cycled a few miles out of Basel and felt like we could not justify spending a whole day off the bikes after covering such little distance. We thanked her for the kind offer but politely declined and cycled off.

It took all of ten minutes before we regretted the decision. We had turned down an offer of hospitality and missed an opportunity to meet someone new. For what? To bring our journey to an end one day sooner? The whole point of our trip was to explore the world. It was not about cycling, the bike was just our vehicle for exploration, and what better way to explore than to meet people and see inside their homes. It was not a mistake that we intended to repeat. From that day on, we vowed never to turn down offers of hospitality.

Chapter 2

"This saddle", says a Frenchman to his son as he gives mine a tap,
"is the best in the world". (A Brooks B17 since you asked). – Tim

'Lunchtime in a village square with baguette, the sweaty remains of
some cheddar and pate. Decided against what was sold as pate du
tete.*' – Laura*

Planning our route for the rest of the day, it was impossible to ignore
the fact that we were getting close to the Alps. Ever since leaving
home there had been a nagging worry in the back of our minds
because we knew that had to cross those mountains.

Crossing the Alps meant cycling up two thousand vertical metres
of mountain. We had never cycled up a mountain that high, let alone
on such heavily laden bikes, and the thought of it was daunting.
Besides, if we could not get over the Alps, then what hope would we
have getting across the mountains of Turkey or Central Asia?

When the morning of our ascent arrived, I woke with a mild sense
of foreboding that, although unspoken, I knew was shared by Laura.
Ignorant to our fears, the sun shone brightly from a clear blue sky.
We cycled along empty roads, through the pretty village of Amsteg
and across a small bridge when, without warning, the road turned
sharply uphill and we passed a sign indicating that there were no
exits until the summit. I did not feel ready. There was no chance to
mentally prepare myself or even drop to my lowest gear, but like it
or not, the climb was upon us.

It was hot, even first thing in the morning, and sweat soon
appeared on my forehead. I reached for my bottle but immediately
worried that I would run out of water if I drank too much so early in
the day. I put the bottle back in its cage and gazed ahead of me. I
wanted to gauge how far it was to the top but it was impossible. I

could not see further than the next turn in the road, let alone to the top of the pass all of those miles away.

While my mind was racing with calculations of water supplies, distances and times, I subconsciously changed gear on my bike. I must not have been finding the cycling that difficult because, without realising it, I had actually moved up a couple of gears. A few bends later, I realised that the gradient we were cycling up was not actually that hard.

After half an hour of pedalling in silence, mentally debating whether we would be capable of cycling over a mountain range, it dawned on me that the Alps would be no different from any other hill we had cycled. I had imagined it to be a gruelling experience, but by pacing ourselves, it was just the same as cycling anywhere else. I could take in the views and had enough air in my lungs to hold a conversation. The anxiety slipped away and I started to enjoy the ride as, from the grin on her face, I could tell Laura was too.

In fact, the mental challenge of passing the time probably required as much effort as turning the pedals. We started playing some games to distract ourselves, like trying to work out how many Queen songs we knew. I had barely got as far as naming two when Laura cut me off.

'You can't just name them. You've got to SING them, mate!'[1]

And so it was that we made our way to the top of the Gotthard Pass, at 6,915 feet above sea level, in the fine company of Freddie Mercury and friends. Before we reached the summit however, we were rudely interrupted halfway through a breathless rendition of 'We Are The Champions' by some other cyclists: two young Brits who were riding to Malta. One of them was towing a trailer.

[1] Despite having been married for several years now, Laura and I still have a tendency to call each other 'mate' whenever one of us is taking the mickey or winding the other up. I get called 'mate' quite a lot.

'It's pretty heavy, particularly on the hills, so we take it in turns. One day each,' he explained. 'I drew the short straw today.'

They were raising money for charity, and they gave us some stickers and postcards with their website address on. They were clearly excited and told us what route they were taking, how far they cycled each day and when they would reach Malta.

'Where are you guys headed?' they asked. Laura and I exchanged an awkward glance.

'Probably Italy next,' Laura said.

'Cool. Then where?'

'Er, maybe down through Croatia. We're not sure yet.'

The obvious answer was 'Australia,' but we could not bring ourselves to say that out loud. It sounded absurd. That was partly because you cannot actually cycle all the way to Australia: the land runs out in Southeast Asia. But you cannot reach Malta by land either, and that did not stop these two guys declaring it as their ambition. The truth was that we found it embarrassing. It felt like putting on running shoes for the first time and announcing that we would run an ultramarathon. Australia was certainly our destination but we did not yet feel worthy of sharing it. Who were we to think we could cycle half way around the world?

We left the two Brits taking photos and continued our steady ascent. The idea of the Alps had been scary; the reality was anything but. The sun shone the whole time and the views were beautiful. It was a long, slow slog to the top but nothing that warranted more than a passing thought in advance. Indeed, a month later we stopped at the top of a hill and were baffled to find ourselves surrounded by ski lodges and chair lifts. We did not believe the sign giving the resort's altitude, but later confirmed it on a map. Without realising it, we had reached the same height as we had in the Alps.

Chapter 3

'Either I unzipped them unconsciously on my way to the toilet or I just crossed the Alps with my flies undone.' – Tim

'Winner day, stunning scenery and two lake swims. Cooking dinner with a sunset view of the lake and several 3,000m peaks.' – Laura

Crossing the Alps marked an important watershed for us. We started to believe that, having made it over those mountains, we might eventually make it to Australia. After reaching the top of the final pass, I paused to take in the view across Switzerland. When Laura caught up, she found me inhaling calories in the form of butter spread across a slab of chocolate. We still had a long way to go, but at least we knew that the next few miles would be downhill.

We flew down the far side of the mountain at speed, erasing two days of height gain in a matter of hours. We stopped at the small town of Faido and parked outside a supermarket. Having stocked up on food before leaving France, we had not yet needed to go shopping in Switzerland, and having just cycled over a mountain, we had hoped to indulge a little. As soon as I saw the eye watering prices however, it was clear that treats would be off the table. Instead, I reverted to my 'calories per pence' calculation. I walked the aisles looking for the total energy provided by various packets of food, and divided that by their cost. That told me how many calories I could get for every penny that I spent and allowed us to maximise how far our money went.

'The best I've got is eight calories per pence, for this bag of pasta,' Laura said, approaching me with an otherwise empty basket.

'These biscuits work out at about eleven,' I replied.

And that is what we ate in Switzerland: biscuits and pasta. We left the supermarket with a giant bag of each.

We were determined to stick to the budget we had set ourselves and had allowed ourselves nine euros per day for Western Europe. In France, with its proliferation of hypermarkets, nine euros had been enough to pay for muesli and milk for breakfast; baguette, brie, salami and tomatoes for lunch; and a dinner that often involved meat or fish. In Switzerland, however, items like meat, cheese and fresh vegetables were out of the question.

Sitting on a quiet promenade on the shores of Lake Lugano the next day, we cooked the expensive pasta on our camping stove while, on the other side of the street, smartly dressed locals drank red wine with their restaurant meals. As the sun set, we clambered down onto the beach and swam in the soothing waters of the lake. Once it was dark, we pushed our bikes further along the shore until out of sight. We unfurled our bivvy bags and went to sleep beneath an open sky.

The weather changed in the night and a thunderstorm struck. By the time we had jumped out of our bivvy bags, the storm was in full force. Conveniently, we had left our bikes fully loaded and ready to roll, so we were mobile within seconds. Laura made a dash for the wooden door of a shed beside the harbour and found that it led to an underground boathouse. We threw our stuff inside and lay down between two boats, dusty but dry.

Despite our disturbed night, we woke early, fearful that someone would find us sleeping in their boathouse. It happened to be my birthday, and as a present, my mum had booked us a hotel for the night, half a day's ride away in the historic town of Agno, near the Italian border. After checking in, and washing our clothes and ourselves, we spent the afternoon pootling around town and generally enjoying not being on our bikes.

Since it was my birthday, we felt like we should celebrate. However, we were still in Switzerland and our daily budget could not afford it. Nine euros would barely get us a lemonade to share, let alone a meal for two. Thankfully, we had a special reserve for just such an occasion.

Running alongside our daily budgeting system was our 'luxury pot': money we had been given specifically for treating ourselves. On Laura's last day at work, her boss had given her some money as a leaving present. She thought that a year of riding a bike and sleeping in a tent sounded awful so had insisted that Laura use the money for 'something nice, like a hotel or a spa'. Instead of adding it to the money we had been saving for the trip, we honoured her wishes and set the money aside for a rainy day.

Later in the trip, we used that money for the days when we were knackered, freezing or fed up and, for the sake of a few quid, could get ourselves a hot meal or a bed for the night. It was a brilliant idea. We would never have allowed ourselves such frivolous expenditure otherwise (or, if we had, would have felt guilty for days afterwards) but this was a guilt free indulgence. We were just carrying out Laura's boss's wishes.

So, on the evening of my 31st birthday, we decided to dip into the luxury pot for the first time, particularly as Laura's mum had contributed some extra cash for the occasion. We still shopped around for the cheapest restaurant in town, but the pizzas we enjoyed that night were a lot better than another bowl of pasta.

Rested, clean and well fed, we left the hotel and headed for Italy. There was supposed to be another European cycle route that we could follow in Italy, like the wonderful one that had carried us across France and Switzerland. Sadly, however, the signs stopped dead after crossing the border so we were left to make our own way across northern Italy: skirting the edge of the Italian lakes and dropping into Milan before heading for Venice.

Our time in Italy coincided with the country's fruit harvest and we were treated to the smell of sweet, sun-warmed apples wherever we went. At the end of our first day's riding in the country, we found ourselves rolling through a huge orchard, where the fruit was particularly pungent. We rode along the top of a series of dykes, which provided the perfect vantage point to watch the frenetic activity of the orchard's operations. We stopped to enjoy the warm evening air while we cooked our dinner and absorbed everything that was going on. Trucks went back and forth, ferrying apples from one place to another, and farmworkers loaded and unloaded them, diverting our attention from the sun, which was quietly setting behind us. Tucked away from the road, we pitched our tent to the buzzing of fruit flies and distant whir of vehicles.

Although it was an idyllic scene, something happened that night that still disturbs us to this day. Throughout the evening, a kitten had been pestering us. Neither of us are cat people so we tried to ignore it and went to bed, listening to its meows through the walls of the tent. On waking, we wondered what had happened to our would-be feline friend until we noticed it lying nearby, not moving. We are not sure what happened – it looked healthy enough and we did not hear any cars in the night – but an animal dying right outside our tent was unsettling. We tried to shake off the creepiness and carried on across Italy.

Cycling southeast since leaving home meant that we were chasing the sun across Europe. We knew it would eventually leave us with a cold shock somewhere around Turkey, but until that point, we basked in the prolonged summer, travelling in permanent blackberry season, picking fresh berries right up until November.

Warm and sunny though it still was, Croatia appeared to have closed for the season by the time we reached it. Its roads were quiet and its cafes closed, which made for perfect cycling conditions: great weather, beautiful scenery and no one else vying for space on the roads. We wound our way along the coastline, sandwiched between the sun-bleached rock on our left and the blue sea on our right.

However, we were lulled into a false sense of security because Croatia had a secret weapon: thunderstorms. When the first one struck, we were completely unprepared. We had become complacent and our waterproofs were buried at the bottom of our panniers so just kept pedalling in search of shelter. The first thing we found was a row of beachfront bars that had shut down for the winter. With no one around to ask for permission, we went ahead and wheeled our bikes under the canopy of one of them. The storm showed no signs of abating, and since we were soaked already, we took the opportunity for a swim in the sea.

By the time the rain stopped, we were settled for the evening. We ate our dinner looking out to sea then pitched our tent on the wooden decking in front of the bar. Hidden from any passing traffic, we slept well in the knowledge that it was off-season and no one was likely to disturb us.

The same thing happened the next day: a storm and a dash for shelter. This time, we pitched our tent in a wooden shack, between a pile of deck chairs and a covered up pool table.

When the downpour started the following day, we wheeled into another resort, hoping for more sanctuary and solitude. This one turned out to still be open but the owner – a huge, topless, smiling man standing next to his huge, topless, smiling twin brother – immediately became fascinated by our bikes and offered us an empty workers' dormitory to sleep in. He brought us food from his restaurant and even provided us with a DVD player for entertainment. The experience made us reaffirm our vow to accept hospitality whenever it was offered.

That was the end of the rain. From there onwards, we had nothing but warmth and sunshine, as we had been enjoying almost every day since leaving home. Further down the coast we wheeled our bikes onto a ferry and began an island hopping exercise. We had heard good things about the Croatian islands but we wanted to reach Hvar in particular, because we knew that my grandpa would be visiting the port as part of a Mediterranean cruise.

We arrived at Hvar in bright sunshine and made our way towards the sea, where we found a group of grey-haired tourists getting off a small boat. My grandpa had assured us that the cruise company would have our names on a list and would take us out to the main boat if we introduced ourselves, so we found a man in a bright red polo shirt carrying a clipboard and said hello.

'Ah, yes,' he said. 'Mr and Mrs Moss. Come on board.'

There was a little chop in the waters but it was an otherwise glorious day and we both grinned as we crossed the bay. Our tiny vessel pulled alongside the vast bulk of a cruise ship, a hundred times its size.

'Welcome aboard the Saga Ruby,' said a man in uniform, who was almost as bemused as us. We had just boarded a Saga cruise ship, usually reserved for smartly dressed, retired holidaymakers. Although we had laundered our clothes for the occasion, they were still the same ones that we had worn to cycle every day, and they were already looking a little worse for wear, two months into our journey. Even if our attire had been up to scratch, the fact that we were half the age of everyone else on board would have turned heads. It felt surreal to have been teleported from the ever-changing world of our cycling trip, to the serenity of a cruise ship for the retired.

After a few flights of stairs, we were pointed to room number 344, and when the door was opened, a familiar face appeared. It took him a moment but recognition soon flooded his face.

'Hello Tim!' cried my grandpa. 'Hello Laura!'

The last time we had seen him was on the day we left home and now we were with him, aboard a Saga cruise ship, off the coast of Croatia. We had told him before we left that we would be cycling along the Croatian coast and he had become pretty excited.

'We're going there on a cruise,' he said, handing over a glossy brochure filled with silver-haired tourists, set against a backdrop of

Mediterranean splendour. He went on cruises all the time and I had not thought much of it. The chances of his boat and our bikes being in the same place, at the same time, seemed remote. Remote but not, it turned out, impossible.

'You're looking well, love,' he said to Laura, and to me: 'That beard suits you.'

I had never been on board a cruise ship before, and after two months of camping wild and roughing it, the luxury seemed otherworldly. Well-dressed gents sat on deck watching the world go by and smartly turned-out women sat in the alcoves of the on board library, whiling the hours away with one eye on a book and the other looking out to sea.

My grandpa took us to a large dining room where we were shown to a table by a waiter in formal attire. He handed around menus that made our mouths water. It was probably the smartest place we ate on the whole trip and certainly since we had left home. It definitely beat the budget pasta that we had been cooking ourselves every night for the last month.

After dinner, we had to bid my grandpa farewell. We clambered back onto the little boat and returned to the mainland. We had been given a glimpse of luxury and a taste of home, but we had many more miles to cover before we could get used to either.

We camped that night in a hidden cove, having been tipped us off about it by a cyclist we had met a few days earlier. We may not have had a luxury pool, nor a fancy restaurant, but we had something better: turquoise sea and a beach to ourselves. It was a world away from life on a cruise ship but it was the one we would choose every time.

Chapter 4

'Camped in a quiet bay when the 1992 Serbian road cycling champion wanders over and offers to service our bikes. Good start in Montenegro.' – Tim

'A man flags us down, picking figs. Forces us to eat some then presses us to take the rest. He's offended by our offer to pay. Uncle Niko.' – Laura

After leaving Croatia and my grandpa behind, we followed a series of dual carriageways across Montenegro and made our way towards the Albanian border amidst a blur of cars and concrete.

We had received several cryptic warnings about Albania, including 'Good luck on those roads!' and 'Enjoy the animals!' We had no idea what they meant and thought nothing of them until we crossed the border and immediately found ourselves on a pothole-ridden dirt track with our path blocked by a huge bull. We followed everyone else and went around the bovine blockade but soon found ourselves stopping again for a small goat being chased across the road by a horse, two chickens and a pig.

Such events appeared to be of little interest to the locals. Far more noteworthy to them seemed to be the sight of two foreign cyclists riding through town. Every man, woman and child who we passed wore a big grin and dished out a wave as we cycled by.

After dodging the farmyard animals, we came off the main road and found ourselves on a dirt track that was little more than a mud bath between hedges. We pushed our bikes through the sludge until it became rideable again. Tired and grubby by the time we reached the first town, we were surprised to find that most of the shops were just tables at the side of the road. Each one looked as though the vendor had simply emptied the contents of his or her pockets onto it. It felt more like Africa than Europe and it was hard to believe that Albania was in negotiations to join the EU. Indeed, it transpired that we had missed Tony Blair's advisory visit to the country by a matter of hours.

We eventually found a proper bakery and ordered a couple of pastries. We paid a handful of lek for them and slumped against the shop's window while we shovelled them down. Once the sugar hit my system, I did the maths to work out what I had just spent.

'Those pastries only cost 20p,' I said, feeling like I had just won the lottery. 'I'm going back in.'

I emerged with handfuls of baked goods, my wallet barely having registered the indulgence. Amongst my purchases was a milky sponge dessert with which we instantly became obsessed. We later discovered that it is known as 'trilece', meaning 'three milks', and is an Albanian delicacy.

Sated, we pedalled out of town and soon found ourselves on another dirt track. Approaching a particularly long stretch of deep mud, I pulled on my brakes to stop and, in doing so, instinctively shot my right arm out to one side. Club cyclists often use hand gestures to warn riders behind them about potholes in the road or oncoming traffic. I have never been in a cycling club and do not know the official signals, but Laura and I devised a few of our own. For example:

Roadside arm extended sideways, palm face down, hand flapping: cyclist is stopping.

Following my stopping signal on that dirt track, we dismounted and tried to get past the giant pool of mud that blocked our path. Laura bounded straight into it, looking for stepping-stones. She got about halfway across before plunging ankle-deep into the sludge. She huffed then waded through the rest of it, pushing her bike. Meanwhile, I spent five minutes painstakingly picking my way around the edge. This summed up our approach to many things in life: I faff around, testing the water with my toes, and Laura just dives in headfirst.

After Laura had wiped the worst of the mud off, we approached a large hill. Laura was in front and, as she started climbing the hill, I ducked behind a bush at the bottom to relieve myself. She reached the top of the hill before looking back to see my bike lying on the floor and no sign of me. I emerged from the bushes a moment later to see her riding back towards me looking concerned. I tried waving to show that I was OK but she took it as a cry for help and came cycling down even faster. She was not especially impressed when I shrugged and said I had just been for a wee. Following that, we agreed upon the following:

Tap top of helmet: cyclist is asking if you are OK.

Tap top of helmet in reply: cyclist is responding that they are OK.

Arm waved above head: cyclist is calling for help.

It sounds a bit cheesy or contrived now that I write it down but it was really helpful and we used it all the time. We would rarely go out of each other's sight whilst cycling but we were constantly well beyond earshot. Being able to check that the other person was OK saved a lot of time in waiting for them to catch up or, worse, having to ride back to them. We got so accustomed to using the gesture that I still catch myself tapping my helmet on our morning commute whenever one of us gets left behind.

We climbed the hill, Laura for a second time, and then passed through a small village. As we reached the far side, a dog flew out from behind a wall barking loudly. Panicked, I tried to dismount by swinging my leg over the saddle. Unfortunately, I was going too fast and my bike skidded out from underneath me. I am not sure who was more scared, me or the dog. It backed off and barked from a distance, while Laura shouted at it and I dusted myself down. After that incident, we added another sign to our repertoire:

Arm extended sideways, fingers clapping against thumb in biting motion: warning, dog ahead.

However, this warning gesture was often followed by:

Clenched fist making pulling gesture away from cyclist's neck: relax, dog is chained up.

We left the village and followed signs for Tirana, the capital city. As a whole, Albania was a lovely country to travel through but Tirana was not its highlight: big, busy concrete roads surrounded by big, ugly concrete buildings. The sky had even turned grey to match our surroundings. We arrived during rush hour and so had to contend with bumper-to-bumper traffic. We had been teleported from lovable rural to unpleasant urban. It began to rain and the air grew thick with fumes as we weaved our way in and out of the traffic.

Laura used her phone to try picking the quickest route across town. I followed her along a dual carriageway, dodging slow moving cars all backed up in a stinking traffic jam. We eventually reached the outskirts of the city and were greeted by a long climb. The rain grew in intensity, pouring so hard that it bounced off the tarmac, soaking us from below as well as above.

After two months of wall-to-wall sunshine, interrupted only by a couple of downpours in Croatia, Albania was doing its best to compensate in a single afternoon. We were travelling at a snail's pace up the steep hill and were drenched within minutes. Cold rain water ran down the back of my neck and I could feel it pouring into my shorts. After enduring it for an hour, I stopped abruptly and turned back towards Laura to make a swiping gesture at my throat. That was one gesture anyone could have understood:

No. Stop. Give up.

It was time to call it a day. I pointed ahead to a large workshop with a wall of windows overhanging the road.

'Let's try the magic letter.'

The magic letter is a letter that works magic. We carried a copy, translated into the local language, through every country in which we travelled. We had used it at a cafe the previous night to suitably magical effect. It read something like:

'Hello, we are Tim and Laura. We have cycled 2,000 miles from the UK. Is there somewhere safe we can sleep?'

Without batting an eyelid, the cafe owner from the night before had said yes. So fast did the magic work, in fact, that we were not convinced he had really understood that we were asking to camp in his car park. But he really did understand and we really did camp right out the front of his cafe. As such, we thought we would try our luck with the magic letter one more time to see if it could get us out of the horrendous weather we were experiencing on that hill. But things did not work out quite as we expected.

The man we found in the workshop would later be known to us as 'the uncle', but at that point, he was just a man in a workshop. A short man, with grey hair and a kind face, he stood in his doorway watching two drowned rats wheel bicycles up his drive. I fumbled in my pocket and handed the man a crumpled piece of paper, blotched with rain drops.

'Hello, we are Tim and Laura. Is there somewhere safe we can sleep?'

To our disappointment, he shook his head. It looked like 'no' but then he gestured for us to sit down.

I smiled weakly and sat on a plastic chair. A puddle quickly formed on the floor as water ran off my jacket and out of my shorts. It was getting dark and we needed somewhere to sleep, so we did not really want to hang around if there was nowhere that we could pitch our tent. But if we had had the cheek to ask a stranger for help then it seemed only polite that we should accept his invitation to sit.

He made a phone call then we tried again.

'Is there *anywhere* we could camp?' We tried to communicate with some more hand gestures, pointing at some possible patches of grass and concrete in the vicinity. He just shook his head again and smiled in gentle bewilderment.

A woman in her fifties appeared with two pomegranates, which she handed to us, and we presumed her to be the man's wife. It was terribly kind but did not much help with our predicament. A long period of awkward silence followed as we attempted to extract the tiny pieces of fruit as quickly as possible, without making a mess, so that we could leave and find somewhere to camp. Bottled water appeared too. They were clearly nice people, but if there was nowhere we could sleep then we needed to get going before nightfall.

We stood to leave, trying one last time to convey our helplessness with shrugs, upturned palms and our best attempt at miming 'tent'. The man looked confused but shook his head emphatically. As we made for the door, a girl appeared and I smiled a greeting.

'Hello. How can I help you?' she asked.

'Oh, you speak English!' I replied, pointlessly.

From there onwards, things started to make sense. The girl explained that her uncle was quite happy for us to camp on his driveway and had been trying to convey as much through the Albanian tradition of shaking one's head to say yes. In Albania, it transpired, yes means no and no means yes. However, given the state of the weather, the uncle said that he would really rather we sleep in his house.

Inside their house, Laura and I perched on the edge of a plush sofa in a warm living room. We felt a little awkward and embarrassed about our invasion of a family home but struggled to suppress smiles. Our fortunes had changed so rapidly since we had been fighting our way up that hill in a storm, just minutes before.

The novelty of the situation was apparently not lost on our hosts either. The aunt had immediately got on the phone and called all her relatives for miles around to let them know that a couple from England had just landed on their doorstep. We were introduced to family member after family member, with the girl as nominated translator. Her cousin, a stout young bus driver, was apparently missing his son's first birthday just to see us. The girl, only about 13 herself, had a remarkable grasp of the English language and her bilingualism made our presence much easier.

The cousin spoke to the girl in Albanian and pointed at Laura repeatedly. The girl blushed and tried to dismiss her cousin but eventually acquiesced.

'My cousin,' she said to Laura, 'says your eyes are amazing.'

Laura blushed too, although she does have quite striking blue eyes. The cousin collared the girl again, this time pointing at me through the conversation. She put up the same resistance but, again, lost the battle of wills. Did he like my eyes too? Or was it another of my characteristics that had caught his eye?

'My cousin,' she said, 'asks if they can't cure baldness in your country either.'

He pulled a sad face and slapped his bald head whilst pointing at my equally balding pate.

We were able to luxuriate under hot showers before dinner was served, and when the auntie saw the state of Laura's sodden socks, she was given a fresh pair, which eventually came with us all the way around the world. An hour beforehand, we had been cold and wet, but now we were warmed by showers and kindness. We were fed like royalty and set up with comfortable beds in the living room.

When morning came we packed up swiftly to avoid abusing the family's hospitality. Nonetheless, we were asked to wait for the girl to arrive from her house around the corner. She was driven over by her mum, possibly the only family member that we had not met the night before. I felt bad about the burden that we had placed on the girl for translation – and even worse when we found out that she was missing school to interpret for us that morning – but I asked her to translate one last sentence.

'Please tell your mother that she has a very kind, intelligent and thoughtful daughter.'

She went red and quiet, but after some prompting, she passed on the message.

'And can I say something to you?' she replied. 'You are absolutely the best people I have ever met!'

Laura's eyes welled.

We mounted our bikes and wheeled them back down the drive.

'I hope you enjoyed your stay,' said the girl.

I shook my head. Yes we had.

Chapter 5

"This box of breakfast cereal contains 13 adult portions". *Incorrect.*
It contains two. One for me and one for my wife.
#1000calorieBreakfast – Tim

'Google Translate informs me the mystery dried meat we ate
yesterday was in fact dried cat. Puss jerky. Nauseous.' – Laura

Concrete rushed towards me faster than my eyes could process. I felt a sickening thump as my back wheel crashed into a coffin-sized pothole and was amazed to find myself still upright as I reached the other side. I relaxed but a moment too soon. My tyres skidded across gravel and the next thing I remember is my head hitting concrete.

We were not even supposed to be in Macedonia. After leaving our Albanian family behind, we had planned to go straight to Greece. But when a fork in the road presented itself and a road sign offered the opportunity to visit a country that neither of us had been to before, we went for it. Cycle touring is great for that sort of thing. Since you have all you need in your bags, it does not really matter where you go from one day to the next. It is OK to change route and country on a whim. It is not OK however, to try beating your own speed record on a fully loaded touring bike, going downhill in a country where the condition of the roads is yet to be assessed.

Using the small bike computer strapped to my handlebar, I had clocked myself approaching 45 miles an hour on a steep downhill the day before and was determined to beat it on the descent into Macedonia. Cycling downhill at that speed is not particularly safe at the best of times and it is even less safe when attempted on a bike with four panniers. Doing so whilst also staring at a tiny LCD screen mounted on your handlebars is downright dangerous.

As I hurtled downhill on a juddering bicycle, my watering eyes could just about make out the digits '45.8' on the bike computer. I raised my head with a grin in time to see Laura swerve to the side of the road and wave frantically to slow down. She was pointing at a large black hole in the road that I was heading straight towards. I squeezed the brake levers as hard as I could. My back wheel got through the hole with a wallop but a gravel-strewn curve in the road was too much at that speed and I skidded over onto my side. My panniers dragged diagonally across the road and my head whipped into contact with the concrete. I lay on the floor, dazed, as Laura threw her bike against a fence and ran over to check on me.

'I'm OK,' I said, sitting up slowly, 'but it'll take a minute.'

I shuffled to the verge as Laura wheeled my bike out of the road. My thoughts had slowed but I mentally scanned myself: I was aware of some grazing on my side and a throbbing in my head, but it appeared that I had been lucky. I had landed on my head at 40mph and lived to tell the tale. I dread to think what would have happened were I not wearing a helmet.

I composed myself and took in some sugar to help with the shock. We finished the rest of the descent slowly, both with our hands firmly on the brakes, and I pedalled gingerly for the rest of the day. We stopped that evening at a hotel whose owner let us sleep in the lobby. I popped a couple of painkillers then fell into a deep sleep. My self-inflicted concussion gave me a headache for the next two days.

No further attempts were made to beat my top speed.

Chapter 6

'I'm not saying my bike's heavy but I leant it against a bollard and the bollard bent.' – Tim

'Unexpectedly found ourselves at the top of a 1,650m pass today, complete with ski lifts and chalets. Greece didn't let us in easily.' – Laura

I woke groggily the following morning, head a little sore from the crash. We had just started packing away our stuff when Laura found the large sandwich bag filled with cod liver oil tablets, which she had carried from England. She thought that our knees might appreciate them, in view of all the cycling we would be doing. When we got caught in the rain in Tirana however, her stash had got wet and the pills had started to disintegrate.

'They're not going to last,' she declared outside the hotel that morning, 'but they're not going to waste either! Here, eat these...'

She shovelled a dozen, sticky cod liver oil tablets into my hands. I chugged them down with a gulp of water and retched at the stench of fish.

'That is disgusting,' I said.

Laura rolled her eyes: 'They're just tablets mate, get over it.' She then necked a fistful of tablets herself and performed the same retching action. For several days, we performed the same routine every time we stopped: tablets, water, retch. I am sure our knees had never run more smoothly but I have no doubt that our breath had seen better days. Riding away from the hotel, we followed quiet back-roads around the side of a lake, belching fish flavours all the way into Greece.

It was the end of October and Greece welcomed us with autumn as we zigzagged up a hillside covered in glorious orange and brown.

The heat was fading from summer and it was taking the leaves with it. Aside from the changing season, what struck me most about Greece was how similar it felt to the rest of Europe. It was very different from Albania, of course, but much the same as any other country we had travelled through in Western Europe. Having never been to Greece before and I had imagined its rich history would somehow be visible from street level, but the roads and the shops felt the same as those we had passed on our way there.

Also, visiting as we were in the wake of the global financial crisis and aware of the country's huge debts and unemployment problem, I had assumed it would be a very cheap place in which to travel. It was not. And I knew exactly where it stood in the price hierarchy of Europe because I had tracked it with my own economic scale: the Lidl Chocolate Pudding Index.

Most of the countries we had travelled through across Europe had Lidl supermarkets and we had grown used to shopping in them. Noting their consistent presence in our journey up until that point, Laura wrote the following at the time:

"Lidl has been an ever-fixed mark. We could walk into a store anywhere in Europe and instantly know that we would be eating tinned sardines and chocolate pudding (not usually together), and where to find them in the standard layout. Of course, it is also friendly on the wallet, a key factor for the budget-conscious cycle tourist. Although we are both unsettled by the power and dominance exercised by some large corporates, and would generally prefer to shop at small local stores, we have grown lazy. At the end of a day of cycling, when tired and hungry, we want a familiar option which is as cheap as possible, and Lidl all too often fits that bill.

Before you judge us too harshly, on a trip like this, life is in constant flux. Every night brings a new place to call home, every week a new landscape to look at, and every month a new language

to learn (or at least, resolve to learn). Having something familiar
to cling to helps anchor us, offering some respite from the
onslaught of new experiences. Of course, we love escaping the
tent on occasion to stay with local people and relish the
opportunity to try local foods, but having a couple of standard
things to fall back on offers us a safety net. In Lidl's case, its harsh
strip lighting envelops us and offers a degree of comfort that we
know what we are doing."

One of the standard products available from the same aisle in
Lidl's standard layout was the aforementioned chocolate pudding.
Every Lidl store we had visited from London to Tirana had stocked
the same cheap, little chocolate puddings and we ate them in
abundance. But whilst the product remained reliably consistent, the
price changed every time we crossed a border. It had mostly been
getting cheaper and cheaper as we got further east but Greece's
desserts bucked the trend, topping the Lidl Chocolate Pudding Index.

With summer having given way to autumn, the trees were aflame
with colour and the harvest was coming to an end. Our route across
Greece – from Edessa through Thessaloniki to Alexandroupoli – took
us through large swathes of farmland, with tractors driving back and
forth, gathering what crops remained. Their drivers often waved to
us as we passed. Soon enough however, the fields gave way to
industry as we approached the outskirts of Thessaloniki. My younger
brother was flying out to meet us there but not until the following
day. That meant we had to find somewhere to spend the night before
entering the city. We spotted a patch of grass and went into a nearby
shop to ask for permission to camp.

'No. Gypsies.'

A shake of the head and a quick swipe of the neck. It was the sign
we had used to mean 'no/stop/give up', but in this instance, it

definitely meant 'cut your throat'. Apparently, this was not a safe place to camp because there were gypsies about.

'OK! Thanks!'

We smiled in gratitude and pedalled off, musing about the idea of marauding gypsies targeting the camping cyclist.

We received warnings from locals throughout our journey: there are wolves, it's too cold, what about thieves, it'll be too steep, we have bears, it's raining. We had been warned about wild animals when camped at the side of the road in Western Europe, and when we later reached the Arizona desert, where the temperature averaged 40 degrees Celsius, people would still shiver when we told them we camped outside. Accordingly, a crazy old woman warning us about killer gypsies on the outskirts of Thessaloniki did not faze us in the least. We just pedalled on to a petrol station and asked there instead.

We got the same response though: head shake, gypsies and the cut-throat thing. Laura and I exchanged a bemused look and cycled onward. A lady outside a house by a bridge: the same. A truck-stop on the outskirts of an industrial park: same again. Perhaps Thessaloniki did indeed have a problem with murderous roamers.

In another shop, the owner appeared to say, 'Gypsy Kings'. We briefly wondered if the warnings were actually about the French flamenco band rather than violent nomads but decided that we must have misheard.

We eventually found a cafe whose owner was closing up for the night and said we could camp in his backyard, opposite a factory. It was an uncomfortably hot and sticky evening and the one spot identified as safe from gypsies was next to a large vat of stagnant water, infested with mosquitoes. It would be no exaggeration to say that I hate mosquitoes with a passion. I find it impossible to relax if there is even a slight possibility one might be trying to bite me and I maintain a high state of agitation until convinced that I am free from bloodsuckers. In turn, I do my best to ensure that Laura cannot relax either by constantly tracking them around the tent and clapping my hands loudly and providing helpful commentary like 'Yes! Got the bugger' or 'Ooh, that was a messy one.'

Eventually satisfied that the insect vampires had been vanquished, we lay down on our camping mats. Despite the irritants, lassitude prevailed and I had just begun to nod off when I was rudely awakened by an overpowering brightness. I squinted, picked my way to the tent door and poked my head outside, which, of course, let in more mosquitoes, resulting in a protracted Benny Hill scene of me chasing tiny black flies around the tent with a sock. I did at least ascertain the source of the light. A new shift of workers had arrived at the factory over the road and had flicked the switch on a huge bank of floodlights, which, apparently, pointed directly at our tent. This was helpful as there remained a slight danger that one of us might have got some sleep that night.

I pulled my hat over my eyes, pressed my face into my pillow and tried to force myself to sleep. But before I had a chance to test my sleep strategy, a loud booming noise came out of nowhere. It was joined moments later by a rhythmic hissing then a range of electronic sounds in what quickly became apparent was the music of choice – drum and bass – for workers on the night shift in Thessaloniki's favourite industrial estate. The banging continued for some hours, eventually subsiding shortly before daybreak when it was replaced by the deafening roar of machinery being fired up.

Our alarm woke neither of us at 6am. Laura groaned. That was probably the worst night's sleep of the entire trip. I rolled over in my sleeping bag and gave Laura a shake:

'What?' she grumbled.

'Shall I see if we can stay another night?'

'Piss off.'

Chapter 7

'Wanted: Flat roads. Last seen somewhere near Italy. Reward: The eternal gratitude of my knees.' – Tim

'Reluctantly decided that swimming goggles and cap were not an essential piece of kit for cycling around the world and sent them home.' – Laura

We spent a few days off the bikes in Thessaloniki being tourists with my brother, before waving him goodbye and cycling out of town.

Our route followed a coastal road that swept along cliff-tops, winding back and forth at increasingly steep inclines. Exiting a small village, we searched for somewhere to camp. The roadside gradient was too much for comfortable camping so we had to keep riding, further and further along the cliff's edge. Through a thicket of trees, a large hotel crept into view, set back into the cliffs.

With no sign of life at the hotel, we decided to sit outside and wait. And while we waited, we figured we may as well cook up some dinner on the patio. And once it got dark and still no one had turned up, we decided it would be OK to pitch our tent on said patio. And since it was dark and no one was around and there seemed no imminent threat of anyone arriving, we reckoned no one would mind us taking it in turns to strip naked and scrub ourselves down while standing in a large bowl of cold water. We were a little concerned that someone would turn up in the middle of one of our strip washes but we got away with it (assuming there was no CCTV).

What we did not get away with however, was urinating outside the tent at night. When you need to answer a call of nature in the middle of the night while camping, there is little choice but to climb out of your sleeping bag and go outside in the cold. Camped on open land, this presents little problem. On this occasion however, we were camped on concrete, and that led to some unforeseen consequences.

In the small hours, I heard the tell-tale rustle of Laura extracting herself from the tent. There was a sound of water splashing on concrete then Laura hissed: 'Oh no.'

'What's wrong? Is there someone outside?'

'It's spreading.'

'What do you mean it's spreading?'

'The concrete,' she said. 'It's not absorbing it. And I think we're on a bit of a hill.'

'Oh, for heaven's sake!'

I buried my head in my pillow and pretended that my wife had not just peed on the tent in which we were sleeping.

Seemingly unperturbed, possibly even amused, Laura lay back down and gave me a little shove.

'Do you think the groundsheet's still waterproof?' she asked through stifled laughter.

'You're disgusting,' I replied.

'I can feel it warming me,' she added, before laughing to herself for some time. 'It's like an electric blanket.'

The owner, who had not interrupted us the night before, arrived the following morning just in time to interrupt me with my trousers down as I emerged from a nearby bush after answering an urgent call of nature.

'Good morning!' I cried breezily, emerging from the bush with one hand waving and the other pulling my trousers up. 'I hope you don't mind, but we couldn't find anyone here last night so we pitched our tent on your porch.'

He looked at our tent, our stove and our bikes, and we braced ourselves for a dressing down. To our relief however, he processed the scene calmly, as if it was normal to have two dishevelled foreigners camping on his veranda, one of whom had apparently seen fit to remove his trousers in the surrounding woodlands. In fact, he just broke into a grin and handed out some bottles of chilled water from the kitchen fridge.

'One other thing,' I continued. 'Your toilets were locked so I just made use of your woods back there.'

He looked at me strangely but we had already established that he did not speak a word of English so I continued smiling as I spoke, and he smiled back.

'I don't know what she's laughing about,' I continued, pointing at Laura who was enjoying the exchange. 'She practically wet the bed last night.'

Soon afterwards, the hotelier waved us goodbye and we continued our way along the Greek coast before turning inland. It was a beautiful day and we were able to ride carefree on deserted roads through the countryside. As the sun lowered behind us that evening, we were conscious that darkness would follow shortly. We saw a cottage amidst a small copse of trees and stopped to see if we could fill our water bottles.

An old lady was sitting on a bench outside the cottage and she kindly offered to fetch us some water from inside. Before she returned, a man emerged from the building, dressed in long black robes intricately embroidered with unfamiliar symbols. He wore a large hat and sported a wonderful chest-length beard. A Greek Orthodox monk.

He appeared stern so I extended my hand for a formal introduction, but instead of my hand being shaken, I was handed a Cornetto. He handed another to Laura then started to unwrap one for himself. The glint in the monk's eyes gave way to a cheeky grin and we shared our ice creams beneath the setting sun. He let us pitch our tent in the corner of his garden and invited us to join him for dinner.

Inside, his accommodation was plain but homely. On the table that evening stood large bowls of hearty soup, a basket of bread and individual salads laid out for the three of us. Father Paeseus gestured to sit and we did.

'I no speak good English,' he offered apologetically, though it was far better than our Greek. Throughout the evening, we communicated with broken English, hand gestures and willpower.

We established that he had tended a nearby church for seven years and lived alone, Orthodox monks being celibate. He was learning English with a tutor in preparation for a visit to a Greek Orthodox community in America the following year. On the hill behind his house and church, a monastery was being built and he was overseeing its construction. He unrolled blueprints across the dining room table to reveal plans for a huge, two-storey monastery with lecture rooms, multiple churches, accommodation for no less than 43 monks and an on-site gift shop.

We were tired from cycling and it took a lot of concentration to follow this story spoken in broken English, but we stayed up late into the night hearing about life as a monk and the differences between Catholicism and Orthodox Christianity. When our conversation came to an end, we walked back to our tent in darkness. The air was cool and still.

The following morning, the Father invited us back inside for some coffee. We instantly recognised the elaborate preparation process.

'Ah, Turkish coffee,' Laura said.

'Not Turkish coffee. *Greek* coffee!' Paeseus corrected.

We had always associated that style of strong, black coffee with the Turks but he was adamant that it was the invention of the Greeks. It was our first sign of the long running Greek-Turkish animosity.

The day on which we made our coffee faux pas was a Wednesday and that is significant for the Orthodox Church. Traditionally, its members do not eat meat, fish or dairy on Wednesdays and Fridays. Instead, they give away that which they would normally eat to those in need. We could hardly claim to be needy, but assisting the passing traveller must have seemed a suitably Christian thing to do because Father Paeseus presented us with a parting gift: freshly baked bread, still warm from the oven, and a foil parcel filled with grilled sardines.

We thanked him for his hospitality and he waved us off to continue our journey east.

Chapter 8

'I'm not saying it's a miracle but the fish the monk cooked and packed for our lunch seem to be never ending.' – Tim

'We've started seeing signs for Turkey... Asia is close! Almost crossed our first continent!' – Laura

We were approaching the eastern edge of Greece and that meant we were nearly upon Turkey. We were excited about reaching the gateway to another, more exotic continent but something that Father Paeseus had said was niggling me:

'Very dangerous,' he had warned us sternly. 'Musselman. Very angry.'

We could not decide if this was just naive, paternalistic concern for his guests or an unfortunate closed-mindedness about an alternative faith. It was a common theme on our trip: people who had never been to their neighbouring country, warning us about the dangers lurking across the border.

'Jihad. Very dangerous,' Paeseus had said.

We did not consider travelling through Turkey to pose any notable danger, certainly not from religious extremism. More plausible was a possible prejudice stemming from the tumultuous history shared by the two countries.

Modern Greece achieved independence from the Ottoman Empire (now Turkey) in the early nineteenth century and there has been angst between the two nations ever since. Sufficient angst, that is, to have seen them fight four wars in the intervening years. The most obvious indication of this today is Cyprus, which has been split in half since the Turks invaded in 1974. As recently as the late 1990s there were threats of open warfare over the 'Cyprus Missile Crisis' when, in an historically familiar scenario, a small island installed a bank of Russian missiles provocatively close to a foe. Thankfully, the disputes these days tend to be contested less with bullets and more with coffee and yoghurt. What we think of as 'Turkish coffee', the Greeks, including Father Paeseus, claim is really theirs. Meanwhile the Turks reckon that 'Greek yoghurt' is nothing of the sort. And as we discovered when trying to navigate our way to Turkey using a map picked up in Greece, the Greeks still call their neighbour's most famous city 'Constantinople', refusing to use its modern Turkish name of Istanbul.

None of which is to suggest that any such anti-Turkish sentiment is widespread. We just stumbled across a possible bastion in a small monastery near the border. By contrast, our last night in Greece was spent with someone far more open-minded.

Pedalling on from the monastery, we should not have been surprised that cycling towards a town called 'Panorama' meant cycling up a big hill. We eventually reached level ground at the entrance to a large, deserted resort that was clearly closed for the season. We could see a light in one of the rooms however, so we approached the building and knocked on the door. After a short pause, the door was opened by the caretaker, a middle-aged man with a weathered face and big grin.

'We were just wondering if we could fill up our water bottles.'

We really wanted to ask about camping, but we had learned that it was better to start the conversation with an easier request. That was partly because we are British so do not like to be overly forward or say what we really mean. But it was also because it gave everyone a chance to gauge each other: we could do our best to demonstrate that we were not crazy and, hopefully, we could confirm the same of the other person. On this particularly occasion, there was very little gauging required.

'Hot or cold?' came the reply.

'Cold's fine, thank you.'

'Cold from the tap or chilled from the fridge? Would you like a coffee while you wait?'

We were directed to pitch our tent on the tiled floor at the side of an outdoor pool and found ourselves thankful, once more, that we had chosen a tent that could be pitched without pegs. In the meantime, Panos, the caretaker, set off to make us all coffees. We joined him around a table on the veranda to watch the sunset with the Greek/Turkish coffee he had prepared for us. Two of his friends joined us and we talked politics.

Greece was still reeling from the depression that had hit the country following the 2007-08 financial crisis. At its nadir, the banks closed for several weeks and nearly one in every four Greeks was unemployed. Referred to in Greece simply as 'The Crisis', it led to huge bailouts from the International Monetary Fund and European Central Bank. The bailouts were offered on the condition that the country adhere to a strict programme of austerity, but when the people were asked if they would support such a programme, they voted against. The government was caught between a rock and a hard place: accept the bailouts and insist on austerity against the people's wishes, or reject the bailouts, close the banks and run out of money. While all of these negotiations were going on, the country's debt rose to over €300bn. That was €30,000 of debt per person.

It had been a difficult few years for Greece. Amongst the many side effects of these problems was the rise of the far-right political party Golden Dawn. They gained popularity in part by handing out free food to the needy when times were tough (only 'Greek nationals' were eligible) and partly by blaming others (foreigners) for Greece's problems.

Over our late-night coffees, we discussed these issues with Panos and friends. We asked their view on the state of the Greek economy (not great), whether they wanted to stay in the European Union (they did) and what they thought of Golden Dawn (not a lot).

Father Paeseus' warning still fresh in my mind, I took the opportunity to ask Panos if he had ever been to Turkey. His English was stilted but the sentiment was clear.

'Turkish people?' he asked with wide eyes. 'Turkish people very hospitality! Good, good people. Very hospitality!'

This was high praise coming from a man described by his friends as being 'known throughout all of Greece for his hospitality', and a far nicer picture than the one painted by Father Paeseus the night before.

The next morning, we left our hospitable host and aimed our bikes at Turkey. The midday sun warmed us gently from the right as we pedalled east along the two long lanes of smooth, black tarmac highway that stretched ahead of us. We revelled in the total absence of any traffic, riding with an empty lane each, powering our way towards our next country.

When we reached the border, we crossed a narrow bridge, heavily guarded on either side, and the sky turned dark grey to emphasise the sense of a border that carried a lot of history. We passed rows of impounded vehicles, presumably having failed to meet the EU's entry requirements, including a bright yellow fire engine from Laura's hometown of Bolton festooned with the words 'Aid 4 Syria'. We paid our money for a visa stamp, slapped each other's palm and rolled into a new country.

'Very angry' or 'very hospitality', we had no way of knowing what the Turks would really be like, but as evening drew to a close we approached the Turks as we had done everyone else: with a big smile and a grubby bit of paper.

'Hello, we are Tim and Laura. Is there somewhere safe we can sleep?'

The recipients in this instance were the employees of a petrol station in the middle of nowhere. They had barely read the first sentence when they gestured for us to sit down. Plastic chairs were brought onto the forecourt, followed by teas, milk and sugar. Before we could finish our drinks, we were ushered to a room above the station with two beds and a shower. There would be no need for a tent, they said. After a welcome wash and a change of clothes, there came a knock at the door. The youngest member of the team carried in a tray of hot soup and fresh bread. These men did not seem angry. They did not seem dangerous. They were kind, friendly and welcoming, as was almost everyone we later met in Turkey and just as almost everyone we met in every other country was too. We slept that night surrounded by the dark silhouettes of distant hills, confident that Turkey would be good to us, just as Greece had been.

Chapter 9

'For those that have lost faith in humanity my advice would be this: get on your bike; for cycle touring and cynicism are surely incompatible.' – Tim

'1st night in Turkey: asked a garage for water. Given sweet tea, soup, shower and bed. Are these tales getting repetitive? #kindnessofstrangers' – Laura

'Are you ready for this?'

Headlights blinded me as six lanes of traffic flew along the highway in front of us. I nodded grimly to Laura. We had been making our way across Turkey for about a week by this point and had reached the outskirts of Istanbul, but things had not gone quite according to plan.

Laura wheeled out across the junction first. Horns blared and traffic swerved. We pedalled furiously across the road, desperately trying to reach the other side before another wave of high-speed traffic steamed out and crushed us.

We should not be here. We do not cycle in the dark. We do not cycle on busy roads like this.

Istanbul is notorious for bad traffic and getting across it is something of a rite of passage for long-distance cyclists. Well aware of this fact, we had been at pains to avoid the problem and had actually found a perfectly civilised route into the city centre by following the coast. We had wound our way through suburbs and parks, following marked cycle paths and arrived in the middle of town shortly before sunset without any trouble at all. It was shortly after we had congratulated ourselves on this achievement that we received a message from our would-be host saying that there was a change of plan and we had to meet him on the other side of the city.

We looked at our map in the fading sunlight and were horrified by the sprawl of dual carriageways and major arterial roads that we would have to follow to where we needed to go. The alternatives were no more appealing: we were not about to fork out for a hotel and camping was out of the question in a big city. So, we steeled ourselves for the ride and rolled out onto a pitch black highway, holding our breath every time a car went past, praying that our blinking lights were enough to keep us visible and alive.

After what felt like hours, but was probably closer to 45 minutes, we reached the final junction, powered our way across on adrenalin and hauled our heavy bikes over the barrier on the far side. We pushed the bikes through crowds on the pavement until the beaming face of Hakan appeared, smiling, waving and shouting my name.

For the previous hour, Hakan's name had been mud. It was *his* fault we were in this mess. It was *his* fault that we were cycling at this time of night and it would be *his* fault if we were mown down by a passing truck. Once we had sat down in his kitchen, though, we quickly warmed to him. The change of venue was an innocent mistake and, besides, it is hard to bear a grudge against someone when they have just presented you with a huge plate of homemade kebab and chips at the end of a long day's cycling.

Hakan was a 22-year-old architecture student, cycling enthusiast, amateur photographer, film buff and Wes Anderson fan. We had arranged to meet him through a cycling network called 'Warm Showers'. It is a wonderful network of people offering hospitality to travelling cyclists; much like the 'Couch Surfing' website, but specifically aimed at those on bikes. When we were organised enough to plan our itinerary more than a day in advance, we would send a message to anyone who lived on our route asking if they would be willing to host us. We always knew that we would be passing through Istanbul so we had emailed Hakan a week before our arrival and he had replied with his address.

The reason he had later sent us the message saying that we would be staying somewhere else that night, and therefore had to cycle across town, was because his grandfather had just died. Arrangements with his family meant that he would be staying in his grandfather's old apartment for the next few nights and so would we. It was a remarkable show of hospitality and made our earlier grumbles seem all the more churlish.

Hakan showed us some of his photographs and told us about an apprenticeship he had served in Paris, where he was able to hone his skills. His portfolio was impressive but his enthusiasm for photography had almost landed him in trouble.

One year earlier, on a warm May afternoon, Hakan was taking photos in a central Istanbul park when a wave of bulldozers arrived and sparked a conflict that would soon involve tear gas, riot police, fatalities and, at its height, 3.5 million protesters across the country. The spot that he had chosen to take pictures and stage a sit-in was Gezi Park. It adjoins Taksim Square, whose name, like Tiananmen Square in China, may always be synonymous with protest. What started as an objection to the proposed bulldozing of a park, quickly spread to a wider objection to the Turkish government. The protesters were angry about the suppression of the press and creeping encroachment on the country's secularism through bans on kissing in public and restrictions on alcohol consumption.

Encroachment on secularism may not sound like the kind of thing to excite passions and flare tempers, but it is a central tenet of modern Turkish history, and you cannot get very far in understanding that without knowing one man: Mustafa Kemal Atatürk.

Mustafa Kemal, now known simply as Atatürk (meaning 'Father of the Turks') was a military officer in the Ottoman Empire during World War I. The Empire was defeated by the Allies, but Ataturk led the rebellious Turkish National Movement during the subsequent war of independence. The movement successfully repelled the occupying Allies and ultimately transformed the country into a modern, secular state. Ataturk is revered in the same way as Winston Churchill in the UK or Abraham Lincoln in the US, but perhaps because the things for which he stood and fought are still being debated today, his relevance to modern Turkey and presence in the national consciousness are much greater.

Hakan's brush with the law had no lasting effect other than to amplify his political engagement and it was whilst spending time in his apartment that we began to understand more about Turkey's past and future. It was also in Hakan's apartment that we downloaded a stockpile of films and all six seasons of the Sopranos onto our laptop.

I mention the films because, while I am writing page after page about the various interesting and exciting things that we encountered on our adventure around the world, the truth is that we also spent a lot of time watching TV.

We had been away for three months by this point and I had started to find myself dreaming, with increasing frequency, about sitting on a comfy sofa and watching a good film. It is not that I did not enjoy cycling, exploring and meeting people; it is just that it was exhausting. Our bodies had adapted to the physical hardship but there was no way to adjust to the mental hardship of being forever at the mercy of the elements, battered by winds and drenched by rain, and not knowing where we were going to sleep each night as the sun went down. Being a good guest could also be a strain at the end of a hard day's cycling. We often struggled to stay up late and find things to talk about with strangers whose language we did not speak. All of these things were part and parcel of our tour, and I would not have wanted it any other way, but it did not stop them from wearing me out. So, when the opportunity presented itself to hide away and watch a few episodes of a box set, I grabbed at it greedily. Just as weeks of nine-to-five office work breeds a hunger for adventure and escapism, weeks of adventure breeds a hunger for laziness and escapism of a different sort.

All of which is my way of justifying the fact that, whilst ostensibly circumnavigating the globe by pedal power, we still found time to watch the full 57 hours of the entire Sopranos franchise.

Laura's parents were coming out to meet us in Istanbul. After two nights at Hakan's flat, we pedalled to the hotel where they were due to arrive later that day. At reception, we were directed to an underground car park where we could lock our bikes. In the basement, we were surprised to discover a full- laden touring bike leaned against the wall as if round-the-world cyclists were ten a penny in Istanbul. Delighted to have found a kindred spirit but deprived of the chance to meet them, I slipped a business card onto the rear pannier with our room number on the back and suggested the owner got in touch.

Business cards might not seem like the first thing you would think to pack for a bike trip, but we met a lot of people on our journey, many of whom were kind and interesting. All too often though, our encounters were fleeting. Giving them a card with our email address meant we could stay in touch. Many subsequently followed our progress around the world and we have maintained contact ever since. We clearly were not the only ones who had gone through the same thought process. A cheerful Polish cyclist we had bumped into in Montenegro carried a pack of large postcards with a photograph of himself on the front so that people would not forget him.

After a few days exploring the city with Laura's parents, we left the hotel having never heard from the mystery cyclist. We pedalled cautiously through the frenetic streets of Istanbul and pushed our bikes onto a small ferry packed with locals. On board we asked another passenger to snap a photo of the two of us because that boat trip marked an important point on our journey. We had crossed one continent under our own leg power and were about to enter another.

PART II

Turkey-Iran

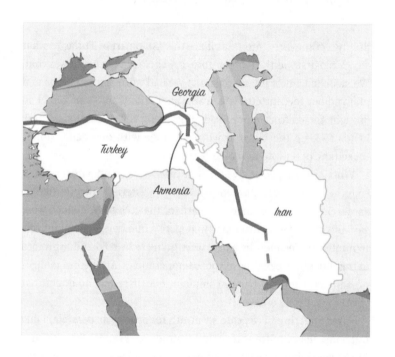

Chapter 10

'Brilliant to see my Mum and Dad in Istanbul, sad to say goodbye. Will be a few months (and a cold winter) before next time.' – Laura

'Snow flurries, frozen turf and water bottles turning to ice in minutes. Real drop in temperature these last few days. Exciting times.' – Tim

Rolling off the ferry into Anatolia – the Asian part of Turkey – what struck me first was the temperature. It was November and it was cold. We switched out of the sandals that we had worn across Europe and plunged our feet into the big, warm boots that Laura's parents had brought for us from home. Pedalling along the coast, I shook my hands to keep the blood flowing and rode with one hand while I tucked the other into my collar for warmth.

When we stopped at a waterfront cafe to warm up with a bowl of soup, a news report showed pictures of Eastern Turkey buried in snow. On the weather map, the parts of the country for which were we were headed were littered with negative numbers from minus five to minus 20. The months ahead were going to be cold and I shivered at the thought of camping at those temperatures. After three months of summer, we could hardly complain, but there was no doubt that winter was firmly upon us.

After lingering in the cafe's warmth for as long as possible, I dug out some fleece mittens from my panniers to keep my hands warm in the cold wind. As well as our winter boots, Laura's mum and dad had brought out a range of other winter supplies for us in their suitcases: down jackets, pile smocks, woolly thermals, fleece hats and a second sleeping bag each. All of this extra kit had to fit onto our bikes. We had each strapped extra duffel bags onto our rear racks and the first hill after that cafe felt especially hard with the additional weight.

We continued following the south coast out of Istanbul before turning inland to head north towards the Black Sea. The paved roads soon disappeared, replaced by tracks of frozen turf. Rolling hills stretched as far we could see and there was something beautiful about the bleak emptiness that surrounded us. We passed the occasional wooden farm building but not a lot else. When we reached a village, we found that it was deserted except for an army of dogs that ambushed us on the main street.

Dogs hate cyclists and, by the time we reached Turkey, we were accustomed to being chased by them. And by 'them', I mean every single four-legged canine between London and Istanbul, plus a few particularly determined three-legged ones. Over time, we learned that what they really like is the chase. As soon as you stop cycling, they stop chasing. Sure, they will still have a bit of a go, creeping towards you and barking at the sky, but you can usually keep edging away on foot and shoo them off when they get too close. The key is to just get off and push.

Even armed with this knowledge, they can still scare the life out of you when they catch you off guard. And even if you dismount in time, it is still a pain in the neck having to keep stopping, dismounting and pushing, especially when it happens 20 times before lunch. What bugged me most though was the stupidity of it. What was the point of charging at us if they were only going to give up as soon as we stopped cycling? I would almost have preferred it if they had been ready to fight to the bitter death.

The dogs in this village were no exception so, when they ambushed us, we got off our bikes and pushed. We shouted, waved our arms and pretended to pick up stones, and the dogs kept their distance, allowing us to walk through town unscathed.

As the sun began to set a few days later, we were looking for somewhere to sleep when we spotted a farmer working his field. He downed his tools on our approach so we showed him our magic letter and pointed to our bottles to ask for water. He walked us to his house and led us inside. We carried our bottles to get them filled up but he gestured for us to sit in his living room. The room was lit dimly with a single bulb shining a weak light on the faded wallpaper. There were three old sofas in the room, each a different colour, and the floor was covered in a patchwork of rugs.

The farmer soon returned from his kitchen with an urn of hot tea, which he poured into shot glasses and served black with sugar. We thanked him with smiles and nods then sat awkwardly in silence, sipping our scalding hot drinks. We pointed again to our bike bottles and indicated that we also wanted to pitch our tent outside. It was all in our magic letter but perhaps he had not read it properly. Once he worked out what we were trying to say, he waved the idea away with a single hand and pointed to the living room floor. We protested that we did not want to intrude but he simply pointed to the floor again. To emphasise the point, he disappeared and came back with some heavy blankets, which he lay on the floor for us.

The farmer's name was Ali and I got the impression that even if he had spoken English, he would have been a man of few words. However, with the aid of pen and paper, we managed to communicate and tell him what we did for a living. We also confirmed that farming was his occupation and that he had a family, including grandchildren, although we did not discover where they were. We drew our own family tree with pictures of our siblings and nieces, and he did the same in return. We also unfolded our map of Turkey, showing him where we intended to go – north to the Black Sea then east until we hit Georgia – and he marked where his friends were in nearby towns. Eventually, he retired and we lay down on his floor to sleep.

In the morning, as we packed our bikes to leave, Ali pointed to another house in the distance and indicated that we should walk over there with him. We wheeled our bikes across two fields to what constituted his neighbours' house. It was much smaller than his was and made of wood rather than brick. Inside, a young couple with two

58

young children invited us to sit down at their kitchen table. Berna, the mother, cooked us all eggs and served them with tomatoes and fresh bread. The couple seemed excited to meet us and we used our new Turkish words to convey as much of our story as possible: teacher, lawyer, husband, wife, England, bicycle, Australia. Aware that our hosts were not wealthy, we tried to offer money for the food but they would not consider it. Berna handed us some more bread for our panniers and Ali wrote down the name and number of a friend in the next town. They waved us off from their veranda as we bounced our way along the track, away from their farms and towards the Black Sea.

We rode in solitude for the rest of the morning beneath a calm, cloud-filled sky. Stopping to scoff the bread we had been given at breakfast, I noticed a funny mark on my back wheel. On closer inspection, I realised it was a crack.

Our bikes had already been heavy when we left home. Apparently, however, the added weight of winter clothes and the additional stress of the potholed roads had been too much for my wheel. The rim was cracked and needed replacing. Unfortunately, we were in rural Turkey and had not seen a bike shop since Istanbul. As such, having identified the problem, there was little that we could do besides keep pedalling, gingerly avoiding any large bumps in the road until we reached Eregli.

Eregli is a port city on the Black Sea coast, best known as the home of Turkey's largest steel plant. Its beaches make it a popular holiday destination for locals, but with the sand beneath several feet of snow, we did not spot anyone enjoying them as we cycled into town. By the time we got to the city centre, the crack had become ten and the wheel had become wonky. We followed directions to the local bike shop, but it did not look promising: a ramshackle building with a few bikes propped outside, each of which slowly fell like dominoes as Laura crashed into them.

The owner came out with a smile, gestured not to worry and began to pick up the bikes.

'Marhaba,' (hello), I said. 'Do you speak a little English?'

He did not. I pointed to my back wheel and he acknowledged that it was broken. Having recently discovered a translation app on my phone, I typed in the words: 'Can you build wheels?'

Instead of replying, he disappeared and reappeared a minute later with a wheel.

'Is it strong?' I asked him, once more using the app. He nodded 'yes' but Laura counted the spokes and disagreed. Another disappearance and another wheel appeared. 'Very strong,' he said of the second wheel, but we realised that it would not work with my brakes. He phoned someone. Can we wait three days?

'If that's what it takes,' I typed into my phone. 'What type of wheel can you get it?'

He showed us a picture. It looked strong and it would work with my brakes, but unfortunately, it was incompatible with my bike's hub. He phoned someone else and so it went on.

The above is a condensed account of our bike shop encounter. Played out in real time through stilted and confusing computer translation, it took several hours. The whole time we were crammed inside a tiny, cluttered old bike shop. Over the course of the afternoon, we were served tea (cooked on a camping stove behind the till) and we distributed numerous packets of biscuits from our panniers in return. Our story was shared repeatedly with a growing collection of men who crowded around us in the miniature shop, apparently without employment or families to occupy their time on a cold winter's day.

Wheel choice is a popular topic of debate among cycle tourists: if you use traditional '700c' wheels, will you be able to replace them when you are on the other side of the world? Or do you need to find a bike with the smaller, stronger '26-inch' wheels, for which replacements are supposedly easier to find?

We had 700c wheels and, like many others, had fretted over our choice before we left home. We were unfortunate enough to have one of our wheels break, but even in rural Turkey, the first bike shop we came across was (eventually) able to source a good quality replacement within 24 hours. When Laura later had an issue with one of her wheels several thousand miles later in Vietnam, we again found a replacement immediately. In other words, we need not have worried. Hundreds of people, if not thousands, have cycled around the world with 700c wheels. Wheel size may be an interesting debate for bicycle enthusiasts, but for the aspiring round-the-world cyclist, it is really not that important.

At some point during the protracted interaction, it dawned on us that we had long since missed any opportunity to depart the town that day and would thus need somewhere to sleep for the night.

As such, our priority swiftly turned from bicycle maintenance to bed acquisition. The default option – camping – was not viable in a town centre and we did not want to resort to an expensive hotel. Our habit of knocking on doors and producing the magic letter was only appropriate in quiet areas, out of towns, where we could ask for somewhere to camp. We had found several hosts in Turkey through the Warm Showers and Couch Surfing hospitality networks, but such hosts really needed to be contacted several days in advance. The chances of there being such a host in Eregli, who happened to be free that evening and who happened to be checking their email at that very moment seemed slim. Nonetheless, while I continued the wheel negotiations, Laura used her phone to put out a desperate plea.

Minutes later a tall, well-dressed man flung open the door of the shop, took one look at us and shouted:

'Tim! Laura! Couch Surfing?'

Our call for help had be answered. He introduced himself, shook our hands and then conversed with the owner in Turkish.

'Your bike will be ready tomorrow. Come with me,' said the man who had just introduced himself as Bercan, a host Laura had emailed just ten minutes earlier in our bid for a bed.

Emotionally unprepared to leave our new friends at the bike shop so abruptly after spending the day with them, we waved an awkward goodbye and uttered our thanks as we backed out the door. We left the bike shop group huddled around our bikes, looking forlorn.

Bercan directed us to his van then drove with some urgency through the town's busy streets.

'You like fish?'

'Yes.'

He screeched to a stop in the middle of the street, leapt out and returned with a bag of fish.

'You like red wine?'

Screech. Leap. Wine.

'You like bread...?'

An hour later, we found ourselves in a plush, modern apartment sipping a large glass of red wine with a belly full of bread and fish. The bike shop, the back wheel, the desperate search for a bed, they all seemed a world away from that relaxed, civilised evening of food and drink. To top things off, our host produced a classical guitar and sang to us in Turkish.

Chapter 11

'Big thanks to the little bald man who caused havoc on the streets of Eregli this evening by driving slowly to guide us to our destination.' – Tim

'This uncertain life makes one crave stability. Today found myself envying our host doing his Saturday wash...until we got back on our bikes.' – Laura

Bercan dropped us back at the shop in the morning and we picked up our bikes, mine complete with new back wheel. As we pedalled out of town beneath a cold, grey sky, my rear wheel spun perfectly and we were back on track. Chilled after a couple of hours on the road, we sought refuge at the next village.

I had never been to Turkey before and had not known what to expect. It was more developed than I had imagined and, even from the perspective of a passing cyclist, it was clearly growing rapidly. Although President Erdogan was a controversial figure, he had overseen a period of stable growth that had helped bring Turkey further onto the world stage. More importantly for us however, the booming economy meant that we were constantly passing supermarkets and petrol stations so were never far from supplies.

Stuffing in some biscuits outside one of those petrol stations later that morning, the owner walked over to us with a tray containing two small cups of tea. It would have been a delightful gesture at any time, but when the only other fluid available was the icy water in our bottles, it was especially welcome. We returned the tray with a 'teşekkür' (thank you) and continued on our way.

Turkey was a cheap country in which to travel. Between its budget supermarkets and its low cost cafes, we were able to eat good food and find regular respite from the cold without breaking the bank.

Stopping in a cafe for hot soup and bread at lunchtime a few days later, two men on a table next to ours arranged for teas to be delivered to us. When the drinks arrived, the men raised their glasses in our direction with a smile. We noticed that they put a sugar cube in their mouths and sipped the tea through the cube. Laura attempted to do the same but, apparently, it was not as easy as it looked. She only got as far as scalding her lips and spitting out a saturated sugar cube.

Riding through the small town of Ovacuma in the afternoon, a shopkeeper leapt from his door when he saw us coming and shouted 'Chai! Chai!' Having been in the country for a couple of weeks, we were growing accustomed to the generous Turkish hospitality and love of tea, but that was the first time anyone had flagged us down in the street to offer it. The day was descending into more of a tea-drinking contest than a cycle tour, but how could we reject such enthusiasm? The daylight hours were now so short that we were hardly making any progress anyway. Not that it mattered; we had long since decided that meeting people was far more interesting than racking up miles.

The shopkeeper spoke English, and as he plied us with hot drinks, he filled in the gaps in our knowledge about Turkish tea. We had already observed that the Turks are a nation of tea drinkers. We tend to think that British people drink a lot of tea but we are not a patch on the Turks. They really do drink a lot of it.

The shopkeeper explained that, in Turkey, tea is not served in a mug or cup, and certainly does not come with milk. It is always drunk from a glass and always served black. Tea is prepared using two metal pots, stacked on top of one another. The larger pot goes at the bottom and contains just water, while the smaller pot sits on top with the tea in (always made with loose leaves). Whereas in England we leave our tea to brew in a porcelain pot and have to insulate it with a tea cosy or let it go cold, in Turkey the tea remains on the heat until the pot is empty.

The reason for having two pots is so that you can adjust the strength to your taste by adding differing amounts of hot water. A brave soul can take the tea straight with no added water. What we call strong tea, they call 'coyu', which means closed. Us softer souls, and this Southern one in particular, would always request it 'acik' (open), with extra water. That word – acik – became one of our most used across Turkey, as we were served increasingly strong tea the further east we went. The only word that might have competed was 'cok', which means 'very'. As in, pleading 'Cok, cok acik,' after spitting out a mouthful of black liquid and tea leaves.

We thanked the shopkeeper for the tea and education then pedalled around the corner to find a bush. After a dozen cups of tea, I was desperate for a pee. Having had a slow, disjointed day of riding, we were keen to make some progress before it got dark – something that was happening increasingly early, as we got further into winter.

The afternoon fell away as we concentrated on covering miles. The world flew by in a blur as I fixed my sights on Laura's back wheel and matched her pace. The morning had been dirt tracks, hills and potholes, but the evening was tarmac, long and straight.

As the sun set behind us, the sky slipped into red, before fading to black. We knew the next settlement could not be far so kept riding through the darkness. Its approach was signalled by the glowing yellow rectangles of houses with lights on and by the barking of dogs, too slow to catch our flying wheels on that particular evening. In the centre of the village, men in heavy coats huddled round small circular tables, sipping tea from tiny glasses. We eased ourselves to a halt.

I ducked under the low frame of a door of what appeared to be bar and entered a room that may have remained unchanged for a hundred years. The walls and floor were bare stone, illuminated by candlelight. The tables and chairs were made of plain wood and the locals propping up the bar wore simple, traditional clothing that showed no influence from modern materials or fashion.

I scanned the room, searching for the proprietor. There was no 'Barista – My name is Brad' badge but the big guy behind the bar looked like he was in charge. Tall, heavy set, thick moustache. I handed him the Turkish version of our letter.

'Hello, we are Tim and Laura. Is there somewhere safe we can sleep?'

Sit, he motioned. And sit we did. Chai? He asked. And chai we took. From his days in Austria and Laura's lessons at school, we were able to communicate in German that his friend, with whom we were sitting, had a niece who taught English and would help us. We drank our tea and were told it was time to leave. The bar owner's friend then led us down a series of unlit back alleys in the dark. Trust can be gained quickly in some circumstances.

We arrived at a three-storey house and were introduced to the English teacher, Gulnur, who showed us to the bottom floor. What was presented was so perfect that we wondered if there would be a charge attached. It was a downstairs flat with freshly made beds, our own bathroom and a kitchen all to ourselves. Gulnur told us to make ourselves at home then come up for dinner.

Upstairs, we were welcomed into a warm, family home and shown to a large dining room table. We sat down for dinner with three generations of the family: Gulnur, her husband, her parents and her son. She led proceedings, translating on behalf of everyone else. Her eight-year-old son did not let the language barrier stop him from interacting with us and took real delight in repeatedly flying his toy plane into my salad.

We ate a huge amount of food. It was impossible not to. The teacher kept offering us extra helpings, and whenever we declined, her mum would chasten her and gesture that we should be eating more. Stuffed full, we waddled back outside and down the stairs to our flat, where we promptly fell asleep.

Morning came, and finding our private kitchen devoid of gas or running water, I heated the water from my bike bottle on our camping stove. I made a pan of semolina but completely misjudged the quantity and produced a huge portion. Even for two hungry cyclists it was a lot of food, but just as we had finished eating the last spoonfuls, there was a knock at the door. It was Gulnur.

'Good morning! Would you like to come upstairs for some breakfast?'

Oh dear. We obviously could not tell her that we had already eaten but nor was the idea of a second round very appealing.

'No, no, no. We wouldn't want to intrude,' I tried, suppressing an urge to vomit at the thought of more food.

'But we've prepared a breakfast for you, upstairs,' she replied. Was that a little bit of hurt in her voice?

I did the moral calculation in my head and quickly concluded that we owed more to our hosts than we did our stomachs. 'Well, that's very kind of you. We would be delighted to join you for breakfast.'

I stole a glance of desperation at Laura, who helpfully mimed sticking two fingers down her throat and throwing up. We shook our heads, steeled our stomachs and followed our host up the stairs, ready to face our fate.

It was tough going but I reckoned we had eaten enough food to be convincing. We thanked the family warmly, pulled some silly faces at the young boy and pedalled off for another day's riding through the Turkish winter. I thought we had got away without Gulnur realising we had already eaten breakfast, but when she later wrote to us, the title of her email was 'Second breakfast'. She had known all along!

We did our best to burn off the extra food over the following days, climbing over big passes and fighting against the cold. We could have followed the Black Sea all the way from Istanbul to Georgia, but that would have meant almost a thousand miles along the same coastline. As such, we had decided to detour inland for a change of scenery. We had lost sight of the sea and were surrounded instead by snow-covered mountains. It was quieter away from the coast too, with smaller roads, fewer cars and longer stretches between settlements.

As our bike computers ticked over the 3,000 mile mark, winter continued to progress. We were well into December by this point and the temperatures dropped even further. It was never above freezing level and frequently ten or fifteen degrees below. The snow piled up at the side of the road, well above head height at times. As it was turning dark on a particularly chilly evening, we climbed a steep hill to a village and knocked on the door of a mosque. We had seen an abandoned building and wanted to check if it was OK to pitch our tent inside. We also needed water since the fountain in the town square had frozen solid. An imam opened the door and gestured that he would help us if we waited outside. Several minutes went by however, and he did not return. We were left standing outside in the freezing cold, jumping on the spot to stay warm in our cycling clothes and watching helplessly as the night grew darker and darker.

When the imam eventually returned, he said it that was OK to camp in the empty building then left. Cold to the bone by this point and unable to think clearly, we frantically set about pitching our tent. Thankfully, our routine was slick enough that we could erect the tent in minutes without saying a word, even with numb fingers. We bundled all of our sleeping kit through the tent door then piled inside to get warm. I started heating what water we had left to make some soup and Laura sorted out our sleeping arrangements.

We had thin foam camping mats that we laid on the groundsheet of the tent. On top of those, we had thick inflatable mattresses filled with synthetic down, which were very warm and embarrassingly comfortable. They strapped together to form a double mattress of sorts. During winter, each of us slept in a silk liner, a thick down sleeping bag and a thinner synthetic sleeping bag over the top. We both slept in merino leggings and long sleeved tops, woolly socks and a hat. It was often cold getting into the tent in the evening and getting up again in the morning, but we were never cold during the night.

Once the bedding was sorted, we took it in turns to change out of our cycling clothes while the other watched the stove. Once the water boiled, we clambered into our sleeping bags to drink our soup and get warm. We had just begun to defrost and relax when we heard footsteps approaching.

'Marhaba!' a shout of hello.

Reluctantly, I opened the tent door, letting in a rush of cold air. A man stood over me and I could see three others busying themselves outside. The man closest to me said something in Turkish and shivered, pointing at us. He was worried we were cold.

'We are OK,' I said, smiling with two thumbs up, pointing to all of the many layers in which we were wrapped. 'No problem. OK.'

He did another pantomime shiver then gestured that his friends were starting a fire. It was unnecessary, but they seemed determined so I just said 'teşekkür' (thanks) and zipped up the tent. We soon heard the crackle of burning wood followed by the smell of burning plastic. Moments later, acrid smoke poured in through the tent door. My eyes began to sting and I started coughing. They were trying to help us keep warm but, frankly, two pounds of the finest goose down was doing that just fine without the asphyxiation. Instead, the building and our tent were both filling with black smoke. It felt more like lynching than hospitality.

Realising that the fire was not going to provide any benefit, they began talking to us again. They kept asking us questions, pointing somewhere outside and trying to get us to pack up our tent. We had just got comfortable and were only minutes away from sleep. The last thing we wanted was to go outside into the cold again, especially when we didn't know why.

They were insistent though and we eventually acquiesced. The tent was hurriedly stuffed into Laura's panniers and we wheeled our bikes behind the men, following them into the darkness. I had to carry the sleeping bags, camping mats and a mug of soup in one hand while the other gripped the handlebars of my bike. We had no idea where they were taking us but it had to be better than a flaming building.

We stopped outside a non-derelict building with no fumes pouring out of it, so things were looking up. It had windows and doors to protect us from the elements, and it had been built on stilts, meaning we would be raised above the cold ground. They put a thick mat on the ground, rigged up a light then brought over a big tray of bread, steaming hot, straight from the oven. No longer freezing cold or in danger of smoke inhalation, we were able to compose ourselves and relax. We thanked them for their help then bid them good night.

Morning came and so did a large portion of semolina, now a daily routine. We packed our panniers and were carrying them out of the front door to our bikes when the previous night's invaders accosted us. They motioned to follow them for some food. We tried to convey that it was not necessary, but our protests fell on deaf ears.

We were welcomed inside another wooden building and climbed the stairs to a family living room. Inside, we smiled and shook hands with various members of the family. The home was more basic than Gulnur, the English teacher's, had been. We were in a smaller, more rural village that appeared notably poorer. The ground floor was reserved for animals and farm machinery. Upstairs, the walls and floor of the house were bare wood, and there was no electricity.

There was a furnace blazing in the corner and the house was boiling hot, but that was not the only thing bringing sweat to our brows. We had polished off a pan of semolina just minutes before but were faced with another table full of food. They were clearly excited to host two travellers however, so there was nothing else for it. Duty dictated that we overeat.

We had learned by this point that money offered for food would not be accepted. However, out of politeness, people seemed to accept gifts so we handed over a box of chocolates and gave them some sweets for their kids.

Plonking our overfull bodies onto the bikes, we rolled back down the hill and out of the village. After a cold week of beautiful desolation, our inland detour was coming to an end and we were about to re-join the Black Sea, but before that, we had one last mountain pass to climb.

Halfway to the top, we stopped to take in the view. The sky was thick with grey clouds and there were fields, white with snow, for as far as the eye could see. Having started the climb shivering, within minutes I was sweating from the exertion. We kept on climbing until we reached a service station a few miles from the top. I wheeled my bike towards the front door and immediately fell flat on my back. Despite being minus ten, some bright spark had hosed down the forecourt, leaving a giant ice rink between the road and the station's front door. Inside, we filled our thermos with hot water and scoffed a few biscuits. I could have eaten a horse at that moment but made do with a quick sugar hit because we were desperate to keep going. We wanted to cross the final pass before it got dark so we could put the mountains behind us.

We pedalled out into the traffic once more and, within seconds, I was shouting at Laura to stop. Punctures always come at the worst moments. We took the panniers off my bike at the side of the road and flipped it upside down. We took it in turns to remove our mittens for the fiddly bits while the other jogged in the snow to stay warm. Reinflated, we hopped back on our bikes and spun the pedals rapidly to warm up. Daylight hours were so short and we wanted to get off the mountain before nightfall. Eventually, we crested the top of the pass and saw what we had long been waiting for: the sea.

Despite the sweat of the climb, I threw on my pile jacket at the summit, put on a second pair of big winter mittens and pulled a

71

balaclava over my face. Cycling downhill at ten below is a chilly business and there were still several miles of descent to sea level from our mountaintop. I swung a leg back over my bike and pushed off towards the coast.

Few things are more satisfying than the descent of a mountain whose every metre you have slogged your way up. I thoroughly enjoyed it and could not tell if my eyes were watering with emotion or just trying to deal with the rush of icy air at high speed. Squinting, it was an effort just to keep them open. This was not helped by the fact that horizontal snow had started to whip through the valley, limiting visibility. Amidst the wall of white that straddled us on either side, a dark object slowly came into view. Gripping the handlebars as tightly as I could through multiple layers of fleece, I pointed across the road to what looked like a small building. I was wondering if Laura was seeing what I was. It seemed implausible up there in the mountains but the sign was unmistakable: kebab.

We slowed to a halt and leaned our bikes against the building's glass front. Apparently, we had discovered a high altitude kebab shop in the Turkish mountains. After stomping some feeling back into our feet, we pushed open the door and were met by a wall of warmth and a lot of bewildered faces. Five young Turkish men in matching polo shirts stared with incomprehension at the spectacle of two tourists appearing from the blizzard on push bikes.

'Hello, we are Tim and Laura. We have cycled from England...'

They may have been baffled at first but once they had overcome their initial shock, we were welcomed like rock stars. We were seated in the middle of the restaurant by the wood burner, and received the full works – soup, bread, tea, meat, salad, more meat, more tea – before being asked to pose for a series of group photos, uploaded immediately to Facebook.

When we stood up to leave and pitch our tent, they looked genuinely concerned. You probably would too if someone stepped out of your kebab shop in the dark to erect a tent in a blizzard, but it seemed perfectly normal to us. We tried to explain that we camped outside most nights (which had been true before we arrived in Turkey) and were prepared for much worse, but they were having none of it and we were shown to a dusty storeroom stacked full of paint where we could sleep.

Morning. Semolina. Pack. Go.

No chance. As we exited the building, the manager appeared and gestured for us to come inside. We knew what would happen next. You would think that we might have learned our lesson after the experience at Gulnur's and in the village, but the problem was that we could never tell when a second breakfast was coming. Setting off for a day's cycling without eating breakfast was not an option, but relying on our hosts to provide it would have been foolhardy, even if it were not presumptuous. Instead, we just had to gamble, make our own breakfast and hope for the best. That morning in the kebab shop however, we were about to get stung again.

We were invited to join the manager and his colleagues at a table loaded with bread, eggs, olives and tomatoes. Bile rose in the back of my throat in memory of the semolina mountain I had just demolished, but the food was presented out of kindness and it would be consumed out of appreciation. We did our duty, thanked our hosts, and then stepped outside to finish our descent.

Chapter 12

'Cycling through Turkey. Every evening is like Come Dine With Me, except that we never have to host.' – Laura

'Yesterday's puncture wasn't ideal but at least it was in a town. Halfway up a snow covered mountain today was definitely sub-ideal.' – Tim

The weather had calmed overnight, leaving behind a brilliant blue sky at the price of even lower temperatures. We started our day with a thrilling, if freezing, descent all the way to the sea, where we re-joined the same coastal route that we had been following before we took to the hills a week earlier. However, the coastal road was much wider now with dual carriageways, lots of tunnels and lots of freight traffic. We would continue to follow it all the way to Georgia.

'I hate those lorries,' Laura declared later that morning, after we had just emerged from one of the many long tunnels that punctuated the coastal road.

'It's not just the size of them,' she said, still shaking her head as our eyes adjusted to daylight. 'It's not even the noise of their massive engines echoing off the walls or the whoosh of air as they go past.'

The trucks were indeed pretty scary when they flew past at close quarters.

'I mean, that's stressful but you can't blame them for it,' she continued. 'What I don't get though, is why they have to deafen us with those reverberating fog horns? It's terrifying.'

The tunnels were not only long – some could be measured in kilometres – but also prolific. They would often run back-to-back with just the briefest glimpse of sunlight in between each one. This sometimes meant we would end up subterranean for quite long periods. In contrast to the tunnels we later encountered in Georgia and Armenia, the Turkish ones were at least in good condition. It is always going to be scary when you are sandwiched between fast moving traffic and a concrete wall, but it is twice as bad when there are no lights and you have to keep swerving to avoid potholes. Turkey's tunnels were always brightly lit with smooth tarmac. Some of them even had speakers in which played music, adverts or the call to prayer. On the downside however, that coastal road attracted a lot of trucks.

It was an unwritten rule that I would cycle at the back whenever we went through a tunnel. I would describe it as a chivalrous effort to protect my wife from overtaking vehicles. She would say that I just couldn't keep up.

Whenever I knew a car was approaching from behind, I would deliberately move into the middle of my lane – there were always two – so there was no chance they would miss seeing us. As they got closer and I knew that we had been spotted, I would pull back to the side and give them plenty of space to overtake.

With the trucks however, I went one step further. I would keep looking over my shoulder until they got within a hundred yards then I would give them a big wave. I did it partly to establish some human contact with the driver and partly because I figured that, if I was in the middle of the lane flailing an arm around, there was no chance they would not see us.

'I hate those bloody horns,' Laura added. 'The only thing they achieve is increasing the chances that I swerve in panic and get crushed by their giant wheels.'

My technique worked though, and I know that because every time I smiled and waved, the drivers would treat me to a long, loud honk of the foghorn.

We followed that road for a month in total and we must have gone through a hundred tunnels. Every single time a lorry passed us by, I would wave. In response, they would blast the horn and I would relax knowing that we were safe, while Laura would flinch in terror, fearing for her life. She is yet to thank me for my chivalry.

The tunnels ended as we reached the eastern edge of Turkey. On our final night in the country, we slept in an empty cafe at the owner's insistence and rummaged through our panniers to see what we had in them for dinner. There was only a tin of tuna fish, a packet of sunflower seeds and some hazelnut wafers, which made for an unusual meal. Our already depleted food store took a further blow during the night when a mouse found its way into our precious Nesquik bag.

Our time in Turkey had been tough. Since leaving Istanbul, the temperature had never risen above zero. Our hands and feet were constantly cold, no matter how hard we cycled, and on the slightly warmer days, our tyres sprayed us with slushy ice. Whenever we were hungry, we had to find somewhere warm to eat or we had to scoff food rapidly at the side of the road before we got too cold.

It was tiring, but after spending almost two months in the country, we had grown very fond of Turkey. We had learned about its history, its customs and its cuisine. We had picked up some of the language and, to this day, we still respond to good food and nice views with a hand gesture we learned in Turkey. No doubt we had barely scratched the surface, but it felt as though we had begun to know the country. Perhaps that feeling was exaggerated by the intensity of travelling through it in winter.

However, the single Turkish characteristic that stood out beyond anything else was hospitality. The Turks could reasonably lay a claim to being one of the most hospitable peoples in the world. They would have a fight on their hands with their Iranian neighbours, as we were to find out later, but I collected evidence on Turkey's behalf to support such a claim. In the seven weeks that we spent in Turkey, we only had to use our tent on a grand total of four nights. Even on those nights, we were well looked after: one was spent in the back garden of a hotel where the owner served us both dinner and breakfast;

another was on the driveway of a house in the throes of wedding celebrations where food was brought to us by a mob of excited children; and the other two involved free kebabs. The rest of the time, people just kept inviting us into their houses.

Sure, we also had four nights in a hotel when Laura's parents came to visit us in Istanbul and one more after we got stuck on the outskirts of Samsun at nightfall after Laura had come off her bike on some ice. But every single other night that we spent in the Republic of Turkey, somebody took us into their home. That is 40 nights with 23 different hosts right the way across the country. That cannot just be luck.

We had contacted in advance some of the people who took us in, but many more were just the unsuspecting recipients of our magic letter and hopeful smiles. We never asked to sleep inside – our letter specifically said that we had everything we needed – but such information was tossed aside like an empty cigarette packet. Our protests that we had a tent were ignored and our suggestion that we could cook the food from our panniers was routinely dismissed too. Indeed, we had to throw away the gone-off food in our bags so many times after families insisted on making us dinner that we stopped buying anything that was not long-life. Instead, we bought boxes of chocolates and other gifts that we could offer as tiny thank you presents for people we had not yet met but who we knew would insist on bringing us into their homes.

Turkey was a friendly place and, as we left the country, we knew that we were going to miss it.

Chapter 13

'Our host is desperate to trim my beard. Clean shaven, he reckons I'd look like Vladimir Putin, Silvio Berlusconi or just "simple".' –
Tim

'I often dry my freshly washed knickers on my panniers. Today they froze. Crispy underwear, mmm.' – Laura

'Three... two... one... drink!' shouted the policeman, and we dutifully knocked back another glass of the spirit he had poured for us. Trying the local liquor was a quintessential experience in many countries that we visited, but it was not usually served at breakfast.

Granny was clearly used to it though. As I reached for some more bread to extinguish the burning in my throat, she topped herself up for a third shot and then a fourth, fixing me with an implacable stare before necking each.

We almost did not get into Georgia at all. We had arrived at the border the day before, after seven wintery weeks of wonderful hospitality in Turkey. The immigration officer had squinted and strained with concentration to recognise Laura from her passport photo. Evidently, she was struggling to match up the fresh-faced enthusiast on the page with the winter weary cyclist in front of her. She eventually let Laura through but then it was my turn. She took one look at my clean-shaven photo and another at the wild mass of hair and ginger beard standing before her at the counter, and didn't even bother trying to reconcile the two. She just laughed, shrugged and waved me through.

Pootling along at sunset that evening, we were stopped by a police truck. The driver hopped out and, speaking faltering English for us, asked where we planned to spend the night. When we said we were looking for a camping spot, he told us that there were dangerous wild animals and that camping was out of the question. He was friendly and seemed genuine, but we were reasonably confident that no such things existed. People often think that sleeping outside is dangerous but it rarely is. Aside from bears, which seemed unlikely so close to roads and towns, there were not that many wild animals in Georgia that we thought would pose a major threat.

That said, it is still unnerving to be told that sort of thing, especially in a new country when it is going dark. He indicated that he wanted us to follow him into town so he could find us somewhere safer to sleep. Eventually, we acquiesced and agreed to tail his pickup truck for a few miles.

'Here!' he proclaimed as he stopped the truck in the centre of town.

'Here?' I replied, 'You want us to camp here?'

Calling it Trafalgar Square would have been an exaggeration but it was definitely the central square and there were definitely a lot of people around. We would have been sleeping in full view of everyone in town, visible to restaurant diners, pub goers and anyone that lived above the many shops that surrounded the square. Every passing pedestrian, shopper, cyclist and jogger would have gone straight past our tent. We had slept in some weird places but this was just about as bad a place as I could imagine.

'You want us to camp here?'

'Yes! Very safe,' he continued, 'but lock your bikes and don't let any belongings out of your sight.' Apparently, even with the police on our side, we would be prime targets for theft.

'I think I'd prefer our chances with the wolves,' Laura muttered.

We compromised with a guesthouse. He felt we would be safe from bear attack and we felt relieved about not having to deal with drunkards in the middle of the night.

The next morning, he picked us up in his truck, complete with flashing blue light, and took us to his home for breakfast where he introduced us to his wife, sister, daughters, and heavy drinking mother. He showed us his gun, posed for a group photo and told us that we needed to come back to Georgia in the summer, when the country was at its best. We thanked him for the hospitality then set off to cycle towards Batumi.

It was Christmas Eve and, mercifully, the weather had turned unseasonably warm. The sun came out and we managed to eat our lunch outside, without our pile jackets, for the first time in two months. We had been following the same Black Sea coast almost continuously since Istanbul but now we were about to leave it for good. To mark the occasion of our separation, Laura and I tiptoed across a pebbly beach and swam in its frigid waters. We would be turning inland from that point, cycling east towards Tbilisi and Armenia.

We spent the night in a tiny hostel in the foothills above the shoreline. The next day, we stocked up on what supplies the local shop had and did our best to prepare a Christmas dinner of sorts. The hostel had an outdoor kitchen and it was dark by 4pm so our meal was prepared in down jackets, by the light of a headtorch. We managed a basic roast dinner of sorts using two large legs of chicken we had found at the bottom of the shop's freezer, some potatoes and a selection of root vegetables. That was washed down with some strong grape liquor, at the insistence of the jovial hostel manager.

It is hard to surprise your spouse with an exciting present when you have not been out of each other's sight or visited any notable shops for several months. Besides, we were on a tight budget. As such, we had allocated ourselves the equivalent of five pounds to get each other presents from one of Turkey's budget supermarkets. We took it in turns to go into the shop while the other dutifully waited out front, watching the bikes. In the absence of wrapping paper, we wrapped our presents in gloves and mittens then stuffed them into our winter socks, which acted as stockings. Alongside the cakes and sweets we had picked up for each other in the supermarket, we discovered that we had both been carrying presents for one another since Istanbul, having separately liaised with Laura's parents to secretly bring them from home. I got a fancy new bike pump to replace the one I had lost, along with a selection economics and politics audiobooks (which I was genuinely excited to listen to). In return, I gave Laura some down slippers to keep her feet warm in the tent at night.

By the time we left our hostel on the 28th, Georgia had returned to winter conditions. Snow covered everything in sight and grey clouds blotted the sky. We pedalled through the Georgian countryside for several days before reaching the foot of the Rikoti Pass on New Year's Eve. Crossing it would mean climbing higher into the mountains, but it was the only way to get to Tbilisi.

Dropping to my lowest gear, I spun my legs round as we inched upwards from sea level. The road wound round and up a steep sided valley, and the snow at the side of the road reached chest height. I pushed hard up a particularly steep stretch, stomping my feet into the pedals and ignoring the rising lactic burn in my quads. Reaching a clearing, I pulled off the road, threw my bike to the floor and collapsed in a sweaty heap.

'Killer,' was all Laura said when she arrived a few seconds later.

Ostensibly, we were outside a petrol station, but it consisted of little more than a tiny, dilapidated stone hut and a single hose. The owner motioned us in and we exchanged apples (his) for biscuits (ours). As we got up to leave, he tried to convince us to stay for the night. We looked around. There was one grubby looking single bed, a rusty chair, four cold walls and not a soul for miles around. It would certainly have been novel, and I could not blame him for not wanting to be alone on that particular night, but we declined politely and resumed our vertical purgatory.

Rounding a corner, the black hole of a tunnel came into view, marking the top of the mountain pass. Unlit, unventilated, filled with potholes and frequented by trucks, the mile-long tunnel was enjoyable only by virtue of indicating an end to our climb. Emerging

81

into wintery daylight the other side, a modern roadside service station positively bustled with people. We looked around for somewhere we might reasonably sleep but there was nowhere suitable. Instead, we pressed on.

It was getting dark by then and we were desperate not to get caught out for the night but we could only descend slowly for fear of ice on the roads. When we eventually reached a town, the streets were lined with drunks. Everyone we asked for help slurred a response or stared through us with glazed eyes. We could pedal late into the evening to reach the next town, but we were keen finish at a reasonable time, given the date. We warmed ourselves with a few routine star jumps then continued rolling downhill.

The hotel, when it came, was nothing special, but it was warm and it had availability. At £15 for the night, it was way over our daily budget, but we decided it was worth dipping into the luxury pot. We checked in, warmed up in the shower and changed into fresh clothes before walking to the nearest shop. It was late but we knew somewhere would still be open that night. Dinner was cooked with our camping stove on the hotel floor, and we ate it while watching a film on Laura's phone, sipping the beers to which we had treated ourselves. As the movie finished, we realised it was about to turn midnight. We clinked bottles. It had been a tough but thoroughly enjoyable day, at the end of four tough but thoroughly enjoyable months.

'Happy New Year!'

'You too, love. Happy New Year.'

The next day, we continued to roll eastwards, through the snow-covered fields of Georgia. At dusk, we reached the quiet town of Gori, birthplace of Joseph Stalin, and pedalled the streets, watching the inhabitants go about their daily lives. Six years earlier those streets would have been deserted, people understandably having been scared off by the tanks.

As countries go, the Democratic Republic of Georgia has to be one of the shortest lived. It lasted just two years and nine months. Prior to the First World War, it had been part of the Russian Empire. It declared independence shortly before the war's end but the Red Army rolled in and claimed it for the Soviet Union after less than three years. It took the fall of the Berlin Wall more than seventy years later for Georgia to free itself once more from Russia's shackles, dropping the 'Democratic Republic' from its name in the process.

However, in 2008, following months of tensions between Georgia and its larger neighbour, war broke out and Russian tanks powered through the streets of Gori. And given the history, you can forgive the locals for not sticking around to find out what was going to happen next. Wisely, they all left.

All of them, that is, except for the nuns. They told us as much when they took us in that evening. They had stayed at the nunnery when the Russians invaded and were unmolested during the occupation. Luckily for us, they were still welcoming visitors six years later.

Staying at a convent was something of a novelty. For one thing, we were given separate bedrooms and slept apart, something we had not done since leaving home. In fact, we were accommodated in different wings of the building and were only allowed to meet in an allocated neutral zone, where intersex mingling was permitted.

The particular quirks of the nunnery aside however, religious accommodation was something to which we soon became accustomed. A range of churches had already hosted us across Europe, including both the Russian and Greek Orthodox. Turkey's imams had given us rooms on several occasions, as Iran's would later do, and further into our trip, Buddhist monks would do the same.

Religion in the 21st century often gets a bad press. Undoubtedly, religious disputes must take a share of the blame for some of the world's problems, but meeting its representatives face to face on a bicycle reminded us of all the positive motivations behind religious organisations, which are often forgotten. Religions vary wildly in their doctrines but almost all involve elements of charity and kindness to strangers, things that are worth their weight in gold to the travelling cyclist. Most people at Friday prayers and Sunday mass have no more interest in extremism or sectarian violence than you or me, but they do know how to be kind to strangers and our journey was all the richer for that.

After sleeping in our separate beds, we joined the nuns for breakfast then continued on our way towards the Georgian capital of Tbilisi. The city gets its name from the Georgian word for warm: 'tbili'. It was anything but warm when we arrived, its famous Leghvtakhevi waterfall having frozen solid, but the name stems from the fact that the city sits on top of thermal springs. For more than a thousand years, Tbilisi has offered its visitors the opportunity to bath in naturally heated sulphuric pools, and that was one tourist attraction that we were quite happy to visit.

Tbilisi is also home to one of the world's largest religious buildings: the Holy Trinity Cathedral. At 101-metres high, its golden dome can be seen from right the way across the city. Interestingly, whereas most of the world's ornate churches are hundreds of years old, this one was only built in 2004. Its construction was planned to coincide with the Georgian Orthodox Church's 1,500th anniversary and 2,000 years since the birth of Jesus. Walking towards it along a huge expanse of polished marble, the scale and luxury of its design reminded me of the modern mosques of the Middle East.

After waiting in the capital for several days for the delivery of some replacement brake pads, we rode our final few miles out of Georgia and crossed the border into Armenia.

Chapter 14

*'Ahead: a huge black wall of snow-capped mountains. That'll be
Armenia then.' – Tim*

*'Frozen water bottles and frozen toes. Battled over a 2,000m pass
today. Bit of a struggle with a cold, sniffling all the way.' – Laura*

On first impressions, Armenia appeared to be Asia's answer to
Cornwall: a place whose roads are all on hills. The new brake pads
quickly earned their keep as we caught our breath on the downhills,
ready for the next short, sharp ascent.

Our route through Armenia took us close to the border with
Azerbaijan. It was a border that carried a lot of tension, as the two
countries are constantly at loggerheads. Large boulders strewn
across the landscape had been painted in the colours of each
country's flag to mark the territory: red, blue and orange on our side
of the valley, blue, red and green on the far side. We passed several
villages that had nothing left but the bombed out remains of
concrete buildings. The military presence was noticeable too, with
training camps at the side of the road and lots of men in uniform.
Mother Nature seemed unaware of the conflict however, and the
scenery was beautiful: steep sided valleys and rolling hills.

A Couch Surfing host had offered to let us stay the night and had
given us directions to her village. Upon arrival, a dozen school kids
ran up to us and started quizzing us in French.

'Bonjour! Ca va? Comment vous appelez-vous? D'où êtes-vous?'

We had no idea how or why a bunch of children in rural Armenia
were speaking French to us but we enjoyed the surreal scene and
Laura was only too happy to answer their questions.

We asked the kids if they knew where we could find our host,
whose name was Marianne.

'Professeur français!'

Evidently, the girl who had offered to host us was their French teacher. A chubby little boy stepped forward and offered to take us to her house. We followed him down the dirt tracks that constituted the village's roads, past the rows of high wooden fences that surrounded each house. He stopped outside the gate of one such building and, without warning, started screaming at the top of his voice. 'Marianne! Marianne! Marianne!'

When no answer came, he picked up a stone and threw it at the side of the house then carried on shouting.

'Hey!' came a cry from inside, at which point the kid ran away as fast as he could. A young girl walked out towards us, introduced herself as Marianne and showed us where we could leave our bikes.

Marianne was on a gap year after graduating from university. Instead of teaching English in China or staffing a youth hostel in Australia, she had chosen to work on an Armenian farm.

'It's hard work. I have to get up at 5am every day, when it's still dark. My first shift lasts six hours then I come back here for lunch. The second shift finishes at 8pm.'

It must have been a lonely existence. Although she was learning Armenian and had been teaching the local children rudimentary French, there was no one who spoke the same language as her. No other gap year students had opted to do what she was doing either, so she was going through the experience alone. She seemed to be enjoying it though, and went out of her way to make us feel welcome.

By the time we woke the following morning, Marianne was several hours into her shift, as she had said she would be. We left her a thank you note and headed back into the cold, to make our way towards Yerevan, Armenia's capital. After Yerevan would come Iran. Getting a visa for Iran had been harder work than it should have been. Iran's diplomatic relations with western countries are variable at the best of times and the visa system was undergoing one of its periodic spasms at just the time we wanted to visit. The rules were changing such that British citizens could only enter the country with a chaperone i.e. someone appointed by the government. We were keen to avoid this restriction so we had been in contact with a range of different travel agencies by email and had eventually found one that was willing to process our application without the need for a chaperone.

An additional complication was that tourists were not allowed to enter Iran on bicycles. In this matter, we opted to be slightly economical with the truth. We never explicitly denied that we intended to cycle across the country but we never volunteered the information either. We submitted our application without mentioning anything about bikes, and to our surprise, the visa was granted.

Despite the hassle with that particular visa, it is worth noting that, during our entire trip, we only had to arrange two visas in advance: Iran and India. For every other country, we just turned up at the border and paid some cash, or were simply given a stamp at the Queen's request, as set out in our passports.

Although we had obtained a visa for Iran, we still had to get across the border, which might be difficult if we were not supposed to enter the country with bikes. We decided that our best option was to book a bus across the border and hide our bikes in with the luggage. And, shortly after arriving in Yerevan, we did just that.

Although we had never planned to take a bus for part of our journey across Armenia, part of me was relieved to do so. I had found the mental strain of travelling through winter difficult: constantly fighting against the cold, always having to be vigilant with keeping hands and feet warm, forever racing against darkness because the days were so short, and spending more time indoors entertaining hosts than outside riding our bikes. The thought of yet more hard graft, cycling through the Armenian mountains, brought flashes of the mental state that I had been in before we left home.

For years, I had railed against the ease of modern life, craving adventure and hardship instead, but when faced with the realities of those things, I was struggling to cope with the stress. It was draining and I was starting to get overwhelmed by the idea of several more months of it. This made a mental battle play repeatedly in my head: I was tired from the months of hardship and felt like I needed a break, but I did not want to admit that to myself, because I was supposed to enjoy the hardship. I believed that admitting I wanted a break would be admitting defeat. In that sense, the requirement that we cross the Iranian border by bus was a convenient excuse: it forced us to rest without me having to admit that was what I actually wanted.

Besides the bus giving us a couple of days' rest, it also changed our perspective on the trip as a whole. Until that point, with the exception of the ferry to France, we had cycled every mile since leaving the UK. That bus would be the first time we had skipped any distance.

On the day of our departure from Yerevan, we woke early and rode down to the bus station, taking care not to skid on the ice that covered many of the roads at that time in the morning. We put our bikes and panniers into the luggage compartment underneath the bus then climbed aboard. As we took our seats near the back, Laura reminded me of a conversation we had had whilst slogging our way up a big hill in Greece, several months before. We had been climbing for 20 minutes already, with no sign of the summit, when a truck overtook us.

'If that truck offered you a lift to the top of this hill, would you take it?' she asked.

We had set no rules for our trip and it did not even take me a second to process my answer.

'No,' I said.

'Why not?'

'Well, why? If I accept a lift to the top of the hill then what was the point of cycling up the first half of the hill?' I replied. 'In fact, why bother cycling to the foot of the mountain in the first place if I could have just got in a truck? What purpose would remain for a cycling trip if I didn't need to cycle?'

I think Laura took a similar view to me – that we should be cycling, not taking transport – but perhaps for different reasons. She liked the image of a line drawn across the globe. A neat, uninterrupted trail that traced the route we had cycled, not a series of dashes interspersed with a footnote saying 'Flew from X to Y'.

On that matter, we were in agreement: no planes, trains or automobiles. Just the bikes. Not that it mattered, of course, because the Greek truck driver was long gone by the time we reached our conclusion. When we arrived in Yerevan however, and discovered that we needed to take a bus if we wanted to ensure safe entry to Iran, it changed the rules. We had already accepted that we would fly across large bodies of water and now we decided that we were happy to accept transport if the alternative was missing an interesting country or drastically changing our route. This was our journey and we would make the rules.

After spending half a day dozing on the bus, the driver announced that we were approaching the Iranian border. It was early evening and pitch-black outside. Our bikes were still buried behind luggage in the compartment beneath the bus. We parked outside the checkpoint and were instructed to get off the bus and join a queue for immigration. As we stood in a brightly lit terminal with our passports and visa stamps, we were happy that we had made the right decision: there was no point trying to cycle across the border and risk getting rejected. This was the safest option and would guarantee that we made it into Iran, without anyone at the border knowing that we would be cycling. Just as we reached the front of the queue however, I heard a shout from behind:

'Sir! Madam! Your bikes!'

It was the bus driver. He was jogging towards us with a smile on his face. With each of his hands, he was wheeling one of our bikes.

He stopped next to us, right in front of the immigration officers, and caught his breath.

'You forgot your bikes,' he said grinning. 'So I brought them to you.'

'Yes you did,' Laura replied through gritted teeth. 'Thanks.'

So much for smuggling them across the border without anyone noticing. We pushed them up to the immigration desk and nervously handed over our passports.

The immigration officers didn't bat an eyelid. In fact, they were delighted to have a couple of Brits to talk to on an otherwise quiet evening. They struggled to type our names using the Roman alphabet so they got us to come into their booth, sit at their computers and fill in the details ourselves. We could have typed anything we wanted; they never checked. Perhaps the warnings from the travel agencies had been unfounded or this particular immigration checkpoint had not got the memo. Either way, there were no questions about our bicycles other than 'Where have you cycled from?' and 'Doesn't your bum hurt?'

We wheeled our bikes to the exit and loaded them back onto the bus. It would drop us at Tabriz, the first town across the border, and we would cycle from there. We climbed the steps again and went back to our seats.

Chapter 15

'Two pouches in the kitchen pannier: one condensed milk, one mayonnaise. One should have gone in the tea this morning and one should not.' – Tim

'Many people we meet are kind enough to give us gifts for our journey. Today's was the oddest so far: leopard print lacy knickers.' – Laura

We arrived at Tabriz. The bus drew to a halt in a dirt-floored car park, and the rest of the passengers retrieved their suitcases and disappeared into the night. Once the bus had departed, we were left in total darkness, two cyclists on the wrong side of the Iranian border. Laur;a shrugged, swung her leg over her bike, and began cycling.

I will admit to being a little nervous. It was the middle of the night, the streets were deserted and we had only just arrived in an unfamiliar country. We had arranged to stay with a local Warm Showers host but we did not know where he lived. All we had was a brief description of his house and the road it was on.

We pedalled aimlessly down empty streets in the city centre with only the occasional loner still lurking on a corner at that late hour. Passing a central square, I noticed a car ease out of a darkened alley behind us. We continued along a high street with four lanes of empty road and rows of closed shops on either side. The car followed slowly in our wake. We turned down a side street on a whim, perhaps subconsciously trying to get away from the car, but it too turned. We took another turn and it followed again. We eventually emerged back on the same high street we were on before, and the car was still behind us. It inched towards us and edged closer to my back wheel.

The experiences of five months on the road should have taught me that 'stranger danger' is something of a fiction but this felt different. We were in the Islamic Republic of Iran: harbourer of terrorists, enemy of the West, Axis of Evil, developer of nuclear weapons, home of the crazed ayatollahs. This was a place to tread carefully.

I knew that the media portrayal of Iran did not give the complete picture and that a country cannot be judged by its government alone. I also knew friends who had been there before and who had told me how great it was. As such, I was confident that the people on the streets would be no more interested in atom bombs than I was and that I was no more likely to meet a terrorist there than I was in Cambridge.

But with a darkened car tracking me down the empty streets of Tabriz at 3am, I wasn't thinking about any of that. All I could think about was Ben Affleck. Much of my knowledge of Iran was derived from the film Argo. In summary, it is a movie in which Ben Affleck has to rescue a bunch of skinny white guys with beards from a mob of angry Iranians. It may not have been the most historically accurate film ever made but I could not help but notice that I was a skinny white guy with a beard. Was I about to be mobbed?

The car pulled up alongside me. I stared straight ahead and pretended it was not there. The window wound down. I looked ahead at Laura and gritted my teeth. A face appeared inches from mine. I tensed. 'Hello!' cried the driver. 'Welcome to my country! Welcome to Iran! I am Hamid. This is my wife,' he continued, gesturing to a small waving figure in the passenger seat, 'and this is my son.'

A small boy beamed at me from the back of the car. 'Please, you must come to our house for tea!'

'It's three in the morning, mate!' I wanted to say back. 'Why are you roaming the streets with your family inviting grubby looking strangers on bikes to come round to your house for a cup of tea?'

Instead, I smiled with relief. It appeared that our friends were right. Iran was a friendly place after all.

'Stuff Khameni! Stuff religion!' Sam announced, before necking a shot of vodka at the breakfast table.

We had declined the invitation for a late night cup of tea with Hamid and his family, generous though it was, and eventually found the house of the host with whom we had originally arranged to stay. Sam was a university student. He explained that, technically, Iranians are not supposed to host foreigners in their homes although it happens all the time. He had been warned by the police on two prior occasions so now had to be a little secretive in his arrangements. This is why he had told us that his name was Sam and had not given us his address before we arrived. Judging from his drinking habits, accommodating tourists was not the only rule he was willing to break.

'You want some?'

He offered us the bottle. We declined and stuck with the fresh bread he had picked up from the local bakery and a small pot of jam.

Given the country's reputation, it is easy to assume that everyone who lives in Iran is deeply religious. It is certainly a more religious place than the UK (though perhaps not much more so than America), but as our shot-slamming breakfast companion was demonstrating, not all Iranians are the same and not all of them are enthusiastic about religion.

Sam's view was that religion caused more trouble than it was worth. He did not have a lot of time for all the rules and regulations it created. Why could he not watch an American TV channel? Why was he not supposed to host foreign tourists? What was so bad about holding someone else's hand in public?

A girl came in the back door, plonked herself down on the bench opposite, and huffed and puffed as she unwrapped the layers of her headscarf, muttering 'Stupid thing,' under her breath.

'I just got stopped by the police,' she said, stopping her disrobing for a moment. 'Do you know what for? Riding a bike.'

Iran used to be a liberal place. From 1953 until 1979, society in Iran was modern and westernised. Women could dress as they wanted, sexes mixed together freely and people could largely say or do what they liked. In contrast to today, the country was closely allied with the US, enjoying friendly relations and absorbing many of its cultural influences. Men wore suits and flares, women wore skirts, rock and roll music was big, and there was even a dance routine called the 'Tehran twist'.

That period was short lived, however. It had only started when the US and the UK instigated a coup in 1953. In doing so, they overthrew a democratically elected prime minister and replaced him with an autocratic monarch: Mohamed Reza, known as the Shah of Iran. He was popular at first, overseeing a period of economic growth, modernising the country and granting women's suffrage, but he was also seen as extravagant, corrupt and brutal. Over time, people grew to resent the perceived influence of foreign powers and what they felt was enforced secularisation. A campaign of civil resistance was started and it eventually led to a popular revolution. Mohamed Reza fled the country and, into the void, stepped Ayatollah Khomeini.

Khomeini was a cleric who had been in exile for the past 15 years due to his vocal opposition to Reza's westernisation of Iran. When Reza left, Khomeini was invited to return. A referendum followed, turning Iran into an Islamic Republic and crowning Khomeini as Supreme Leader. In the years that followed, universities were closed and books proscribed. Women were encouraged away from the workplace and restricted in their access to education, and the veil was mandated once more.

Khomeini died a long time ago but his legacy remains pervasive, most visibly in the huge posters of his face that plaster every town. Ayatollah Khomeini's successor, the confusingly named Ayatollah Khamenei, has maintained most of the country's stricter rules. They include widespread censorship of most forms of media (out of 179 countries, Iran currently ranks 175th for free speech and a free press) and particularly restrictive rules for women (such as the requirement to cover everything but their face in public, not being able to leave the country without their husband's permission and, oddly, a ban on entering sports stadiums). And, apparently, they were not allowed to ride bikes.

'That is ridiculous,' said Sam. 'Why the hell shouldn't you ride a bike?'

'I just wheeled it out of sight then cycled the rest of the way here,' continued the girl who, by this point, had let down her long brown hair. 'I was scared but I was angry too.'

For better or for worse, there was no such rule against foreign women riding bikes. The other anti-women rules were slightly less stringent for tourists too but there was still strict guidance on what Laura should wear. She was not allowed to expose any flesh besides her hands and face, had to wear a loose top that was long enough to cover her down to mid-thigh (in addition to trousers) and needed to cover her head with a scarf at all times.

For us, these were minor inconveniences. For our hosts however, they were pervasive restrictions on their everyday lives.

'You sure you don't want a drink?' asked Sam, having poured one for his friend.

'Nah, we better get going,' replied Laura.

We left them discreetly holding hands in the doorway of Sam's house and pushed our bikes out onto the street. At that very moment, a cyclist appeared around the corner. He had a long beard, big panniers and the kind of crusty dishevelment that indicated he, like us, had cycled a long way.

It turned out he had cycled to Iran from Spain and, like us, had arranged to stay with Sam. We engaged in some typical, cycle tourist small talk – like which countries had the best roads and worst drivers, the relative merits of Turkey's discount supermarkets, what the Iranian word for 'bread' was and whether southern Pakistan was safe for cyclists – before we prepared to set off again. Meetings with other cyclists were rare and it seemed a shame to separate so quickly. I suggested that we exchange email addresses to see if we could meet up further down the road.

'Have you got a pen?' he asked.

'Actually, let me give you a card.' I dug one out of my handlebar bag and handed it over. He took one look at it and his face fell.

'Oh, no,' he replied and smacked his forehead, looking forlorn. 'I'm so sorry!'

Laura and I exchanged a confused glance. Had we made some sort of faux pas? Unclear what had caused such consternation, we watched the cyclist rummage through his own handlebar bag and, to our complete bewilderment, pull out one of our business cards. How on earth had a Spanish cyclist in Iran got a card with our contact details on?

'Istanbul. The Best Western,' he said, as the penny began to drop. 'You left this on my bike. I kept meaning to email you but I never got the chance and then, well, it just seemed too late.'

We marvelled at the coincidence. We were a thousand miles from Istanbul. We had been cycling for more than two months since then and passed through three different countries. But the three of us had wound up at exactly the same spot at the same time. Apparently, it is a small world when you are cycling it.

'This time, I'll email you,' he shouted after us as we pedalled away.

He never did.

Chapter 16

'Iran. Home of competitive hospitality.' – Laura

'This morning's send off from our Iranian host family was as big an event as the day we left home!' – Tim

We followed a quiet road out of Tabriz and made our way up a huge valley. While ascending it, we were treated to some of the best scenery of our journey to date: snow covered mountains on either side giving way to gravel plains below. The mountains were larger and more spread out so the scale felt bigger than it had in Armenia. We could also see a long way between and beyond the mountains, giving a greater sense of space.

In contrast to Turkey, where we had spent most of the winter, Iran felt wilder and more remote. Because we had largely followed the Black Sea coast through Turkey – a major thoroughfare between Europe and Asia – it was well-developed, with regular shops, settlements and freight traffic. There is no such concentration of activity in Iran. That is partly due to its geography and partly due to politics, with international sanctions drastically reducing trade activity.

The net result of all of this was that Iran immediately felt very different from the previous countries through which we had cycled that winter. When we booked the bus out of Yerevan, I had hoped to escape winter. That had not happened but the change of scenery seemed to relieve me of a feeling of claustrophobia that, unbeknownst to me at the time, had dogged me from Turkey to Armenia. My head felt clear and I was excited by the prospect of exploring a new and fascinating country.

Towards the end of our first day's riding in Iran, we knocked on the door of the only building we could find outside Bostanabad and were welcomed into a small family-run office. We were invited to sit by the fire whilst three brothers finished their day's work at their desks. They glanced up occasionally to exchange a chuckle with us at the incongruity of the situation: them carrying on their normal lives, typing away at their computers, whilst two strangers in smelly clothes huddled around a fire in the corner of their office.

When their work was finished, we were shown to a room at the back of the building where we could stay. Soon afterwards, one of the brothers knocked on the door and presented us with a huge bag filled with steaming curries, rice and fresh bread from a local restaurant. Well sated, we climbed into our sleeping bags, glad to have escaped the cold, and already confident that Iran would be good to us.

We woke to glorious blue skies, which would have made for perfect cycling weather if not for the fact that it was absolutely freezing and there was a ferocious headwind. That was one day on which Laura had no objection to the requirement for women to cover up. Indeed, I pulled my hat down to my eyebrows and a scarf over my nose to create a sort of voluntary burka of my own. Wrapped up in thick jackets and big mittens, we got our heads down and battled the wind. Adding to the difficulty of cycling into a headwind was the terrible condition of the roads.

Along with the open landscape, another big difference in Iran was how poor it felt. Turkey, our primary host for the winter, was a country on the rise with a booming economy. In contrast, Iran was crippled by international sanctions. There were no large, brightly lit supermarkets, just small, dilapidated, local shops. The cars were old and rusty, clinging onto life because sanctions stop spare parts and newer models from reaching the country. For us, that often meant inhaling noxious fumes whenever we were in a city, and as noted on that windy morning, road surfaces were often poor; little more than a dusty patchwork of potholes.

The sanctions have hit Iran in other ways too. It was one of the few countries we visited in which internet cafes still proliferated, the rest of the world having moved on to wifi. It is also entirely cut off from international banking networks, which meant we could neither pay for anything with a credit card nor withdraw money from an ATM. Instead, we had to carry a large wad of US dollars into the country and change it into local rial. We also noticed how rarely we saw any familiar brands in the shops or on the clothes people wore.

The absence of cash machines and designer trainers was, however, of little concern as we battled into the headwind. When it reached a particular crescendo, we climbed underneath a bridge and sought refuge from the onslaught behind its walls. The bridge spanned a dry, stony riverbed, with a view across a dusty plateau towards distant, snow-capped mountains. We hunkered down to shelter from the maelstrom and shared some dry bread, cream cheese and an Iranian staple, carrot jam, before venturing back onto the road.

A week or so later, riding along a quiet and potholed road, the silence was interrupted when a small truck caught up with us from behind and screeched to a halt at the side of the road. The driver jumped out, ran towards us and shouted 'Are you Olly and George?'

It was hard to know how to respond. Apparently, the driver, Hadi, had bumped into two foreign cyclists here five years ago. He had bought them a cup of tea and spent a few hours hearing about their journey. Seeing us pedalling fully loaded bikes all these years later, he got excited thinking that he might have bumped into his old friends. Quite why the same two cyclists would still be in the country after five years is unclear. However, I suppose that while long distance cycling seems quite common to me, I could understand some people not imagining that more than two people would ever do such a thing. Having later seen a photo of the very hairy Olly and George, it still does not quite explain why he was asking Laura if she used to be a man with a beard.

Hadi gave us his phone number and told us to call him when we reached his home town of Qom, a few hours' ride away. We did so and he came out to meet us and walked us back to his house. Compared to most of the people we stayed with in Iran, Hadi's family were comparatively wealthy. They lived in a nice, modern home with a big TV. They were incredibly generous too. Like every other house we visited in Iran, we were greeted with a plate of sunflower seeds and fresh fruit. Hadi's family also prepared several delicious meals for us during our stay, including the pomegranate and walnut stew known as 'fesenjan' and plenty of Persian 'tahdig' rice, all crispy at the bottom. They even put on a big spread at breakfast: fresh 'sangak' bread, baked on a bed of small stones, served with carrot jam and cream.

Qom is home to a sacred shrine and is thus considered one of the most holy cities in Iran. That is quite a big deal for a country that takes its religion so seriously. As an Islamic Republic, although Iran holds parliamentary elections, the government is overseen by its Supreme Leader, Ayatollah Khamenei. That means the highest ranking politician in Iran – Khamenei – is a religious figure. It is the equivalent of the Archbishop of Canterbury being able to overrule the British Prime Minister or the Pope doing the same in Italy. As such, religion plays a big part in the daily lives of Iranians.

We had read that the shrine was not normally open to non-Muslim tourists, but Hadi said he could get us in because his brother was in the Revolutionary Guard, the elite military force charged with defending the Islamic system of Iran. The guards have a fierce reputation, but his brother seemed perfectly friendly when he joined us for dinner one evening and said that he only joined the Revolutionary Guard as it was a good job that would pay the bills.

Hadi drove us to the shrine where we joined a throng of people gathered outside the building, taking photos and queuing to get in. Amongst the crowd were several imams, easily identified in their long, brown robes and white turbans. The shrine itself was part of a huge, ornate mosque. It had marble floors, elaborate water fountains, towering minarets and a giant gold dome. To enter, Laura had to wear an extra veil, covering her from head to toe and leaving just her eyes visible. Hadi's sister took Laura into one entrance while Hadi and I used the door reserved for men.

Inside, the shrine was heaving. Masses of people moved around the graves of the various clerics, prime ministers and members of the royal family buried there. When visible between the feet of the crowd, the floor was an intricate mosaic of tiles. The many tombs were covered in gold paint and brightly coloured jewels, and the walls were hung with paintings of religious figures.

It was a confusing place to navigate but spotting the main tomb was not hard. The size of a small room, its bright gold walls rose above head height and it was surrounded by a large crowd. Worshipper performed ritualistic circumambulations, walking laps of the tomb as part of their pilgrimage. Others clung to the side of it, reciting prayers or simply weeping. I had never seen anything like that level of religious fervour before, but this was one of the holiest shrines in Shia Islam.

Although almost 90% of the world's Muslims belong to the Sunni branch of Islam, Iran is a Shia country. Other religions are represented in Iran – notably Christianity, Judaism and Zoroastrianism – but Islam is the official religion and at least nine out of ten Iranians identify as Shia.

Islam split into its two schools, Sunni and Shia, over a thousand years ago following the death of the Prophet Muhammad. They may have had a long time to get used to each other, but as with Catholics and Protestants, western democracies and communist states, the differences between the two groups still cause conflicts in the modern world. The bloody eight-year Iran-Iraq war that claimed a million lives in the 1980s was partly fuelled by Sunni Saddam Hussein's fear of his neighbour's newly found Shi'ism following the Iranian revolution. The current civil war in Syria has largely devolved into a battle between the ruling Shia government (with support from Iranian 'Shia militias') and the majority Sunni population. Shia Iran is also fighting an ongoing proxy war with Sunni Saudi Arabia, most recently in Yemen.

I thought about all of this after becoming separated from Hadi inside the shrine, and I considered myself lucky to not be caught up in any such complicated religious issues. Looking around for my host, I spotted a bearded a man walking towards me. He looked me up and down then asked if I was Muslim. I hesitated, unsure of the etiquette, and then muttered an apologetic 'no'. In my pontification about the conflict between Sunni and Shia Islam, I had forgotten that Islam and Christianity have not always lived in harmony through the years.

He pointed at me and shouted: 'Infidel!'

Heads turned and I froze on the spot. Before I could work out what to do, a younger man quickly appeared at his side, slapped the angry guy on the back and said: 'Sorry, my brother does that to all the tourists,' before they both collapsed in laughter.

Back at Hadi's house that evening, I asked him about a picture of the Prophet Muhammed that we had seen hanging in the shrine.

'A picture? No, no, no,' he chuckled. 'The Prophet lived many years ago, long before there were cameras or mobile phones. There are no photographs of him.'

'Yes,' I replied, 'I know that. It was a painting. I was just under the impression that it was forbidden to depict the Prophet, but now I'm wondering if that's a rule in Sunni Islam rather than Shia?'

'No, really. It was many hundreds of years ago. Nobody has taken a photo of the Prophet Muhammed. There were no cameras back then.'

He gave me a patronising smile before turning to the rest of his family to share our presumed stupidity in whispered Farsi, barely concealing his mirth.

He must have thought we were really stupid. You can insert your own jokes, but this was a surprisingly common assumption by people we met while travelling. I think it resulted from a combination of our inability to speak the local language and the fact that we were often unfamiliar with local customs. Time and again, people would extrapolate from our unfamiliarity with a country and its language, and conclude that we were a bit thick.

Some months earlier, a host on the Black Sea coast had been educating us on the various foodstuffs of Turkey when Laura asked him about a particular green drink she kept seeing in the shops.

'That sounds like shampoo,' he said, as if we needed a full comprehension of the Turkish language to differentiate between fizzy drinks and hair care products.

'No, it's a drink. It's in the fridge next to the Coke and Fanta. I just wondered what it was, that's all.'

'You have seen shampoo. There is no drink like this in Turkey.'

Similarly, several hosts felt that it was necessary to teach us how to drink hot beverages. We would raise a cup of tea to our lips ready to sip but be stopped before making contact and told that it was too hot and that we would burn ourselves. The host would then wait for several minutes to pass before telling us when it was safe to drink.

I think the British tradition of repeating English sentences to foreigners, loudly and slowly, stems from the same implicit assumption that if someone does not speak your language then they are probably not that bright. It should have been funny, and often was, but it was also frustrating. We knew that people thought we were being stupid but we were not smart enough to prove them wrong in their language.

Hadi's family recovered from laughing at the idea of the Prophet Muhammed having indulged in selfies, and served us a final breakfast before we got back on the road.

As we prepared our bikes for departure, Hadi approached Laura and said: 'It is a very busy road out of the city. I can ride your bike for you. It will be safer. My brother will drive you in his car and we'll meet outside of town.'

It was nice for our host to think about our safety, and kind that he and his brother were willing to give up their time to ensure it, but how did he think that we had tackled every other busy road between England and Iran? Had he not already witnessed us navigate the exact same city to reach his house? Was there some reason that Laura would be more susceptible to traffic incidents than me?

The idea that it would be safer for a less experienced male cyclist to ride Laura's bike through a city was farcical but such treatment was common across many countries we visited. Men looked at me during conversations (even when Laura was doing the talking) and people routinely assumed that Laura did not know anything about bikes.

Laura bit her tongue and politely declined the offer. We thanked Hadi and his family profusely for their kindness. We then did our best to resist the masses of food that they tried to thrust into our hands, but following their insistence, we still came away with a large tin of pineapple and several cans of high-caffeine energy drinks. Panniers bulging, we set off out of Qom, me riding my bike and Laura riding hers.

Chapter 17

'Two apples, Two bananas, some sweets, hot tea, bag of dried fruit, two cakes, chocolate milk, and two more oranges. One day's roadside gifts.' – Tim

'Watched Laurel & Hardy this evening with our hosts. A little bit of Lancashire in rural Iran, they loved it.' – Laura

Leaving Qom, snow began to fall, coming down in huge flakes. When we reached a small town that evening, several locals shouted 'Hello!', 'Welcome to my country!' and 'I love you!', as we cycled past. We stopped at a tiny bakery where 'lavash' was being made. Iran has several types of unique bread, of which lavash is one. It is a very thin flatbread, made in huge rectangles that can be wrapped around sandwich ingredients or folded flat for easy storage. It has a remarkable shelf life but unless eaten fresh it is as dry as a bone.

We stood in front of the counter for several minutes admiring the production process before the owner greeted us. We got talking – by which I mean we mimed a lot, showed him our magic letter and occasionally typed things into Google Translate – and eventually asked if there was somewhere we could sleep. There was, he said, and led us to an abandoned shop next door. It comprised a small, empty room with floor to ceiling windows onto the high street. It was sparse and piled with junk but infinitely preferable to the horizontal snow outside. We wheeled our bikes inside, rolled out our camping kit and fired up our stove.

The town in which we had stopped was small, but once night fell, we drew quite a crowd. The spectacle of two Westerners holed up in an empty shop, cooking noodles on a camping stove from the comfort of their sleeping bags was probably a fairly odd sight. Thankfully, the baker came back and strung up a curtain so that we could get some privacy. Whilst doing so, he noticed that we were reading our books by headtorch so disappeared and came back with a light bulb. He slipped on a pair of rubber marigold gloves, grabbed two wires coming out of the wall with a pair of pliers and attached them to the bulb. Sparks flew and he jumped back in shock but, sure enough, the light bulb illuminated. The baker grinned, pleased with himself, and left us to read. We had no intention of attempting to detach the wires ourselves so slept with the light on all night.

The baker woke us with fresh lavash, half of which we ate for breakfast and the rest we folded into our panniers. The overnight snow had not settled on the ground and the roads were clear but the morning was colder than previous days. We delayed our departure by wheeling our bikes through the local *souk* market. A carpet salesman there tried to convince us that we could strap a full size Persian rug to the back of our bikes, but we resisted the temptation of souvenir shopping and instead shared some tea with him. The temperature was only marginally warmer, when after an hour's delay, we pedalled out of the village towards the mountains that lay ahead.

We soon began climbing into mountains. A little more snow fell and the frozen particles scattered across the tarmac, swirling in the wind and around our bikes. As we climbed higher, getting further and further from civilisation, the temperature plummeted and the water in our bottles froze solid. We could see the plains below us, now distant and calm, a reminder of how far we had cycled and how far we were from the nearest town. We stopped to check the map and realised that the next settlement was much further than we could manage before dark.

Turning a corner with dusty snow spinning up from the ground around me, I was surprised to see a petrol station in the distance. We had everything we needed to survive a night in the wild, but when it was that cold, shelter and running water were always welcome. We pushed our bikes up to the shop, where three sets of eyes widened at the sight of us appearing out of the gloom on our bikes. We were desperately cold as well as hungry and thirsty. It had been a long day of riding and, although we carried both food and water, stopping to eat or drink in those temperatures had not been appealing. Wonderful, hot, sweet tea was brought to us immediately and then we were left alone in a back office while one of the garage attendants spoke into a radio. Warmed slightly, we were directed back outside and pointed towards a large building across the road. No explanation was given – we shared no common language – but Laura and I had learned to just accept situations like this and go with the flow. We climbed some steps to an anonymous door and knocked. It was opened by a man in bright red overalls who had clearly been expecting us

'Salaam,' he said. Hello.

'Salaam,' Laura replied.

We were led into a surprisingly modern building, which turned out to be the headquarters of the local Red Crescent, the Islamic equivalent of the Red Cross. Apparently, their job was to rescue cars and people who got stuck in the mountains and caught out by the snow. We were shown to a mess room where three uniformed young men were sitting on the floor, typing into their phones. Our arrival sparked their interest and we began a long conversation with them, communicating by passing a phone back and forth, typing translated messages. They peppered us with questions:

'What religion are you?'

'Where are your children?'

'What do you think of Ayatollah Khamenei?'

'What is England like?'

'What do you think of Ayatollah Khomeini?

'Why don't you have any children?'

'Who do you prefer: Khomeini or Khamenei?'

'Will you have children soon?'

After a lull in conversation, I was handed a screen on which the following words were displayed: 'Do you like table tennis?'

Downstairs in the basement was a full-size table-tennis table and tonight it was Iran versus the UK. They took it in turns to tag team us in doubles matches, but after a few games, I paused to let Laura play on her own. I took a step back and enjoyed taking in the scene. We were in deepest, darkest Iran, halfway up a mountain in a blizzard, tucked inside the overheated basement of a branch of the Red Crescent rescue team and we were playing ping-pong. At that particular moment, my wife, dressed in a long brown robe and wearing a headscarf, was shouting 'You're going down, Iran!', to a large group of young men dressed in red overalls who were cheering on their teammate as he aced a serve past her. I stepped back into the fray and we did our best, but we were outclassed that night and no match for the Iranian Ping Pong squad. We lost, five games to two.

After a warm and cosy night inside the Red Crescent facility, we woke to find that the snow had stopped and the sun was out. We continued our progress through the mountains, emerging onto a wide gravel plain with the dark silhouettes of distant peaks on either flank. The road we had been following was largely deserted, but that afternoon I became aware of a vehicle behind us. I turned to discover it was a police car. The man in the passenger seat gestured for us to pull over. Two officers opened their doors simultaneously and walked towards us.

'Where are you from?' one of them asked.

'England.'

'Where in England?'

'Bolton,' replied Laura, 'near Manchester.'

'United or City?'

'Er, United.'

'Manchester United! Oh, I love Manchester United!'

Neither of us knowing the first thing about football, we proceeded to blurt out the names of random football players from the Euro '96 squad in the hope that one of them played for Man United and was recognisable to an Iranian policeman. It didn't really matter what we said, though. The fact was that we were from England, near Manchester. As far as they were concerned, we were in the first eleven. They were over the moon, peppering us with questions and asking us to pose for selfies on their phones. Suddenly, though, the driver became very serious.

'Alex Ferguson,' he said gravely and looked Laura dead in the eyes. 'Alex Ferguson,' he repeated, this tall, serious man in his policeman's uniform. 'Alex Ferguson, I find her *very* attractive.'

And with that, they left. As we had stopped already, we took the opportunity to have some lunch and wheeled our bikes over the stony ground to sit down in the sunshine. Half way through stuffing our faces with some of the lavash from the bakery of two days ago, the police car re-appeared at the side of the road. The Alex Ferguson fan club emerged and sheepishly shuffled back towards us and asked to see our passports. In the excitement, they had entirely forgotten the reason they had been told to stop us in the first place.

Shortly after lunch, we set up a tripod at the side of the road to take a photograph of the two of us cycling past. Photos with both of us in were few and far between, and with such picturesque surroundings, we thought we should make the effort. Amusingly, just minutes later, we cycled past a huge sign saying 'No Photography'. It seemed like an odd sign to erect in the middle of a deserted mountain plateau.

Later in the afternoon, another police car stopped us and went through a similar routine to the earlier one: some cursory checks of our passports followed by a series of questions about the Premier League. After our third questioning by police, we began to wonder what was going on. Had word spread that members of the English football team were riding through town? Or had they finally caught onto the fact that our visas did not cover us for cycling?

Pedalling onwards none the wiser, some unusually shaped buildings started to appear on the horizon: tall, thin structures with large, black objects jutting out of the top. As we got closer, they slowly became recognisable from the computer games of my youth. For reasons that were yet to become clear, we were surrounded by a large bank of surface to air missiles.

A little unnerved, we stopped to look at the map to work out where we were and discovered that we were near a place called Natanz. The name rang a bell in the back of my head, which, when I saw the little picture next to its name on the map, began to ring a bit louder. The picture was the distinctive black and yellow circle of a nuclear sign.

Without realising, we were cycling past one of Iran's largest and most controversial nuclear enrichment sites. The International Atomic Energy Agency estimates that the site contains no less than 7,000 centrifuges capable of enriching uranium for use in nuclear weapons. To keep it safe from the many world powers that would rather Iran was not developing its nuclear abilities, the facility was originally built eight metres beneath the earth. Above ground, the bunker was further protected from prying eyes and probing planes with an additional three metres of concrete wall. In 2004, however, the authorities decided that still was not quite enough to keep it safe so they buried the whole thing under another 22 metres of soil. Add to that the impressive arsenal of anti-air defences that were on ostentatious display for miles around and you should have a reasonably secure research base. Except, of course, that two hapless British cyclists appeared to have inadvertently cycled through the middle of it, posing for photos with the local police.

I would be lying if I said that I knew all of those facts at the time, but I knew enough to make me a little nervous. In many ways, until that point, we had felt safer in Iran than anywhere else in the world. Almost every person we met had treated us like long lost relatives, and we practically had to fend off invitations for tea and accommodation. Even the police were friendly. However, the nuclear signs and missile banks were starting to undermine my confidence, as was the appearance of a masked motorcyclist behind us.

Historically, Iran had always had a reputation for hospitality and kindness to travellers. Unfortunately, that message has become clouded by events such as the 1979 Iran hostage crisis and its inclusion by George Bush in his 'Axis of Evil'. As a result, we in the West now tend to associate the country more with terrorism than with hospitality. The Iranians that we met were acutely aware of this and did their utmost to demonstrate that they did not deserve the label. I lost count of the times that, after stuffing us with food and preparing a room for us, a host would ask us: 'What did you think of Iran before you came here?' followed by, 'And what do you think of Iran now?'

When we gave our invariably positive responses, they would immediately say: 'Please go home and tell your friends that Iran is a nice place.'

After a week or so in the country, we became so comfortable that we routinely left our bikes and bags unattended outside shops and cafes. We knew that if one bad apple made a grab for them, a dozen of his country folk would be so appalled at the idea of their nation's reputation for hospitality being tarnished that they would have our stuff back in seconds.

The evidence was clear: Iran was one of the friendliest places we visited. However, when you are in the middle of a hotly debated Iranian nuclear facility being tailed by a police bike and surrounded by rows of giant missile launchers, it can be hard to remember all of that.

The motorcyclist, dressed in black with an impenetrable visor covering his face, overtook us then motioned for us to follow him. He paused at a large gate in the side of a chain-link fence we had been following for some miles. Two military personnel with rifles slung over their shoulders opened it and we were led through, followed by two police vans, which had also appeared. The gate slammed shut behind us.

We found ourselves in a military compound. There were a range of low buildings, all fenced off with barbed wire, and a selection of military vehicles parked in neat rows on the gravel floor. Several armed men in military fatigues stood behind us, holding their weapons. We stayed put, clutching our bikes, and watched the helmeted motorcyclist disappear into a building. Moments later, another man in formal military dress walked towards us. He had the gait and hat of a man in authority.

'Your passports, please.'

We rummaged through our handlebar bags to extract from their waterproof pouches the passports that we always kept close at hand. The man nodded.

'United Kingdom?' he asked

'Yes,' we replied emphatically, as if our enthusiasm would underscore our innocence.

'Very good,' he said. 'Team?'

'I'm sorry?'

'Team. What football team?'

'Manchester. I'm from Manchester,' Laura blurted out with relief.

'Manchester United! David Beckham! Wayne Rooney!' he cried with enthusiasm. We should have known better than to worry. We may have been in an Iranian nuclear complex, but like so many people back home, these guys were much more interested in football than their jobs. We did our best to keep the conversation going, giving the impression that we were close personal friends of Sir Alex and ate, slept and breathed football.

The atmosphere had changed so quickly from one of tension to one of conviviality that we largely forgot we were surrounded by armed Iranians, locked inside a nuclear facility without a soul in the world who knew where we were. In fact, the interaction was going so well that we may have pushed our luck a little. It was getting dark and we were a long way from any towns so I caught Laura's eye and made a little gesture. She nodded in reply and I thought it was worth a try.

'Hey, nice chatting about the football and all. But it's getting kind of dark and it's an awfully long way into town. I don't suppose you'd mind if we put our tent up and stopped for the night would you?' I said, pointing at an empty patch of ground inside the compound.

The officer looked at me with complete bewilderment before replying slowly, enunciating his words as if speaking to a child: 'Sir, this is a military base. You cannot camp here.'

Slightly disappointed that the legendary Iranian hospitality had stopped short of allowing two bumbling Britons from pitching their tent within the confines of a top-secret nuclear enrichment facility, we shook some hands, posed for some photos and made off into the sunset.

The sunset was beautiful and provided a dark orange backdrop to the mountainous silhouette on our right, but, ultimately, it left us in darkness. There was plenty of open land on which to pitch a tent, but we were still within spitting distance of the military base and there was something unsettling about erecting a tent so close to all that uranium. We decided it would be safer to get to Natanz. Unfortunately, reaching Natanz meant heading deeper into the mountains and cycling through the night. While we debated our options, our pedals kept turning and we crept higher.

Situating the nuclear compound so far from civilisation had the pleasant side effect of keeping light pollution to a minimum. As we climbed further into the mountains, the sky filled with the white markings of the universe, which gave me a welcome distraction from my empty stomach and the worry of reaching safe haven. However, the loud rumbling of a large truck soon punctured the tranquillity when it appeared from behind. It overtook us then continued at a snail's pace, a few yards in front. We tried to wave the driver ahead but he maintained his speed and it appeared that we would have a guide through the mountains. It was frustrating at first, but curiously, the lorry began to provide us with some reassurance. We were not alone out there in the mountains.

We knuckled down, climbing higher as the air grew cooler with the fading memory of daylight. In the darkness, there was no way of telling how far we had come or how fast we were travelling. The noise from the truck's engine blocked out all thoughts and I focused solely on moving my legs. After an unknown period, the truck drew to a halt as we crested a final rise. Beneath us in the distance, were the unmistakable lights of a settlement. Our anonymous guide gave a wave from his window then drove off. We watched his tail lights disappear into the distance and allowed ourselves a smile of relief. We had made it. We gave our bikes one final push then let gravity do the rest.

Chapter 18

*'Yesterday I announced our arrival in the desert. This morning it
rained. Tomorrow snow is forecast.'* – Tim

*'Memorable birthday in Isfahan today, with parades to celebrate 35
years since the Islamic Revolution. Most popular sign:* Down with
USA.' – *Laura*

It was very late by the time we reached Natanz and few places showed
any sign of activity. We spotted an attendant outside a garage set
back from the road and rode across the dirt to get his attention. The
man was old and wizened, and wore grubby grey overalls. We greeted
him with a smile and a 'salaam' then handed him our magic letter,
but he just waved it away. It was not the first time that had happened
when we presented someone with the letter. We take literacy for
granted in the UK but it is not a universal fact. It is estimated that
one in ten men in Iran, and two in ten women, cannot read (in India,
where we found ourselves later on the trip, it is reckoned that fully
40% of the female population cannot read or write).

The garage attendant did not need a letter to explain the
situation. He motioned us towards a building with a light on and
pointed towards two beds at the back of the room. They were bare
and well-worn but they were beds and they were indoors. The only
food in our panniers was the stale lavash the baker had given us a
couple of days before. We shared it with the attendant, who produced
a few triangles of spreadable cheese in return.

The room reeked of diesel and the rusty metal beds made for
disturbed sleep, particularly when combined with the constant
interruption of trucks arriving. They came throughout the night and
the old man would rise slowly from his bed to fill their tanks. To this
day, the smell of diesel fumes takes me back to that dark room.

Waking groggily after a short and fitful night, we thanked the attendant and set off in search of breakfast. It was a cold and windy morning, and too early for any shops to be open, so we pressed on to the next town. With the roads deserted that morning, we both took the opportunity to distract ourselves from the hunger and cold by listening to an audiobook: Andrew Marr's 'A History of the World'.

We had started listening to podcasts and audiobooks a couple of months after leaving home. I would never have dreamed of using headphones while cycling back home, but we spent much of our time on quiet roads with minimal traffic. We found that a single earphone in the kerb-side ear, playing talk radio, generated little interference with road awareness.

The audiobooks were initially prompted by a craving for intellectual stimulation. Whilst life on bikes met many of our needs – being outside, getting exercise, meeting people and exploring the world – there was little to keep the mind active during long days in the saddle. Our interactions were all with strangers and usually conducted in broken English. As such, whilst we might talk about politics, religion and other big issues (like the English Premier League), we could only do so in the simplest terms.

Over time, it felt as though my brain was atrophying. Being able to listen to books during the long hours of cycling solved that problem. I also found that my capacity for tackling weightier tomes – like A History of the World – was much greater than it would be back home. I read more, and heavier, books in the year and a half that we were away than in any other comparable time before or since. In fact, we got through so many history books, economic texts and political podcasts while cycling that it almost felt like studying for a distance-learning course.

However, a highbrow audiobook was perhaps not the best thing to be listening to when cycling through an icy crosswind on an empty stomach. My hands and feet had gone numb and I was low on sugar so finding it difficult to concentrate. I watched Laura trying to shake some warmth into her hands as Andrew Marr prattled on about the Jacobite rebellion of 1745. She was obviously struggling to follow the history lesson too, because moments later I watched her tear the headphones from her ear shouting: 'Oh, piss off Andrew Marr!'

'My feet are freezing,' she said through tears when I caught up with her. 'They're killing me.'

Mercifully, a settlement had come into view ahead. There were the now usual cries of 'Welcome to Iran!' from everyone we rode through town, and we stopped at the first cafe we saw. As we waited for our coffees and eggs to arrive, Laura took her boots off to rub some life back into her feet. Seeing this, the owner brought out a lit camping stove and placed it on the floor for Laura to warm her feet.

While Laura's feet defrosted over an open flame, we discussed where we would head after Iran. Three countries lie on its eastern border: Turkmenistan, Afghanistan and Pakistan. With the aftermath of the 2001 invasion still playing out, Afghanistan was out of the question so our options were Pakistan to our east and Turkmenistan to our north.

Unsure of the safety of independent travel in southern Pakistan, we had done some research before leaving home. A friend, Emily Chappell, had recently cycled there and she told us about her experiences. She described a fascinating country where she had received remarkable hospitality, never once needing to use her tent at night. She also talked about passing burned-out buses at the side of the road and various reports of violence in the towns that she passed through. That was enough for us to make our decision. We would have loved to visit Pakistan but had decided before leaving home that it was well beyond our safety threshold. As it happened, shortly before we stopped in that cafe, a Spanish cyclist (not the one with our business card) had crossed the border from Iran into Pakistan and been attacked. He survived with a shrapnel wound but six police officers died in the incident.

With Afghanistan and Pakistan both ruled out on the grounds of safety, our only overland option was Turkmenistan. We had no safety concerns over Turkmenistan but going there would have other implications. Firstly, heading north into the mountains of Central Asia would mean a continuation of the winter conditions that we had already been enduring for three months. The northern route would also commit us to travelling through China, a country that we had both visited before and that we could not possibly cross in the 30 days allowed by a standard tourist visa. In contrast, had we been able to stay south (by travelling through Pakistan, for example), we would reach warmer climes and be able to visit India, somewhere that we were excited to explore.

When we planned our route across the globe from the comfort of our own home, it had been simple: Turkmenistan was the only option. However, since taking that bus in Armenia, our minds were open to other possibilities. We no longer felt constrained by the need to cycle every mile. The freedom allowed us to see an alternative that would have been heresy before we left home: we could take a boat to Dubai. From there, we could cycle to Oman, then hop across the Arabian Sea to India. In other words, we could still follow the southern route across India and into Southeast Asia, but we could bypass Pakistan. Plus, having previously lived in Oman, it would be a chance to catch up with old friends and have a few weeks of familiarity in a year of constant changes.

By the time we reached the decision, feeling had been restored to Laura's toes so she put her boots back on and we headed out into the morning light. We continued cycling to Isfahan, where we stopped in a hotel for a couple of nights to celebrate Laura's birthday, and then pointed our bikes south, towards the coast and a ferry to the United Arab Emirates. Armed with the knowledge that we were aiming for the sunny Arabian Peninsula, we cycled with a renewed enthusiasm, excited by what lay ahead.

Once we had escaped the horrendous traffic in Isfahan, we found ourselves once more riding through vast gravel plains that would go on for several days. At some point along that road, we noticed a car parked in a layby ahead of us. A couple emerged from the car and waved for us to stop. As we pulled into the layby, the woman ran up to Laura and handed her a baby. The dad then pulled a phone from his pocket and indicated, excitedly, that he wanted to take a photo. We duly obliged, the two of us in our thick, winter jackets, holding a tiny baby for an unexplained photo opportunity. The couple thanked us, took their baby back and drove off.

After spending the afternoon pedalling along a deserted road with Andrew Marr talking me through the Haitian Revolution, we stopped at the quiet town of Sistan to order a lunch of kebab and rice. We washed it down with hot tea, and Laura drank hers through a sugar cube nonchalantly held in her teeth, gaining a nod of approval from a man on the neighbouring table.

When sunset arrived several days later, we wheeled our bikes over an embankment and erected our tent. Laura trudged back across to the other side of the road to fill our water bladder from a pond she had seen on our way past. She had to break the ice on the surface but returned with enough water to see us through until morning. Still feeling chilly after a dinner of noodles, we climbed into the tent to warm up in our sleeping bags. We wrote our diaries and read our books then fell asleep to silence.

I woke to a solitary beam of sunlight, penetrating the morning haze and illuminating our tent. Inside, the tent was lined with the frozen breath of our sleep, which showered us whenever we moved. I brushed the ice from my sleeping bag and rummaged inside for the clothes I had kept warm overnight with the heat of my body. Laura rolled over in response and pulled her hood tighter against the cold of morning. I unzipped the tent door, put one foot after another into my frozen boots and stepped out into daylight.

It was a glorious morning. The sky was an electric blue, under which even the barren rocks and dried up scrubs looked beautiful. In preparation for the morning's cooking, I dropped a gas canister down my top to warm it and flinched at the touch of cold metal. I set up the stove ready for a brew but discovered our water bladder had frozen solid in the night. It took some minutes to beat its contents into chunks of ice that were small enough to shake into a pan. I removed the gas canister from my top, lit the stove then jogged on the spot to stay warm.

Laura emerged having packed the contents of the tent away into their neat little packages. I poured our drinks – tea for me, coffee for Laura – and left them to steam while we took the tent down. Despite staying regularly with hosts across Turkey and Iran, our tent still felt like home. Performing that same routine day after day – erecting the tent and unpacking our bags at night, striking the tent and repacking our bags in the morning – sometimes felt like a chore and exactly the kind of monotony we had tried to pedal away from back home. Other times however, it was more like meditation. A ritual performed without thought, a dance that was second nature. That morning it was the latter, and we parcelled away our home without exchanging a word.

Tent stowed away, we sipped our drinks in comfortable silence, Laura perched on a rock, me sat on a pannier. It was cold, but swaddled in all our layers after a burst of activity it was pleasant enough to sit in the sunshine, which we did until we had finished our breakfast.

I lifted my bike from the ground and held it upright with one hand while I bent down to pick up my panniers one at a time and hook them onto their racks. I then lifted my duffle bag onto the back of the bike and clipped on my handlebar bag while Laura did the same. We pushed our bikes back towards the road we had left the night before, our tyres crunching through gravel, and positioned them on the smooth tarmac pointing south towards the coast. They were prepared for departure, but our feet were firmly planted in the dirt, not quite ready to leave. I knew we had a ferry to catch but I also knew that such moments did not come around every day. I turned to Laura, her face illuminated by the sun on our right, and smiled.

'Morning, love,' she said.

'Morning,' I replied.

PART III

Dubai-Japan

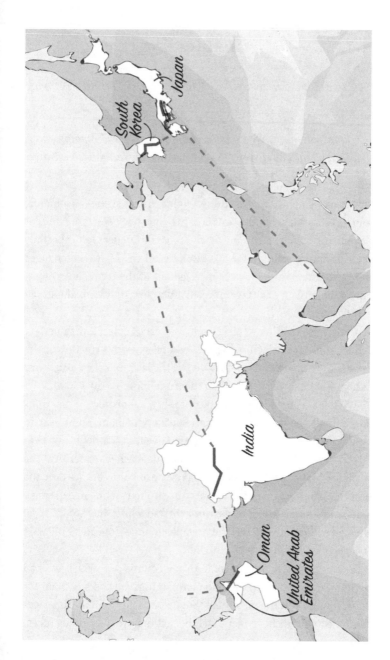

Chapter 19

'The ferry from Iran to the UAE. Flips flops go on, headscarf coming off. What a relief.' – Laura

'Camels on race tracks, omnipresent heat, 4x4s off-roading and camping in sand dunes. This is cycle touring in Arabia.' – Tim

Fast cars, smooth roads, traffic lights, road signs, pavements, roundabouts, glass buildings. It is hard to imagine two more different neighbours than Iran and Dubai, and those differences felt especially acute from the saddle of a bike. Rolling off the ferry, the changes were like a slap in the face. We cycled out of the terminal, straight onto a main road, and it was immediately clear that we had entered a different world.

Gone were the dusty tracks and rusty cars, replaced with perfect tarmac and huge machines, polished and powerful. In Dubai, the drivers were predictable and obeyed traffic laws, but they also drove at higher speeds, far scarier than the trundling mayhem of Iran.

We had emerged from a country sadly encumbered by sanctions and behind the curve of international development, to appear in another that was at its shining zenith. Love it or loathe it, nowhere else in the world quite matches Dubai for unabashed modernity. The roads are brand new, the shops are pristine and the cars are only the best that tax-free wages can buy. Expats strolled around in expensive suits and Emiratis floated past in robes so white they would have shamed a Persil advert. We had travelled in time from ancient Persia to a peculiar vision of the future.

The cries of 'Hello! Welcome to my country!' to which we had become so accustomed, were no more. In Iran, we had stood out for being foreign, but the only thing that made us different in Dubai was the state of our dishevelment and the fact that we were riding bikes.

It was hot, too. Just days before, we had been camped at the side of the road forcing chunks of ice from a frozen water bladder. For months, we had been shoving numb fists into giant mitts and jumping on the spot to bring back feeling to our lifeless feet. In contrast, within minutes of getting off the ferry I spotted a guy wearing nothing on the top half of his body but a pair of designer sunglasses. I buried my pile jacket at the bottom of a pannier, unzipped the legs from my trousers and dug out my baseball cap to shield me from the sun. Winter was over, and we had skipped spring and hopped straight into summer.

With the benefit of hindsight, I can happily say that those winter months were some of the best of our trip. However, I will just as freely acknowledge the sense of relief and elation at having escaped them. My bike was still laden with the trappings necessary for camping in winter, but on the day we rolled off that ferry it felt a lot lighter.

Bewildered and elated, Laura and I set about riding to our friends' house. It was a glorious day without a cloud in the sky and the heat, although a shock to our unacclimatised bodies, was welcome as we enjoyed the ease of cycling in a developed country. Having arrived in the morning, we had several hours to kill before our friends would be home from work. We stopped outside a shopping mall and Laura decided on a whim to indulge herself with a visit to a hairdresser. Being able to sit outside and read a book for an hour was treat enough for me. It had been a long time since it was warm enough to do that.

I got into conversation with two Philippine security guards outside the mall. Fascinated by our bikes, they took it in turns trying to lift them, without success. We could not lift them ourselves when we first left home but had soon developed the technique and strength to do so. When Laura emerged with her freshly coiffed hair and effortlessly lifted her bike down some steps, the two guards found it hilarious.

We looked at the map on our phones and plotted a route to our friends' house with a sigh. It was going to involve crossing some big roads. We wheeled our bikes to the edge of the road and waited for our moment.

'OK, after this car... go, go, go!'

Laura's words ringing in my ears, I heaved my own body weight in bike over a barrier and ran frantically across three lanes of overpass. My eyes were fixated on the bend to my right, certain that an overpowered sports car was about to screech around it and bring our holiday to an end.

Dubai: fantastic for cars, not so great for pedestrians or push bikes. This was no surprise to us. When we had lived in neighbouring Oman a few years beforehand, it was only possible to walk to our nearest supermarket by crossing over two highways, jumping some barriers and hiking through large stretches of barren wasteland. This would all happen in blistering heat and unrelenting sun, leaving you a sweating, dust-covered wreck by the time you had made it to Carrefour for some milk. The cities of the Arabian Peninsula are not designed for walking or cycling.

After hurdling countless barriers and dodging far too many fast cars, we arrived at a gated community. We gave our names and intended destination to an attendant who raised a barrier and let us inside. Pedalling through unfailingly rich green lawns with rows of matching trees and regular water features, it felt as though we had entered the set of the Truman Show. Everything was perfect. Everything that is, except for us.

I had worn the same pair of trousers and the same shirt every day since leaving home. I had not cut my hair, or shaved my beard, for six months. Our bicycles had been pushed through thick mud, ridden down endless dusty trails and regularly sprayed with mushy, grey snow. Our panniers were dropped into the dirt most days of the week.

Loitering outside our friends' house waiting for their return, we were lucky not to be arrested as vagrants. Families emerged from neighbouring houses to pile into their bright white SUVs (it is against the law to have a dirty car in the Gulf) and turned their heads with absolute bewilderment. I could just imagine the well-spoken young girl asking: 'Mummy, what happened to that poor man?'

Our friends returned, welcomed us into their house, pointed us towards the shower and gave us instructions for the washing machine. We enjoyed a few days with all the trappings of the modern world. We went out for dinner and drank cocktails; went to coffee shops and to a house party. We shopped in well-stocked and brightly-lit supermarkets with areas selling Marmite, Weetabix and PG Tips, just for the expats. My parents and younger brother came out to visit too. Having been away for six months by this point, their visit was nice in itself, but it also meant we could give them all of our winter kit to take back home, lightening our load for the warmer months ahead. In exchange for the winter clothing that had been strapped to the back of my bike, my brother brought out my ukulele. We had a delightful few days of rest and relaxation but we knew it had to end. After a week, we threw all of our belongings back into panniers and headed off towards Oman.

Having listened to our complaints about the danger of cycling on the Emirati roads, our friends told us about a new cycling loop that had been built, straight into the desert. After leaving their house, we made a beeline for it. It was a wonderfully surreal experience, cycling through wild desert on a tiny strip of perfectly flat tarmac, exclusively for the use of bikes.

By the time we regained the road at the far end of the cycle path, we had escaped the city traffic and saw more camels than cars. At sunset, we wheeled our bikes into the dunes and slept beneath a clear sky. The following morning we passed an encampment of tents in the dunes at the side of the road. Not all Emiratis live in the city; here several Emirati families lived in tents, selling food and drinks at the roadside. They invited us in and gave us breakfast.

Before the sun got too high, we bid our breakfast hosts goodbye and continued on our way towards the Omani border. Oman is unique in the Middle East for its neutrality. It maintains peaceful relations with both of its quarrelling neighbours – Saudi Arabia and Iran – is frequently involved in brokering Arab-Israeli peace initiatives, and is a solid friend of the west. It is also an oasis of peace in a turbulent part of the world, with a score of zero on the Global Terrorism Index.

Although Oman is technically a dictatorship, Sultan Qaboos is a much-loved leader. We lived in Muscat, Oman's capital city, during the Arab Spring. While other countries were rocked by massive protests and their leaders ousted or killed, the only demonstration we came across in Oman was in support of Qaboos, not against him.

Politics aside, it is also home to some of the most stunning scenery you could imagine: pristine sand dunes, lush green wadis and vast rocky mountains. Although it has developed at an electrifying rate since Qaboos seized power from his own father in 1970, it has avoided the brashness of Dubai, opting for a gentler approach that leaves even Muscat feeling more like a friendly town than an anonymous city. Best of all, it is still not a major tourist destination so many of its best swimming spots and most beautiful mountains are entirely devoid of people.

By the time we reached the border, the heat was oppressive, the sun unrelenting and the shade non-existent. We sought refuge at every opportunity that afternoon: ice cold lemon-mint drinks at a roadside cafe and lingering beneath the air conditioning unit of a supermarket. For the most part however, we were out in the hot daytime sun, cycling next to scorching sand that radiated yet more heat.

It was tiring work, and when evening arrived, I was ready to collapse at the side of the road and inhale some calories. However, Laura had a different idea. 'Let's ride out to the coast,' she said. 'It's not far, it'll be fun,' she said. But starving hungry and surrounded by empty desert an hour later, as far I could tell, we were not at the coast and we were certainly not having any fun.

I will admit that I am not always the best of company when hungry, and that evening was no exception. Having to cycle more miles than I deemed necessary was not helping the situation and nor was the heat.

'We're not getting anywhere. Shall we just stop here?' I tried.

'Come on! It's got to be close now,' she replied with her usual indefatigable energy.

This sort of thing was a recurring theme of our trip. Laura frequently wanted to make detours to see a landmark or follow a more scenic but longer route. She would often see something interesting on the map that was a few miles out of our way and suggest we check it out, but I would invariably just want to get to wherever we were going. On more than one occasion, having cycled thousands of miles from the UK, we would pass within an hour's ride of a world class tourist destination and I would put up a fight when Laura tentatively raised the subject of our visiting.

This was partly because, from my perspective, seeing specific things and visiting specific destinations was not the main reason for undertaking the trip. The joy was in the journey: the experience of a year on the road; the ever changing cultures and scenery; the people, the food, the shops, the roads. It was also partly because I tended to fixate on a plan and not like to deviate from it.

So, when Laura suggested pedalling out to the coast, I did what any other grown man would do: grumbled under my breath then followed behind her in a hypoglycaemic funk feeling sorry for myself.

Sunset came and went. Dusk set in with fatigue. Eventually, a speck of town came into sight on the horizon. We dragged ourselves there with one final push. Upon arrival, a road sign read: 'Beach eight miles'. Too far.

I gave Laura my 'unimpressed' face then wheeled my bike off the road and pushed it through sand to the very first house I could see. We would not be getting to the coast and we would not be having any fun. Instead, we would be looking for somewhere to sleep that did not require any more cycling. Laura rolled her eyes and pushed after me.

'Hello, we are Tim and Laura. We have cycled 5,000 miles from the UK. Is there somewhere safe we can sleep?'

With the owner's permission, we began to pitch our tent outside a large, walled house. Before we even got as far as choosing the best spot however, three children appeared from inside the house. My stomach was now beginning to digest itself and all I wanted to do was climb inside our tent, eat some noodles and fall asleep. But I felt we had a duty to entertain the kids outside whose house we were pitching our tent.

First, a tour of the bike, the bike computer and the bell before hoisting up the older boy for a go at pedalling it around the courtyard sans panniers. Second, a brief ukulele concert, encouraging the little girl to strum the strings while I held the frets. Then, a slideshow and some videos of our trip shown on my phone (although the middle child was more interested in opening every single app on the screen in case any of them turned out to be games. They did not). Finally, a lengthy England vs Oman football match complete with half-time and changing ends.

By this point I was running on fumes, desperate to get some sugar into my system. The only food we had in our panniers needed cooking, and just as I thought there was a lull in the evening's entertainment that might have allowed some surreptitious cooking, the entire extended family descended upon us.

In urban areas of Oman, men and women effectively have a uniform. They all wear the same thing. For men it is white robes and for women it is black. Away from the cities however, the women's outfits were a kaleidoscope of colours with a brightness matched only by their characters. They took it in turns to fire questions at us, laughing constantly. Laura showed off her knitting to widespread acclaim whilst I smiled weakly from a corner, mouthing the words 'feed me'.

It was late enough by this point that we figured we could reasonably excuse ourselves, pitch the tent and, crucially, cook some dinner, but as we stood to leave there were loud protestations. They could not let us sleep outside. We should take a room.

Under normal circumstances, such an offer would be most welcome, but sleeping in their guest room meant using our camping stove was out of the question and that meant no food. As our hosts closed the door behind them, I lay my head down on the floor and asked Laura to read my last rites.

'Drama queen,' she muttered while shaking her head and getting her sleeping bag out for the night. As I sat contemplating my demise there came a knock at the door. It was the mother of the three kids we had been playing with earlier in the evening.

'Sorry it is late,' she said, as she handed over a huge tray piled high with hot, steaming curry, rice and naan. Perhaps the detour had been worth it after all.

We reached Muscat a few days later and once again rode on the roads we used to ride on with our racing bikes when we had lived there some years earlier. We stayed in the apartment of an old friend and still look back on it as the fanciest accommodation of our entire trip: high ceilings, marble floors and big balconies overlooking the city. She was kind enough to let us stay for several days, enjoying some downtime in the beautiful surroundings while we sorted our visas for India. She was also gracious enough to not bat an eyelid when I inadvertently left our tent to dry on her priceless Persian rug.

We caught up with friends, visited our old haunts and then, well rested, packed our bikes into big boxes ready for their first flight: to India.

Chapter 20

'Heaved 60kg of luggage through station, stored bike boxes vertically in train corridor, then had to share a tiny bunk bed, but made it to Jaisalmer.' – Tim

'Monkeys, buffalo, goats, rats, boar and of course cows. All roaming the streets of India.' – Laura

India was a remarkable place, full of colour and chaos. Women strolled around in bright saris, men wore big turbans and elaborate moustaches, and large animals mingled freely with traffic. The roads were a free for all, with cars, bikes, motorbikes and pedestrians all vying for space against cows, fruit carts and the occasional camel. The food was good, when we could get it, and the scenery beautiful. The dusty streets and old sandstone buildings often made it feel as though we had travelled back in time.

Our route took us from the inhospitable desert of Rajasthan on the west into the busier, buzzier Uttar Pradesh. We started in rural wilderness, with goat herders and water buffalo on otherwise deserted stretches of road, and ended in the hustle and bustle of busy towns, crammed full of people and monkeys. We had the beautiful emptiness of the Thar, with its dusty roads and remote villages, and we had the splendour of the Mughal palaces and imperial forts.

We loved the madness of it, constantly surprised and never quite knowing what was going on, but India presented its challenges too. We were constantly the centre of attention, far more so than anywhere else we had visited and far more so than when we had previously visited more touristy areas of India, without our bikes. We could handle a bit of attention but being repeatedly mobbed and stared at became trying. We also got sick a lot, which was doubly hard when we had to keep cycling in the heat, dehydrated and drained of energy.

Despite being as careful as possible with what we ate and drank, we spent most of our time in rural areas where we could cycle for several days without being able to buy any food apart from crisps and biscuits. When we did find a cafe, it was often nothing more than a roadside shack with an open kitchen, offering vats of dahl that had been sitting around for hours. The constant attention and illness made India a real struggle.

Before any of that however, we landed in Rajasthan full of excitement and ready to embrace a new country.

As soon as we left the airport, we were mobbed by taxi drivers. Or, to be more accurate, auto-rickshaw drivers.

'Autos', as they are known, are motorised tricycles. They are found everywhere in India and are the country's standard form of taxi. Used by millions every day for routine journeys, they have space for two or three people to sit in the back. What they do not really have room for however, are seven-foot-wide bike boxes. Game for anything that would earn them a few rupees, the drivers insisted that the bikes would fit on-board just fine.

I lifted mine onto the back of one, pushed it in from one side and watched it fall out the other. The problem, of course, was that the bike was longer than the auto was wide. I lifted it back up from the other side and we eventually got it to balance. Laura did the same with her bike on another auto.

The bikes protruded some distance out either side of the autos making for a hair-raising journey. Oblivious to our concerns, the drivers put pedal to metal and screeched through the narrow winding streets of the golden, sand city of Jaisalmer. Objects flew past me at breakneck speed: motorbikes, school children, tea sellers, fruit stalls and other autos. With one hand I clung to the seat and the other to my bike box. Ten yards ahead of me I could see Laura doing the same. We were flying down steep hills, through marketplaces, over cobbles and along roads, in a constant cloud of dust. Despite the fear, when Laura caught my eye from the back of her auto, I could not fight the grin that spread across my face. We were in India and we were having an adventure.

Our world had been growing slowly more exotic since leaving home: the muddy, animal filled roads of Albania; the mosques and call to prayer in Turkey; and the unfamiliar rules and customs of Iran, but India seemed exotic on a different scale from anywhere else we had been. The roads were utterly chaotic, a mass of autos, bikes, pedestrians and cows. The people behaved completely differently, seemingly at home amongst huge crowds, wobbling their heads rather than nodding them, and staring unremittingly without embarrassment. The Hindi script was like no alphabet I had seen before and the English people spoke was like a comic version of a period drama. Jaisalmer, where we started our journey, looked more like the set of an Indiana Jones movie than a functioning 21st century city. It is surrounded by high sandstone walls and the whole town sits atop a huge rock, like a medieval castle.

The sense of bewilderment was no doubt heightened by having arrived there on a plane rather on our bikes, but I feel like nothing could have quite prepared us for the shock of excitement that India delivered. Exhilarated, we put our bikes back together and reloaded our panniers before cycling out of the city.

We followed a black tarmac road that snaked its way out of Jaisalmer, writhed across the yellow sand of the Thar Desert and continued towards a blue horizon. Some miles into the barren landscape, we found our path blocked by water buffalo. There were five of them, stepping out from the sand to cross the road in front of us. They were preceded by four goats and two camels, and followed by a woman wrapped in a bright purple sari. She gently goaded the herd through the desert as we slipped past her and continued threading our way between the empty dunes.

After a few hours' riding, we took the opportunity to seek solace from the sun under the shade of a khejri tree. Rajasthan was hot. I tipped up my sun-soaked bike bottle and squeezed tepid water into my mouth before we continued on our way.

Empire-built roads gave way to ancient dirt tracks over the coming days, as we bounced through dust and potholes. Arriving into the outskirts of a small village, we consulted the free map we had picked up at tourist information. It had delightful drawings of cartoon camels but was a little lacking in other areas: for example, the existence of this village and any roads leading into or out of it.

We wound our way through narrow streets and blind turns, dodging children and the odd goat on our way towards the centre of the village. The stone buildings were all cream-coloured, bleached by decades of bright sunshine, and the streets were unpaved. A muster of peacocks clustered around a brightly painted statue of Ganesh, the elephant-headed Hindu god, discarded in a pile of rubbish. Pausing at a junction to work out where we were going, we caught the eye of man with a turban and the most magnificent moustache.

'Jodhpur?' we asked, pointing in the direction we thought it should be. He tilted his head to one side then back upright again.

'Chai,' he responded and motioned us to sit down. It seemed like a surprisingly quiet spot in a busy village so we accepted his offer. He brought out two plastic chairs from his house before taking his facial hair inside to make some tea.

I stand by my claim that the Turks are the true tea kings of the world. They drink more of it and more frequently than any other nation we visited, but when it comes to quality, the Indians take the top spot. Even in the most ramshackle wooden shed propped up at the side of the road, miles from the nearest town or water source, tea will be cooked up in front of you with loose leaves and all manner of spices. Served hot and fresh, it makes a Tetley tea bag and kettle look positively amateur.

Whilst Mr Moustache went through the elaborate chai preparation ceremony indoors, a crowd of some thirty-odd onlookers formed around us in a semicircle. We sat still, not really knowing what to do with ourselves but enjoying some respite from cycling. Our fan club grew to several rows deep and each member stood calmly and motionless, watching the two white folks sit in awkward silence.

Moustache emerged with two small, steaming paper cups. He handed them over then shooed back the crowd who responded by taking two steps backwards before resuming their staring. We leaned back into our chairs and sipped our tea, hiding behind our sunglasses and doing a pretty bad job of stifling grins. We were total novelties in this town, and unlike in most other countries around the world, no one displayed the slightest inhibition in observing us. They were quite happy to stand and gawk at two entirely average Europeans having a cup of tea. We finished our drinks, thanked our hairy host for his hospitality and did our best to part the crowd. In doing so, we found a layer of children hidden at the back. They grew excited at finally being able to see the foreigners so chased after our bikes as we cycled out of town, two pied pipers with all the village's children in pursuit.

That was our first taste of what was to come in India, always attracting a lot of attention. When we had visited India previously, we had stuck to touristy areas and no one had paid us much notice. In contrast, in the rural areas we passed through on our bikes, we were constantly the centre of attention.

The roads we followed over the coming days were perfectly straight and only wide enough for a single vehicle. They had no markings or pavement; the concrete just gave way to sand at the edges. Cars were extremely rare. More common were motorbikes, pedestrians leading herds of animals and the occasional cyclist.

At one point, we found ourselves beneath another khejri tree, once more hiding in the shade. As we shared a few dry biscuits, I noticed a farmer a quarter-mile away in the distance. He downed his tools and began a slow walk towards us. Leant against the tree, I surreptitiously followed his progress from the corner of my eye as he grew steadily closer until he was within a few yards. He stopped there, folded his arms and began to stare.

'Namaste' (hello), we said, with a smile and a nod. We received a minute wag of the head in response but he was otherwise undeterred from his staring. Three boys on bicycles arrived out of nowhere then a moped dropped off a passenger. We were in the middle of a desert that had been entirely devoid of life just moments ago, but now we had attracted a small crowd. We tried, unsuccessfully, to engage them in conversation and offer them biscuits, but they just wanted to observe us and did not stop even when I had need to relieve myself.

And so it went on. Everywhere we stopped, even in a seemingly deserted stretch of empty sand, people would find us. Even when we were not stopped, but riding our bikes, we still attracted people's interest. Motorcyclists would frequently ride right next to us for miles at a time, uninterested in any interaction, content only to watch us.

Most of the time, this kind of staring was harmless. Sometimes, however, it could be frustrating or even intimidating. This was especially the case when we were hot (as we always were in India) and hungry (as we often were because proper food was hard to come by).

As the landscape grew less barren and slightly more developed, we arrived at a small but busy town. Distracted for a moment, I was forced to stop in my tracks as an auto-rickshaw appeared out of nowhere and braked within inches of my front wheel. Two other autos took the opportunity of my braking to overtake me, cutting Laura dead in her tracks in the process. A large bus appeared behind us and sounded its horn, which simply drew attention to the fact that it had been the only vehicle on the road not already doing so. I wheeled my bike through a gap between two other autos, skirted around the nonchalant cow that appeared to be acting as the village roundabout, and followed Laura behind a motorcyclist whose rider was obscured behind a huge wall of empty petrol canisters strapped to the back of his bike. Spying a fruit stand and an opportunity to escape the melee, Laura cut across five oncoming vehicles to bring her bike to a stop.

We were hungry and this was the first chance in some time to buy food. The fruit seller began filling a bag with bananas for us, and as we negotiated our order, neighbouring stallholders left their stands to gather around us. We pointed towards some oranges. Auto drivers hopped out of their vehicles to see what the commotion was and found two white people buying fruit. They did not seem disappointed.

We tried to collect our fruit but were blocked by the crowd. I smiled politely and gestured with my hand to indicate the direction in which we wanted to travel: 'Excuse me. Thank you. Just coming through, please.'

No one responded. They just stood in our way, entirely unperturbed. It was hot and the never ending chorus of car horns made for a stressful environment. We gave up on the fruit and focussed on escaping instead. 'MOVE!' shouted Laura, as she pushed her bike into the crowd. She made some progress and we managed to wheel our bikes back into the traffic and start riding again. We left a trail of grown men staring after us as we pedalled out of town, hungry and harried.

I think we could have learned to live with all this attention even when we were hot and hungry, if we had not been forever getting ill.

We did our best to avoid dodgy looking food and sometimes sterilised even the bottled water, but there was never anywhere to eat that even approached western standards. The choices were sketchy looking cafes, packets of biscuits or going hungry. Having failed to get fruit from the town where we were mobbed, we spent the rest of the day hungry. By nightfall, we gave up and tried our luck with a roadside cafe serving dahl in bulk to truck drivers.

There were swarms of flies on the tables and the chef kept wiping a running nose with his hands. I was ill that night and spent two days in a hotel bed afterwards. By the time I felt strong enough to get back on my bike, Laura fell ill and we stayed put for another two days.

Chapter 21

'Within seconds of stopping anywhere we are surrounded by curious Indians touching every part of ours bike or just staring at close range.' – Tim

'Been offered children to take home with us twice so far in India. It would be funny if they hadn't been so serious and it wasn't so tragic.' – Laura

When we both felt we had enough strength back to get on our bikes, we returned our key to the hotel's reception.

'OK, 500 rupees for your room,' said the hotelier.

'We paid last night,' I replied, puzzled, 'and it was only 200 rupees.'

'OK then, 200 each. You give me 400 rupees.'

'But we've already paid,' I said, still baffled.

'OK, OK. You pay 200.'

'We paid you 200 last night,' I repeated.

'OK. Thank you.'

Paying for things in India is not as straightforward as it is at home. Everything is a negotiation including, it seemed, whether or not you have already paid for something.

Initially, we were at a distinct disadvantage because we would never know what constituted a reasonable price, and some shopkeepers regarded us as tourists ripe for exploitation. Reaching a small shop later that morning, we noticed with some relief that all of the drinks had the price printed on the back: 15 rupees. We checked the packet of biscuits we had picked up and that too had the price on its packaging: five rupees. We added some crisps to our basket, ten rupees, and headed to the till happy for once that we knew how much it would all cost.

I put the three items on the counter and watched the shop owner write '100' on a piece of paper. As a former maths teacher, I was only too happy to write out the addition in column method to produce the correct total of 30. I gave him a 50 rupee note but received no change so I wrote out another sum: $50 - 30 = 20$.

He smiled, wagged his head and handed over ten rupees in change. I pointed at the sum again and held up two fingers (the polite way). He smiled, wagged his head and handed over the remaining ten rupees.

Every transaction in India was the same and numbers were seemingly plucked out of thin air. We would respond by demonstrating the 'correct' total with paper, calculator or fingers and then begin a protracted negotiation. On a good day, with a friendly shopkeeper and high spirits, the game was baffling but amusing, carried out with smiles and laughter. On a bad day with a bad sport, it was infuriating.

By late afternoon, we had run out of water again so stopped at a roadside shack to pick up a bottle. The bottle's price was 15 rupees, so I gave the shop owner a 50-rupee note and waited for change, but he just sneered and refused to give me any. I pointed to the price printed on the back of the bottle and wrote out the sum on a scrap of paper. He had attracted a crowd of grinning men by this point and was clearly enjoying his power over us so would not negotiate. I tried to keep cool but the smugness of his power trip was infuriating. Eventually I shrugged, said 'dhanyavaad' in thanks and helped myself to two more bottles from his fridge and stormed off. The crowd loved it, and I think even he may have cracked a smile. I had not done it for show, though; I was at the end of my tether.

Economists may say this is a wonderful demonstration of a free market system, but grossly overcharging flew in the face of my understanding of right and wrong. Interestingly, there seemed to be no shame attached to the process. If I 'caught' someone overcharging us, there would be no embarrassment or guilt from the vendor. That was just how they did business in India.

Knowing this did not make it any easier. My sense of fairness was being challenged and all I wanted was a bottle of water. Maybe I should have just accepted that things worked differently in India but I was struggling to.

My frustration was probably exacerbated by the fact that we stayed with very few local hosts in India so there was no one who could explain things to us. In every other country, we had largely wild camped or been hosted, but in India we primarily stayed in hotels. They were only hotels in the loosest sense – often little more than an empty room with a mangy bed and no running water – but it was still a commercial exchange and that gave our stay a different feel. We were cut off from our surroundings and had fewer opportunities to get to know people.

We made the decision to use hotels in part because India is a densely populated country and we knew our tent would attract a lot of unwanted attention. It was also because we had heard that just weeks before we arrived, a Swiss couple who were cycling across the country had been attacked in their tent at night. Although we preferred camping out, we decided it was safer to stick to hotels. However, we did manage to find one willing host in Jaipur.

Jaipur is the capital of Rajasthan and often known as the Pink City after many of its streets were painted that colour in 1876 to welcome Edward VII. Alongside Delhi and Agra (home of the Taj Mahal), Jaipur is part of India's 'Golden Triangle' of tourist sites, and visiting the city marked a rare overlap of our cycling route with a popular holiday destination. The city is awash with ornate palaces and huge forts dating back to the 18th century, and like all Indian cities, its streets throng with people. Fortunately, we managed to dodge most of the chaos and navigated our way to a quiet, well-to-do suburb, where we parked our bikes outside a large white townhouse and rang the doorbell.

Our host, whose name was Hemant, was a tall, gangly man with a pot a belly and, naturally, a moustache. Hemant was another long-distance cyclist so we were surprised when he asked us whether we could fix a puncture on his bike. He had had a flat tyre for months but did not know how to repair it.

'Haven't you cycled across Australia?' Laura asked.

'Yes,' he replied. He had also cycled the length of South Korea and a thousand miles through the US. Apparently, however, he had never needed to repair a tyre before.

'I didn't get many punctures,' he said, 'and when I did, I just pushed my bike to the next bike shop.'

Hemant was a member of his local Lions Club. It is an international network, a bit like the Rotary Club, which helps local communities and generally tries to do good stuff. The Lions hold an annual conference in a different part of the world each year and Hemant tried to cycle to all of them. He did not start from his home in India but picked a point in the country that was a few hundred miles away from the venue and pedalled from there.

What made Hemant's story particularly interesting was that he was not a cyclist when he first came up with this plan. He did not even have a bike when he started. He just flew to wherever he was going and then went to a local bike shop and picked one up. When he was done, he would sell it or give it to the local Lions Club. Apparently, he did not even own a tent.

'You don't own a tent?' Laura asked. 'Where you do you sleep?'

'I just lie on top of a picnic bench and, if it rains, I lie underneath it.'

I loved this. We had spent ages worrying about what camping kit we needed for our trip and here was a guy who had been all over the world without carrying any kind of shelter. And he had done all of this without ever learning how to change a tyre.

The bike he now owned at home in Jaipur had been sitting in the porch with a flat front tyre for three months. We were only too happy to repair it for him while he told us all about cycling in South Korea.

It sounded remarkable. He described a brand new cycle way running the length of the country, made with smooth tarmac and almost entirely traffic free. He said you could collect stamps every few miles to prove you had done it, and he showed us the certificate he had received for completing the whole route. We made a mental note to add it to our list of future cycling trips.

We spent the night in his spare room, but in a depressingly familiar routine I woke in the early hours of the morning and had to run to the toilet. With nowhere else available on our way into Jaipur, we had eaten lunch at a cafe where we saw cockroaches run across our table and a bird defecate into a cooking pot.

This was the third time in three weeks I had been ill and it was worse than before. I was bed bound for three days. Tired of it, frustrated at the amount of time spent inside when we could be out cycling and worried that I might have something worse than food poisoning, Laura put me in an auto and took me to hospital.

They put me on a bed and hooked me up to an intravenous drip. I lay down feeling sorry for myself as electrolytes drained from a bag and flowed into my veins. I closed my eyes and listened to the sound of rats crawling through the air vents. Laura took photos of me looking pathetic to share on Facebook.

After another day in bed, I started to get better just as Laura started to get worse. She crawled from the bedroom to the bathroom, delirious with a fever, and we spent another few days locked inside.

On the one occasion we ventured outside together, we were followed by auto drivers and shopkeepers trying to proffer their services and wares. We clung onto each other for strength and focused on putting one foot in front of the other. Crowds thronged, autos whizzed past and a monkey ran across the rooftop above us. We found a fruit seller and paid significantly over the odds for a bunch of bananas. Neither of us had the energy to haggle.

Walking back along a narrow street, there was a commotion and the rustle of a carrier bag before Laura yelped loudly. The bag she had been carrying was gone and we watched with dismay as the monkey climbed a fence onto a nearby roof then made its way back to the fruit-seller, carrying the bananas we had just bought from him. We went back to Hemant's spare room miserable.

When we eventually felt able to get back on our bikes, we breakfasted on fresh coconut water before setting off gingerly. Our energy had been sapped by several days of illness and not eating. What we needed was a nice, easy day of riding, but there was little hope of that in India. We got as much attention as always, and later that day I ended up snapping.

Exiting Jaipur had been hectic. We were swamped by vehicles on a huge road with a dozen 'lanes' of traffic travelling in both directions and, of course, there was the usual mix of farmyard animals to add to the excitement. A few hours later, we stopped for some tea at a tiny roadside shack but found it hard to relax with people surrounding us and fiddling with our bikes, so we necked our drinks and continued on our way. Then, as we pedalled along a narrow tree-lined road that afternoon, I saw Laura draw to an abrupt stop at the side of the road, turn angrily and cry out.

'That guy on the moped just hit me!'

I saw red. The heat, the crowds, the staring, the traffic, the sickness, the noise. It was all stressful but I had constantly tried to rationalise it and put it down to cultural differences. But in no culture is it acceptable for a grown man to hit a woman in broad daylight. I had had enough. I spun my bike around and pedalled back after the moped as Laura called out 'Don't!' He was faster than I was, but for once I was thankful for India's absurd traffic. I caught him when he got stuck behind a truck and I tapped him on the back.

'YOU HIT MY WIFE!' I shouted. 'HOW DARE YOU!'

He gestured that it was just a joke. A light tap.

'A joke? Do you think it's funny to hit a people in public!? What the hell is your problem!?'

He shrugged.

'Don't shrug! You can't attack people in the street then act as if nothing happened!'

I continued shouting but it was pointless. He didn't speak English and there was nothing to be achieved anyway.

'Don't EVER do that again! Do you hear me?' I shouted pathetically and wheeled back to Laura, still feeling angry but also now a little foolish. Further up the road, after we resumed cycling, a teenager on a bicycle pulled alongside me and followed me, staring. He rode next to me like that for some time, his bike a few inches from mine, just staring and cycling.

'Hi,' I said wearily with a wave. He did not respond. 'How can I help?' I offered with wide eyes and an upturned hand but got nothing in response. I cycled faster and he cycled faster to match me. I slowed down and he did the same. I stopped and he stopped with me. I resumed cycling and so did he. 'Mate, I'm not in the mood. Just give me a break.'

I knew he could not understand me but I did not know what else to do. I needed him to leave me alone so I cycled as fast as I could but it was easy for him to catch me on a bike without panniers. I was panting by this point and the adrenalin had started to flow.

'WHAT!?' I shouted. 'What the HELL do you want!?'

The boy stared back impassively and continued following me for another 15 minutes.

Chapter 22

'0630: wake. 0800: start cycling. Stop every hour for cold/sweet drinks. ~1400: 40-50 miles done. Our daily routine in a hot India.' –
Tim

'Quoted hotel price was just for four hours. Do most people who pay for hotels by the hour turn up on bicycles? Perhaps it's the stilettos.' – *Laura*

A few days later, we were trying without much luck to find a hotel for the night. The first place said it was not open to foreigners and the second just offered us the floor of a store room that was piled high with rubbish. The third place looked like a prison – long, dark, narrow corridors of bare brick, and concrete floors with rooms whose only windows were internal and barred – but at least it had a bed. We would not have minded the conditions if the proprietor had been even remotely friendly, but sadly he was not. Specifically, he is noted in my diary as being 'an obstinate w****r'.

'1,200 rupees,' he insisted. Four times the going rate. I tried and tried to get something more reasonable but he would not budge. We were weary after my hospital visit and we just needed to lie down. Having been through the haggling charade twice already that day, we acquiesced and paid the money. Inside our room, Laura was just starting to change her clothes when I noticed three boys huddled at the window staring in at us.

'Hey!' I shouted and closed the shutters. As I switched from my cycling shorts to my evening shorts – which were identical other than for that fact that the latter were more recently laundered – the doors swung open and a man walked in to fiddle with some dials on the wall. I hurriedly pulled my shorts up, but the man paid no notice. He flicked some switches and walked out again leaving the door wide open. The familiar heads of three small kids appeared in the doorway shortly before I slammed it.

I took my shirt off, sat on the edge of the bed and let out a heavy sigh. I put my hands behind my head and made to lie down when I noticed three pairs of eyes staring at me. I had not actually locked the shutters when I closed them earlier, so the boys had managed to open them again and resume their observations. The interruption was probably in my best interests however, because it was at that moment that Laura pointed out what was on the bed: rat poo, all over it. As if on cue, a large grey rat scuttled down some shelves and ran across the bed to the bathroom.

Wheeling our bikes back along the corridor to the front door wearing the international facial expression for 'unimpressed', the owner jumped out of his office looking puzzled.

'Price very good,' he said.

I could not think of a way to act out 'Yes, but the bed's covered in rat poo,' so we just waved him off and got back on our bikes.

We pedalled away from Hotel for Rats feeling drained and desperate for somewhere to sleep. We had given up all hope of finding somewhere in town and – fed up with the whole thing – just started cycling out into the desert. Something would work out.

We paused at the side of a dirt track to let a herd of goats stream past us, followed patiently by a wizened old man with a wonky wooden walking stick. Behind him in the distance lay some white buildings. Upon arrival, the village appeared deserted but for one man.

'Hello, we are Tim and Laura. We have cycled 6,000 miles from England. Is there somewhere safe we can sleep?'

He smoothed the long ends of his moustache as he thought. We followed him into the village and met with three other turbaned men who joined him in the pensive act of moustache stroking before agreeing on something. They upped sticks and walked further into the village where they convened a meeting of a dozen more men. All with turbans. All with taches. There was much debate whilst we stood, wilting in the sunshine. It felt as though hours slipped by as we tried not to pass out, but no conclusion seemed to be in sight. Finally, a woman turned up, took one look at us and made us sit down immediately while she ran off to fetch some tea and biscuits.

At some point during our rapid consumption of their offerings, some children arrived. Perhaps 50 of them. They had a ball and it was not long before they were throwing it around. It was not long before we were too. And it was not long after that Laura and I found ourselves running around the school playground, chased by a mob of enthusiastic kids, flinging a tennis ball high into the air and seeing who could catch it first. The kids must have ranged from five years old to fifteen, but they were united, as we were, in the love of a good ball game. The laughing was almost as hard as the running.

We snuck back to our bikes exhausted, but the boys were not sated. They wanted more entertainment. Thankfully, strapped to the back of my bicycle was the ideal tool for situations like this: my ukulele. I doubt I will ever perform a ukulele concert to a larger audience than I did that evening. I suspect it may also have been the only time that Hey Jude's been sung and no one joined in for the chorus.

Laura eventually tagged me out for a break and provided entertainment of a different sort with her knitting. The kids were less impressed by her needles than my Beatles, but since they were being chased away by their parents anyway, that left the village's women to crowd round in amazement at the apparently universal language of cardigan knitting.

The sun fell and the people drifted away. Dinner was brought to us on a roof terrace and eaten by the light of the moon. Stars shone and we watched them from our rooftop bed.

That night we made a plan. India was an exciting and intriguing place but it was getting the better of us. We counted the number of days we had spent riding our bikes and the number we had spent ill

150

in bed and found them to be equal. Fifty percent sick days was not a good ratio. Friends and family had written to us urging us to get out, get better and start enjoying ourselves again. Perhaps they were right.

We always knew that we would have to fly out of India. The Burmese border was closed and the only way to reach Southeast Asia was on a plane. Rather than keep cycling to the eastern edge of India before taking a flight, as originally intended, we decided that we would jump on a train to Delhi and leave the country at the earliest possible convenience.

It had taken us some time to reach that conclusion. We had been looking forward to India for a long time and leaving early felt like quitting, but there was no joy to be had from constant bouts of illness and that showed no signs of abating. When we reached the next city, we found an internet cafe and planned our escape. As we searched for cheap flights to Vietnam however, something caught Laura's eye.

'It doesn't cost that much to fly to Seoul,' she said.

'Seoul? As in, South Korea?'

Hemant had made South Korea sound like a cyclist's paradise. It was not exactly on our route, but when would we next have the chance to go there? So, on a whim, we booked ourselves two tickets to the South Korean capital and started researching ferries from Korea to Japan.

Chapter 23

'I sometimes wonder if cycle touring is just a good excuse to read more.' – Tim

'I love sleeping under the stars. Seeing the Plough here in South Korea, home feels close: same view from Lancashire to the Far East.' – Laura

They were not on the baggage carousel and the 'oversized baggage' area was dormant. I found someone who looked official and used gestures to indicate that we were looking for two bicycles. He radioed a friend, turned and waved. At the other end of the baggage hall were two more officials waving back at us. They were holding what looked distinctly like two bike boxes. We had last seen them in Delhi airport and were relieved to find that they had made it to Seoul in one piece.

Remove packaging, inflate tyres, load panniers, depart airport.

Although flying with bikes can be a pain, the ability to ride away from Arrivals on your luggage almost makes it worthwhile. You do not have to interpret a train time table in a foreign language, work out where the bus leaves from or negotiate fares with a taxi driver. You can just start pedalling.

Outside the air was cool and fresh. The oppressive heat of India was a thousand miles away and I felt freed. The modern skyline of central Seoul was visible in the distance and we made a beeline straight for it. A few hundred metres down the road however, a police car appeared from behind and pulled us over.

'You can't cycle here. It's dangerous.' The policeman spoke kindly in flawless English with an American accent. I looked around baffled. Dangerous? It was an empty road, perfectly finished and with a huge shoulder for us to cycle on. There were no raging auto drivers with their fists rammed into their horns and no cyclists dodging between them. There was no oncoming traffic on our side of the road and there were no potholes or giant cow pats to dodge. There were not even any water buffalo. How on earth could this be dangerous?

South Korea was not India however, and the rules were different. The road leading out of the airport was deemed too big a road for cyclists, so the policeman directed us to a quieter route.

Hungry after the long flight, we stopped at a cafe to buy some food. I paused before ordering, hesitant about getting sick again, but a cursory glance around reminded me that we were not in India any more. The streets were pristine and the cafe looked cleaner than our own kitchen. We ordered some combination of vegetables and rice, and never looked back.

From the cafe, we wound our way through the Seoul suburbs. The roads were clean and well maintained. There were road signs and traffic lights again, and, unlike in India, road users obeyed the rules.

We followed the directions we had been given, to a tall tower block in an undistinguished neighbourhood, where we pushed the buzzer for number 137 and waited for the response.

'Yeoboseyo!'

The enthusiastic 'hello' through the intercom confirmed that we had found the right place. The door was buzzed open and we found ourselves in the brightly lit hallway of a huge apartment complex. In our scruffy state and with our bicycles in tow, our surroundings made us feel somewhat out of place.

The lift doors opened and a little old lady waved us inside then introduced herself as we ascended the building. We had been put in touch with her by a local cyclist and she had kindly agreed to host us. We emerged on the 13th floor and wheeled our bikes into a compact apartment. We were shown to a room which had two beds made on the floor and a note on the table, which read:

'Hello Tim Moss. Welcome to my home. Make yourself at home :)'

The note was attached to a giant pink bouquet of 'Hello Kitty' Ferrero Rocher chocolates. To me it seemed like an odd gesture, but it was a kind one. We put our bags down then went to join our host in the kitchen where we helped her make noodles from scratch and prepare a feast for dinner, which was served with liberal helpings of her own, homemade 'kimchi' pickle.

We bid farewell to our host the next day and, after a morning spent wandering around the national Korean War museum, we pedalled out to the start of the cycle route that would take us all the way to the south coast.

The route followed the Han River and took us back through the middle of Seoul. It soon became clear that we would not escape the city before nightfall so we stopped by a huge crowd of tents that were pitched in a park by the river. It seemed unusual to find a campsite in such a central location and there did not appear to be any way of paying for a pitch, but we soon found that a lot of things in South Korea were pretty unusual. We pushed our bikes to a convenience store, bought pot noodles and filled them with hot water from an urn. We slurped our noodles as the sun set and watched, with mounting as concern, as each of the tents around us was taken down and packed away. By the time we had finished our dinner, there were no tents remaining. Apparently, they were just pitched for the day. That left us in an empty park in the middle of a capital city, in the dark.

We decided that our best bet was to forget about the tent and hide away in our bivvy bags instead. We waited for a quiet moment, when no one was around, then wheeled our bikes behind a bush. Quietly, we unfurled our bivvy bags in the darkness, the lights of skyscrapers visible above us.

It was easily our boldest suburban bivouac. We were a hundred yards from the Han River that runs through the heart of the city, fifty yards from the nearest shop and ten from the national cycle route. We cleaned our teeth, climbed into our sleeping bags and lay down on the grass, staring at the night sky and listening to the sounds of the city.

'Is this a bit weird?'

'Yup.'

We grinned, closed our eyes and fell asleep. I awoke some hours later, still in darkness, with a sense of foreboding.

'Lau!' I whispered. There was a vague rustling noise from the form of Laura's sleeping bag then silence. 'Lau!' I hissed again.

She rolled over in the darkness to meet my eyes and I pointed her silently to my right. No more than ten feet away was the silhouette of a man carrying a golf club. He walked towards us, raised the club and.... thwack!

The club swung through the darkness, connecting smoothly with a golf ball, which flew into the distance and disappeared from view. The late night golfer paused for a moment to watch his ball land then continued strolling on his way.

It seemed odd to be playing golf in total darkness in the early hours of the morning, but then he may have thought that it seemed odd to stumble across two fully grown adults lying sound asleep in central Seoul. As we watched his shadow retreat into the distance I looked up at the glorious skyline that towered above us, all bright lights and modernity. I marvelled at the privilege of being able to wild camp somewhere like this.

Weird? Yes, but without doubt, wonderful.

We could hear traffic pass and the occasional distant sounding of sirens, but aside from the midnight golfer we had the place to ourselves and the overriding sensation was one of tranquillity. We slept soundly, tucked away in our little corner, and woke with the sunrise to begin our journey south.

Chapter 24

'Irish soda farls with black bean spam. Reckon tonight's dinner could be the first of its kind.' – Tim

'Camped under a pagoda at the top of a mountain pass 'so high even the birds need a rest'. Fantastic views and clear air, brilliant.'
– Laura

When former South Korean president Lee Myung-bak announced his ambitious plans to revitalise four of his country's largest rivers, I imagine that creating the world's longest bike path was quite a long way from his mind. His intention had been to improve water quality, provide a secure water source during times of scarcity and help reduce flood risk. But like so many great plans, this one did not go according to it.

From the outset, Mr Lee's project was dogged with criticism: it was damaging the environment, it increased the risk of flooding rather than reducing it, it made water quality worse, it was too expensive, it was undemocratic, it was illegal and so on and so on. This was not what Mr Lee had planned. He thought his idea would bring adulation, but in fact, it had resulted in the opposite. He needed to salvage the project and his reputation. But how?

The epiphany came one evening when Mr Lee sat down at his desk with a bottle of soju and scratched his head (at least that is how I like to imagine it happening). The answer, he realised, was bicycles. Specifically, he would create a bike path that ran the length of each river and, in so doing, win round the public.

It worked. The path eventually stretched the entire length of the country, from Seoul in the north west to Busan in the southeast, and it is this path that Hemant had told us about in Jaipur. We planned

With friends outside Hampton Court Palace, ready to start cycling.

Hampton Court Palace: before and after cycling 13,000 miles around the world.

Preparing to descend the Alps.

Camped beneath a beach-front bar in Croatia;
and wheeling through mud in Albania.

Snowy roads in Turkey.

Sleeping in the store room of a Turkish kebab shop.

The second breakfasts: Gulnur and family, the family who fed us after their neighbours started a fire outside our tent, and the kebab shop employees.

Beautiful mountains and cold conditions in Iran.

Playing table tennis with the Iranian Red Crescent.

Being plied with food was a daily occurrence in Iran.

Laura with Khomeini and Khamenei; and a poster we found after stumbling into a 'protest' in Iran (the protesters were really friendly and handed out sweets).

Indian women in the village where we were served tea in front of a crowd.

Attracting attention in India and communicating with the Google Translate app.

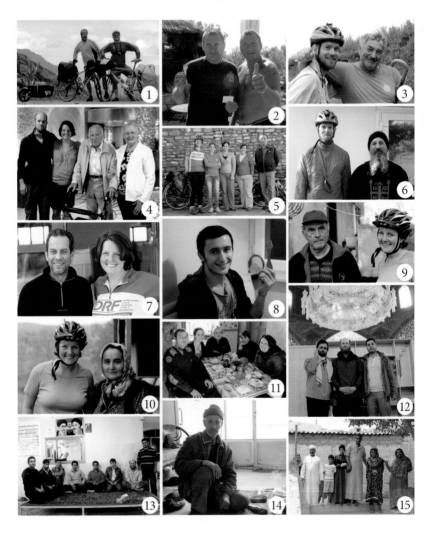

The people we met while cycling around the world.
See the appendix for an index of who's who.

Washing in India was often done al fresco, and usually with an audience.

Entertaining the kids in the Indian village where we were put up for the night.

Collecting a stamp for our 'passport' on South Korea's Four Rivers cycle path.

The hill-top pagoda where we slept until woken by cries of 'Fighting!'

Sleeping in a Korean toilet cubicle; and our shirts after a year on the road.

Boarding a ferry across the Mekong Delta in Vietnam.

Exploring quiet roads in Cambodia.

Sleeping in a Malaysian bike shop.

Big skies in Arizona.

Testing guns in New Mexico, with a 'Federal Agent'.

Warnings near the Mexican border; and jazz in New Orleans (*Nor'lins*).

Camped beneath a house on stilts on Dauphin Island, Alabama.

Reaching the Atlantic coast after 13,000 miles of cycling.

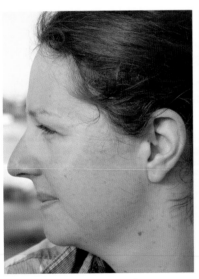

With the sun on our right.

to follow it all the way from our city centre bivouac to the south coast, where we would catch a ferry to Japan.

At the start of the path, we were given free maps along with a novelty passport for which we could collect stamps. Shortly after packing away our bivvy bags and pedalling along the river, we stopped at what looked like a telephone box. Inside, there was an ink pad and stamp, which we used to mark the appropriate section of our toy passport as evidence of the route we had followed.

That day's ride was on perfectly smooth tarmac and entirely free from traffic. Approaching the edge of a rock face outside the city that afternoon, I imagined the route would have to join the road for a short section. Instead, the Koreans had dug a tunnel. That is the only place in the world where I have seen tunnels that have been specifically constructed just for bikes. We passed through the rock and emerged the other side by a tall bridge.

Cycling up onto the bridge was clearly too steep and my heart sank at the sight of several flights of stairs: hard work when carrying a fully laden bike. When we got closer however, we saw there was a handy little groove running up the side of the steps enabling us to easily wheel our bikes without having to lift them. We later passed a bike pump at the side of the road. Not your regular push-pumps but an actual pressurised air pump like the ones you get at garages for cars. They really had put a lot of effort into this cycle route.

We stopped for lunch at a camping area – a real one this time – whose onsite cafe had giant urns of boiling water for hot drinks and instant noodles, clearly designed to cater for large numbers of cyclists. And the numbers of cyclists were indeed large. We saw husbands, wives, families and children sharing the path. There were young couples wobbling on tandems and lycra-clad roadies shooting past at speed, waving their fists and shouting 'fighting!' We met a hand-cycling team out training and fellow tourers tackling the entire route's length.

In short, though the path may not have been part of Mr Lee's original plan, it was a roaring success and we were delighted to have found it.

Combined with the temperate climate, the lack of food poisoning and the fact that not every member of the public felt the need to follow us around, Korea was a welcome change from India. The well-signed, family friendly bike route made for the most blissfully easy cycling of our entire trip. After the trauma of India, we lapped it up.

That night we stopped beneath a pagoda, cooked ourselves some noodles and fell asleep as it got dark. I woke to the early morning sun, the world around me quiet but for birdsong, and happily dozed back to sleep, safe in the knowledge that we had nowhere to be and no miles to cover that could not easily be made up later.

When we later dragged ourselves out of bed, Laura decided to try making her own bread on the camping stove. With flour, water and baking powder, she made fresh dough then cooked it in our pan. Served hot, with generous helpings of jam, it was delicious. We sat around reading our books long after we had finished eating, oblivious to the day's ticking clock, unworried about mileage or making the next town before nightfall. Breakfast spilled into elevenses as we devoured bread with paperbacks and watched fellow cyclists meander past before eventually rousing ourselves to action.

'Shall we do some cycling today?' Laura eventually said, with some reluctance.

'I suppose,' I replied.

Laura slipped her world map bookmark back into her novel and we eased ourselves onto our saddles and pootled on to the next picnic bench for more bread, jam and laziness in the sunshine. Unfurling our sleeping bags as the sun set on another pagoda at the end of the day, Laura paused for a moment and said: 'This is exactly where I want to be right now.'

As the name suggests, the Four Rivers cycle path largely follows the flow of four different rivers. As such, the vast majority of the route is flat. However, a single mountain stood in the way between us and Busan, and it was one of the few times that the bike path joined a road, the mountain being too big even for the Koreans to tunnel. We spent an entire afternoon climbing before reaching the top of the pass early in the evening.

We stopped under a particularly large and ornate pagoda, which afforded us a fantastic view into the valley we would descend the following day. I cooked up some noodles then promptly poured half of the pot into the dirt as I tried to drain them. The last time I had done that was in France and it still hurt me to think about it – all of that effort wasted. A young group of Koreans had just pulled over on their bikes, having conquered the climb themselves. They witnessed my clumsiness and gave me two replacement packets of noodles before starting their descent.

The wind had picked up so we strung part of our tent to one side of the pagoda to act as a windshield. We were woken twice in the night. First, a young man on a bicycle appeared in the darkness at the foot of the pagoda and said:

'I sleep here?' he looked genuinely puzzled, as if it was us that had suggested it.

'Yes, of course,' I replied, 'there is plenty of room.'

A look of anguished confusion passed over his face before he turned and cycled away.

Sometime later, we were both awakened by the sound of rustling in the bushes. There are bears in the South Korean mountains. Given that Laura worries about bears even in the UK, I was pretty sure this would be the first thing to cross her mind. We soon heard voices however, and the sounds of general merriment. The lights of half a dozen torches came into view as a small group of hikers marched past our pagoda. They all carried bottles, of what we later discovered was rice wine, which, when they saw us lying in our sleeping bags, they waved in our general direction and shouted 'Fighting!' This might sound threatening, but we had gathered that it was just a word used for encouragement. I waved back and gave a half-hearted 'fighting' in return before falling back asleep.

The previous evening's wind had brought a change in weather by daybreak. It was cloudy and wet. We rolled down the mountain and re-joined the riverside path. It was an uneventful day that would later become memorable for one thing only: Laura and I spending the night in a disabled toilet.

Before resigning ourselves to the prospect of sleeping on the floor of some public toilets, we had been looking for another pagoda under which to shelter from the rain. I cannot speak for all cycle tourists, but as far as we were concerned, pagodas were just about the best thing since sliced bread. Their key feature was rain cover. Our tent, of course, was waterproof, but it is pretty miserable being cooped up inside a tiny nylon shelter: cooking dinner in the porch is awkward, sitting up straight is a pain and everything gets slowly wetter than when you arrived. With a roof over your head however, you can spread your stuff out, leave plenty of space for the stove and hang up your kit to dry on a makeshift washing line.

Just as importantly, pagodas give you a bench to sit on. That might not sound like much, but sitting on the floor every day gets tiresome. Until arriving in South Korea, if I were allowed one luxury on a cycle tour, I would have chosen a picnic bench. Now it would definitely be a pagoda.

However, pagodas came to be a crutch. It got to the point where I would not contemplate stopping for the night if we were not under one. It had rained constantly the day we came down from the mountain and it showed no sign of stopping so I was particularly keen to find a pagoda.

'Mate, let's just put the tent up,' Laura shouted after me.

'We'll find a pagoda soon. We always find one!' I shouted back.

We did not find one. Instead, we found a sheltered walkway leading from a car park to a museum. The museum had closed for the night and the car park was deserted so we settled under the shelter of the walkway to cook some noodles and drink some tea. It was better than nothing, but it was no pagoda: rain kept blowing in from the side and there was nothing to sit on. Besides, it was the main entrance to a museum and not really an option for sleeping. The curator probably would not too be impressed by two bivvy bags blocking her path in the morning. It was getting dark so we needed to find somewhere else to sleep. There was a toilet block outside the museum that had been left open.

'We may as well clean our teeth in there while we're here.'

Stepping inside together, it was impossible not to notice the difference: there was no wind and no rain. It was dry, perfectly quiet and spotlessly clean. Although Laura had not said a word, I knew that she was thinking exactly the same as me: we could sleep in here.

The first thing we did was double check outside that the place really was deserted. It was.

Then we stood really still for a minute to see if the automatic lights would go out. They did.

Then we checked whether the disabled cubicle was big enough for two camping mats. It was (if we bent them round the toilet bowl).

And that was that. Warm and dry, we spent a night in a disabled toilet. It provided proper shelter from the elements, hot and cold running water, en-suite facilities and at least one comfortable seat. As such the disabled toilet is in many ways the ideal spot for travelling cyclists. In fact, if until arriving at that museum, I would have chosen a pagoda as my one luxury on a cycle tour, now...

We woke early in the toilet cubicle to avoid giving the janitor the fright of his life. Outside, the rain had stopped so we sat in the sunshine, reading our books while bread baked on the stove. Sleeping in a public toilet was a slightly surreal experience, but as it happened, Korea had something far weirder in store for us that evening.

We were nearing the end of our route and we had not yet visited a Korean sauna (known as a 'jimjilbang'). We had been told that we should not leave the country without having experienced one so, when we saw one sign posted that afternoon, we took our chance. To get to the entrance, we had to haul our ten-ton bikes up three flights of stairs. We had been assured that sleeping in a sauna was standard practice in Korea so, huffing and puffing after the climb, we wheeled our bikes straight up to reception and asked how much for the night.

In exchange for our *won* we were handed six hard boiled eggs and what looked like a prison uniform each, then pointed towards some double doors. I followed the signs for the men's changing rooms in which I found several rows of hand held showers with plastic seats in front. The routine, it appeared, was to lather oneself with soap from head to toe then scrub vigorously for some time before finally rinsing and heading to soak in a communal bath.

Emerging from our separate shower room experiences – Laura's, apparently, involving more group scrubbing than mine – we stood and marvelled at each other. We were both cleaner than we had been for months, but we were also wearing matching prison outfits, me in orange, Laura in blue.

We walked along a corridor clutching the eggs (about which we were none the wiser) and stopped when we came to a group of locals, all wearing identical uniforms to our own. They were gathered around a TV and seemed transfixed by what appeared to be a live broadcast of two people playing the board game Othello. Catching us staring, they pointed us towards a hall. We entered to find a middle aged man lying flat on his stomach snoring. The only other object in the hall was a large hot water urn perched on a table with a woman sat next to it, eating some noodles in the same blue get-up as Laura.

She gestured us over and we joined her on a gym mat, where we ate our boiled eggs. Even with a common language, I felt that the situation had veered so far from normality that words could never quite offer a full explanation. We made ourselves some noodles, watched a bit of Othello then fell asleep on a gym mat. The following morning we handed back our uniforms and continued on our merry way. Subsequent conversations with expats confirmed that this experience – the scrubbing, the uniforms, the boiled eggs, the gym mats – was a common activity in South Korea, but for us, like so much in the country, it was pure, bewildering, novelty.

We reached Busan the following day and made a dash for the ferry terminal. At the ticket booth, we handed over the last of our *won*, which was not quite enough, but the lady smiled and waved us through. We said our goodbyes to South Korea – a country we had never expected to visit but were thoroughly glad we had – and looked across the East China Sea to Japan.

Chapter 25

'Thanks to the girl at the checkout who dug out 500 won (3p) from her purse to pay the remainder of our ferry ticket.' – Tim

'Oh Japan, with your heated toilet seats and 'mechanism to wash buttocks', you are spoiling us.' – Laura

The ferry to Japan was notable for a number of reasons. For starters, the sleeping arrangement was a single large room shared with a dozen other people, all sleeping on mats on the floor. Had such an option been available on a British ferry, I might have baulked, but in East Asia, it was a delightful experience: immaculately clean with well-behaved roommates.

I was also entertained by the discovery of a vending machine serving pot noodles, having never previously come across a venue with sufficient demand to warrant such a thing. Most significant of all however, was the availability of an on-board hot tub. I struggled to believe that our budget tickets qualified us for entry, but sure enough, we were waved through and able to enjoy a jacuzzi with sea views before going to sleep. The boat also had a karaoke room, but we gave that a miss.

The ferry brought us into Fukuoka port early on a Thursday morning. The first place we visited in the beautiful and culturally rich country of Japan was the convenience store 7-Eleven. It was breakfast time, and having not seen a 7-Eleven since my childhood, I felt an odd sense of nostalgia. Unable to even understand the alphabet here, let alone the words, we selected an unidentified range of baked goods for our breakfast and took them outside to sample:

'Urgh. I wouldn't recommend that one.'

'Ooh, this one's amazing.'

'What is it?'

'No idea.'

From our spot, sitting on the floor of a 7-Eleven car park, I surveyed my surroundings. It took me a moment to work out what felt so different. In South Korea we had spent all of our time following a river, tucked away from civilisation, with nothing but greenery and other cyclists for company. Now, we were in the middle of a town, surrounded by shops, cars and people.

The calm of Korea had been wonderful for its contrast to India, and it was just what we needed at the time. However, following the riverside cycle path had meant we had little exposure to society. After a few weeks of solitude, we were ready to be immersed in a culture again. There was no cycle path to follow in Japan, so we would once more be making our own way across a country by road. Having a flight booked out of Kyoto gave us a focus for our time in Japan, and after devouring our pastries, we set off to make the most of it.

We rode out of town and spent the morning navigating through terraces of paddy fields, stretching up the hills that surrounded us. In the afternoon we were climbing a small, tree-covered hill when another cyclist passed us. Having recently learned the lingo in Korea, Laura waved her fist and shouted 'Fighting!' at him, but received only a bewildered look in return.

We were repeatedly told during our stay in Japan that we were unlucky to have arrived just after the cherry blossom had finished, but that day we did not feel unlucky. The scenery was beautiful, the weather was fine and the cycling excellent. We descended into wide-open fields of green and yellow.

Stopping at a junction of rural lanes to check our map later that afternoon, a car pulled onto the grass verge next to us, and its driver walked towards us.

'Can I help you with directions?' he asked in stilted English.

We got talking and he asked about our trip, where we had cycled from and where we were going. To each answer, he responded with the same incredulous 'Is that right?' spoken with an accent straight out of an American detective show. Instead of directions to where we were going, he gave us directions to his house, where he and his wife awaited our arrival with fresh tea.

The house was set back from the road, surrounded by woodland and with no neighbours in sight. It was quite the opposite of the Japanese stereotype of a cramped cityscape with business people sleeping in coffin-sized booths. There was greenery, space and calm. Inside, their house was filled with a lifetime's accumulated belongings, but all of it kept in neat order. The living room had bamboo matting on the floor and paper walls that slid to and fro, serving as doors that made it possible to shrink or enlarge a room as required. Other than that however, it could have been a cottage in the South Downs.

The man was a flower seller and he showed us around his garden after we drank our tea. We told him that we had just arrived in Fukuoka port that morning, and he told us about a boat that had docked there 30 years earlier. It was a 'book boat', which sailed around the world, taking its floating library to different countries. He showed us the book he bought all those years ago, written in English. That coming weekend, he told us, the very same boat would be coming back to Fukuoka three decades after it had first visited, and he would be there to meet it.

We were invited to stay for the night, and they suggested that we go to their favourite restaurant for dinner. They drove us there after dark, and conveniently, food was served buffet style, which enabled us to avoid the difficulty of ordering from a Japanese menu. Everything on offer was unfamiliar so we had to ask our hosts repeatedly what we were eating. Not that it mattered because it all tasted great. They would not accept our attempts to pay for dinner in thanks for hosting us, nor even split the bill. We slept on mattresses laid on the floor of their spare room and left the following morning with the directions he had offered to give us when we first met.

As we rode away on another delightful spring morning, we commented on the pleasant surprise of having been invited into a home on our very first night in Japan. Invitations are always nice, but this was especially so, because we had not expected such hospitality in Japan.

We had received so many acts of kindness in almost every country we visited. Some countries, like Turkey and Iran, stood out for their willingness to help strangers, but none stood out for being unfriendly. Despite that, we had still arrived in Japan with the preconception that its people would be reserved and unlikely to invite strange cyclists into their home. It was great to be proved wrong within 24 hours of arrival.

Interestingly, when we tell Brits about the hospitality we received in other countries, they often reply: 'I doubt you'd get that in England.' However, our experience has been that British people are indeed hospitable to strangers

Of course, part of the reason people took pity on us was precisely because we were foreign. We were clearly a long way from home and thus more vulnerable and more in need of help. However, we had experienced similar levels of hospitality in the UK before leaving home. On our practice ride from Cornwall to Scotland, we were invited in by complete strangers and given a room for the night. The circumstances were particularly striking because the couple who invited us in were on their way out for dinner when we knocked on their door to ask for water. Rather than turn us away, they left us in their empty house for the evening, despite only having just met us. On the same trip, we were also invited to sleep in several pub gardens, one of which brought a complimentary Full English to our bivvy bags in the morning.

It had been nice to have our assumptions challenged before leaving home. Nicer still to be having those assumptions challenged almost a year later. Japanese society is undoubtedly very different from Britain's – and most other countries' – but it has one thing in common with all of them: the people are kind.

Chapter 26

*'I'm long past feeling any shame about sleeping in public places,
but waking up surrounded by a Japanese women's baseball team
was a little awkward.' – Tim*

*'Japan, you beauty. One of the most beautiful days of the trip so far,
winding between the forested hills of Honshu.' – Laura*

From the rice fields near the flower seller's house, we continued
cycling east, enjoying the novelty of a new country and the
cheapness of the sushi. We had contacted a cyclist who lived a few
days' ride along the coast and arranged to stay with him. We made
slower progress than we had anticipated however, so on the day we
were due to arrive, we had to phone and let him know that we would
not reach him.

'Don't worry, I'll come and pick you up.'

'Oh no, you really don't have to,' I protested. 'We're quite happy
camping out. Besides, our bikes are pretty big. I'm not sure you'd fit
them in your car.'

'No problem. I have a big car,' he said.

I acquiesced and we settled down on a bench with our paperbacks
to await his arrival. A few cars came and went, but none were our
guy. A school bus pulled in and I carried on reading my book. I
noticed the driver walking in our direction out of the corner of my
eye.

'Tim? Laura? It's me, Yoshi.'

Yoshi, our host for the night, was quite accurate, understated
even, in assessing himself as 'having a big car'. He apparently owned
a school bus. We wheeled our bikes down the central aisle and set off
for his house.

His young son sat in the front seat of the bus with a bag of shopping at his side. After I had exhausted my repertoire of silly faces to make him laugh, I picked a potato out of the shopping bag and tricked him into thinking I had thrown it out the window. His mouth widened with horror then switched to a mischievous grin. My sleight of hand may have been a bit too convincing however, because the boy quickly began removing potatoes from the bag and throwing them out the window. I think I had just got him to stop throwing away his dad's weekly food shop at unsuspecting pedestrians when Yoshi turned and said:

'You like raw fish?'

Back in his apartment, we sat cross legged on the floor around a small table, six inches high. We were talking to Yoshi's wife as he brought out several long white plates, one by one, with rows of thinly sliced fish.

'Mmm, this is delicious. What is it?'

'That one is yellowtail.'

'This one's good too,' Laura chipped in, passing me the plate.

'That's snapper.'

One small round plate had a delicate looking fish sliced onto it, the colour of pale flesh. I had not tried it yet so took a few chunks with my chopsticks and popped them in my mouth.

'What's that one?' Laura asked, gesturing to the plate I had just sampled.

'Fugu,' came the reply. I stopped chewing.

'Fugu?' I mumbled with what I feared may have been my last breath.

'Isn't that pufferfish?' Laura asked, looking like she had seen a ghost. Or, at least, that episode of The Simpsons where Homer eats fugu pufferfish and is told that he has only 22 hours to live.

For a moment, I panicked. Did I have a mouthful of poisonous tetrodoxin? My only knowledge of the fish comes from that episode and I was worried I had only 22 hours left. However, having survived

170

the incident, I have since researched the topic and am happy to report that The Simpsons was woefully inaccurate about the symptoms of fugu poisoning. If you eat the wrong part of a pufferfish, you would never last 22 hours.

Mercifully, the only pufferfish that is sold to those without a licence has already been prepared safely, with the dangerous parts removed. Yoshi knew that, his wife knew that, and they both guess correctly that we did not. They had a good laugh as I regained the colour in my cheeks.

The following morning, we got back in the school bus and were taken to a natural disaster information centre. It seemed like a strange choice of tourist destination but turned out to be the perfect insight into Japanese society. They live with the constant threat of natural disasters, and they love health and safety. The centre was half museum, half theme park and the highlight was a simulated earthquake. We were given hard hats, then directed to sit at a table in a pretend kitchen and hold on for our lives as the room shook with increasing violence. It was terrifying, but everyone else seemed to find it hilarious, including Yoshi's five year old son.

The bus's next stop was an unremarkable back street. We disembarked and followed Yoshi towards a grubby little building with an unmarked door, which he pushed open.

'Lunch,' he grinned.

We were hit by a wall of steam as we stepped into an unlit room with few windows but lots of people. Rows of tables were filled with suited men and women leaning over bowls of noodle soup, slurping their lunches. There was a long line of people, all holding plastic trays and queueing to get access to two huge urns. The choice appeared to be between thick noodles with broth and really thick noodles with broth.

'Just follow me,' Yoshi said, as he helped himself to noodles and requested various extras from an aproned man who stood behind a buffet of steaming food. We tried to replicate his actions as nonchalantly as we could but still required the help of the guy behind us to extract our noodles from the urn.

We joined Yoshi and son on two wooden benches around a wipe-clean table and tucked into our food. It was simple but tasted great. As with the earthquake experience, I might have initially questioned the choice of venue – the cafe was unremarkable from the outside – but we were getting a glimpse of normal life in a foreign land and that, surely, is the reason we travel.

Our noodles consumed, we got back on our bikes. We waved goodbye to Yoshi and his son and pedalled out of town. I could not help but think that, had we stuck to our original principle of 'no motorised transport' and not accepted Yoshi's offer of a lift, then we would have missed out on a wonderful 24 hours' experience. No noodle cafe, no earthquake simulation, no fugu. We had skipped 20 miles of forgettable cycling and replaced it with stories and memories.

Chapter 27

'Happiness is a Japanese supermarket and a weak Yen. (P.S. Woken up by another baseball team).' – Tim

'I can safely say that after 9 months of living outside, I am looking weathered.' – Laura

We continued our route along Japan's south coast working our way towards Hiroshima. It is a town whose name will always be associated with that fateful morning in 1945, when a tiny parachute fell from the sky, turned everything white then ripped the town apart. These days, Hiroshima is a fully functional, modern city, but our first port of call on arrival was still the museum dedicated to the day the atomic bomb was dropped.

Despite effectively being tourists for the entire duration of our trip, it was surprisingly rare that we actually visited museums or other tourist attractions. On most holidays, you hop from one interesting place to another, teleported by bus or plane. The journey is often inconsequential, an inconvenience even. With cycle touring, the journey *is* the holiday. We spent far more time on dusty tracks in the middle of nowhere and in little villages that would not make it onto any tourist map than we did at any honey pot destination. That was not because we were trying to 'get off the beaten track' and deliberately differentiate ourselves from other travellers, it is just that there are a lot of miles between the hot spots. What might be a couple of hours on a bus could be several days' cycling for us. I like experiencing a country through its towns and villages, so the life of a cycle tourist suited me well. However, there were some tourist attractions that I did not want to miss and the Hiroshima Peace Memorial Museum was one of them.

173

We locked our bikes to a railing outside the museum and went inside. The subject matter was dark but instantly fascinating. With only two nuclear weapons ever having been used in anger, the survivors and remnants of Hiroshima and Nagasaki provide the only real examples of their destructive capabilities. No less than 100,000 people were killed by a single bomb dropped on Hiroshima and two-thirds of the entire town were obliterated.

A mesmerising chart in the museum displayed the relative strengths of nuclear weapons over the years and the quantities stockpiled by different nations. Disturbingly, the bomb used on Hiroshima was just a firecracker compared to the weapons subsequently developed. The strength of a bomb is measured by the kilotons of TNT to which it would be equivalent. The Hiroshima bomb was 15 kilotons. A few years after it was dropped, the US army tested a bomb that was equivalent to 15,000 kilotons. In other words, a single warhead with the same impact as 1,000 Hiroshima bombs. It is no wonder that the world was on the edge of its seat for much of the following decades when there were weapons that powerful floating around. But it was never just one bomb the Americans had stashed away. They had a lot. Thousands, in fact: at their peak they had no fewer than 30,000 nuclear warheads in their arsenal. Worryingly, they were not even the worst offenders. The Soviet Union had far more warheads than America. Thank goodness all of that nonsense is long behind us, I thought, before moving onto the next room.

The subsequent exhibit was particularly poignant. It was a wall covered in framed letters written by the various mayors of Hiroshima since 1945. On closer inspection I realised that each letter was addressed to a world leader, written the day after that leader's country had tested a nuclear weapon. The mayor would write to them, remind them of what happened to Hiroshima all those years ago and implore them to stop developing nuclear weapons. The most recent letters were addressed to Kim Jong Un, Vladimir Putin and

Barrack Obama. They were all dated within the last 12 months. Perhaps the nonsense is not behind us after all.

Some have debated whether the dropping of atom bombs was the least worst option when the alternative was a protracted ground invasion, which would probably have resulted in an even greater loss of life. What no one debates however, is that the bombing of Hiroshima was horrendous. The city was obliterated and tens of thousands of men, women and children were killed indiscriminately. Given that, what made the Hiroshima museum particularly powerful was how balanced it was. It did not pull any punches in detailing the horrors that occurred to its citizens, but its coverage of the events leading up to the bombing were impartial and threw no accusations. Visiting the War Memorial of Korea museum in Seoul a few weeks earlier, we had been struck by the same impressive neutrality in its dealing with the Korean War. It was not treated as an opportunity to bad mouth North Korea or China, while making the south look magnanimous. The good, bad and ugly were detailed on both sides and the museums were all the better for it.

I emerged from the museum feeling like World War II had ended just days before. It was something of a shock, then, to find a vibrant, developed city in front of my eyes. It was a complete contrast to the images in my mind of the burned out aftermath of 1945.

We retrieved our bikes and noted, as ever, that all of our panniers were still attached and no one had run off with our stuff. We remounted and rode out of the city, back to the coastal road. As we did so, the clouds darkened and it began to drizzle.

Putting on waterproof jackets and trousers was a faff. We had to stop, find somewhere to lean our bikes, rummage through our panniers, pull the waterproofs over whatever else we were wearing, reseal our panniers and remount before we could carry on. We frequently found that, by the time we had gone through the rigmarole, the rain had stopped. As such, it was often better to not bother, which is exactly what we did when the drizzle started.

Two minutes later the rain was falling so hard it was almost deafening and I was soaked through to my underwear. We battled along a busy highway with our heads down, fighting to ignore the rain and pedalling hard to stay warm. We knew that there was a roadside service station a few miles ahead, which in Japan often meant there would be space to camp. When we arrived however, we found there was no designated camping area. We made a dash for the attached shopping centre but found it closed for the evening. The rain continued unabated, lashing down in huge waves, as we looked out forlornly from the relative shelter provided by the building's entrance.

While we considered our options, we got our stove out and cooked ourselves dinner. The front of the shopping centre had a canopy, which kept most of the rain off. With the high winds, spray still wafted in from the sides, but it was considerably drier than anywhere else in the vicinity. By the time we had chased down our noodles with a mug of hot chocolate, it was dark. There was nowhere obvious to camp and, besides, the prospect of pitching our tent in the middle of the storm was not greatly appealing.

Instead, we hunkered down where we were: in the entrance to a shop. We lay our bivvy bags as close to the front doors as possible to minimise the amount of rain that got onto them. We pushed our bikes out of the way, either side of the entrance, then piled panniers next to our heads to stop the spray from getting our faces wet. The car park next to us was brightly lit and cars came and went throughout the night, but thankfully, no one tried to get into or out of the closed shop. It was not the best night's sleep I have ever had: the storm grew in ferocity, shaking the whole building and blowing clouds of rain onto us from varying angles. We were awake before sunrise and had our bivvy bags packed away long before anyone came to open the shop. When they did, we just smiled politely as they unlocked the front door, then followed them inside for a cup of tea.

The weather cleared by late morning and we set off through the fresh air, dodging huge puddles and watching our tyres spray an arc of water in our wake. We were heading towards Shimanami Kaido: a series of bridges high above sea level which connect half a dozen islands in the Seto Inland Sea. There are two roads that connect the main island of Honshu with the smaller island of Shikoku, but the Shimanami Kaido is the only one open to cyclists. In fact, its specific cycling facilities and great views afforded by its elevation have resulted in the route becoming an attraction for cyclists in its own right.

Shortly after we caught our first glimpse of the bridges in the distance, they were obscured by cloud. Yesterday's storm appeared to be returning for a rematch and we scrabbled in our panniers to get our waterproofs before it struck. The heavens opened and a torrent of water poured forth. We were soaked through within minutes, even with our jackets on. I squeezed water from my gloves like they were sponges. The roads, already saturated from yesterday's downpour, quickly turned into a series of small lakes whose depth was only determined by riding straight through them. It took real concentration to keep my bike within the lines of the hard shoulder and not stray into the moving traffic, as rain hammered the ground around us.

In the midst of this melee, a man appeared at the side of the road with a huge umbrella, and tried to flag us down. I stopped in front of him and said hello through gritted teeth. It was nice that strangers stopped us to talk from time to time, but doing so in the middle of a thunderstorm was not ideal.

'Where you come from?' he asked.

This was not the time for idle chat. I was cold and getting battered by rain. I stared at the floor.

'UK,' Laura said distractedly, a stream of water pouring off her helmet. 'We're from the UK.'

'Where you sleep?' he fired back.

'Tonight? Don't know. Roadside probably.'

We had not given it much thought and, judging from the broken sentences tumbling out of Laura's mouth, we were not capable of doing so right now. My shoulders were hunched and my head ducked down beneath the hood of my jacket. I hoped my face was conveying the discomfort of having to stand around talking to a man who looked perfectly protected beneath his giant umbrella.

'You sleep my house,' he said. 'Follow me.'

If there is one thing that you dream about when cycling in the rain, it is that you are spontaneously offered accommodation.

He drove slowly for us with his rear hazards blinking, stopping at every turn to make sure we caught up. He pulled up to a wooden house surrounded by fields and pointed us towards his garage. In his porch we stripped off our wet jackets and wrung out our socks before he handed us fresh towels and showed us to the shower. This was excellent.

Warm and dry, we floated back into his living room where he brought hot tea.

'English,' he said, opening a DVD case and pushing play on Despicable Me 2. We found ourselves freshly showered in the house of a complete stranger, watching bright yellow cartoon characters dance on screen.

'Wagyu steak,' he said, interrupting the film to show us several cuts of meat, clearly intended for dinner. 'I work chef.' If there is one person that you dream of being hosted by when cycling, it is a chef.

He laughed at the TV while preparing dinner as well as laughing at himself, us and everything else. We rarely knew what was so funny, but it was infectious so we laughed too. Besides, when you had been expecting instant noodles in a tent and instead are being served Wagyu steak, what is there not to be happy about?

'I work chef. What your job?'

'Teacher,' I replied. He clearly did not understand so I did my best to communicate in mime. I indicated the height of a small child, wagged my finger and pretended to talk sternly.

'Ah, sensei!' he said, with a spark of recognition. 'You?' he said to Laura.

'Lawyer,' she tried, before miming the hammer action of a judge's gavel.

'Ah, OK,' he said, returning the hammering gesture.

The man's wife returned home from work and, helpfully, she spoke perfect English. After conferring with her husband and sneaking a few glances at us, she turned to Laura and said:

'So, what's it like being a builder?'

Once we had clarified that Laura was a lawyer not a labourer, we all sat around a dining room table for dinner. The Wagyu he served ranks as one of the top three steaks of my life, all three of which were cooked by strangers who hosted us. The wife brought out a couple of bottles of wine. We drank a little, they drank a lot. After dinner, the chef disappeared from the room then returned a few minutes later wearing a sequined Union Jack t-shirt that belonged to his daughter and a pair of novelty glasses with fake eyes. He loudly sang the words 'Goodbye England Rose!' shouted 'Elton John!' at the top of his voice then fell about laughing with his wife.

In the morning, they were clearly suffering from their excesses, but they dressed for work and left early. We thanked them for their hospitality, and they apologised for having to rush off before handing us a six-pack of ring doughnuts for breakfast.

We cycled a few miles along damp roads before finding a bench to sit on while we ate our breakfast. Doughnuts were surprisingly common in Japan. I had always thought of Japanese food as entirely foreign and other worldly; meals in which you cannot tell if you are eating animal, vegetable or mineral. Japan certainly had that stuff in spades. We frequently bought things from shops without knowing what we were getting. On one occasion we ended up with something that looked (and tasted) like a large dollop of PVA glue on a piece of balsa wood. As well as the weird stuff however, they also had loads of cheap, American-style junk food: doughnuts, hot dogs and synthetic, long-life pastries.

I found it hard to reconcile this 'low culture' with the Japan of my imagination. I had thought of Japanese culture as tiny geishas dancing in silk kimonos and giant sumo wrestlers fighting in their underpants. Also tall temples with curved roofs like square hats, houses divided by sliding paper walls, works of art like The Great Wave, manga cartoons, anime, Judo, karate and Mr Miyagi. All of these things are indeed unique to Japan, and we saw many examples of them, but the proliferation of cheap snacks sold from American convenience stores was quite unexpected. A cursory consideration of the country's history however, gives some explanation.

Japan was almost completely isolated right up until the middle of the 19th century. It refused to trade with other countries or even maintain dialogue. This history is reflected today in its remarkably homogenous population. Whereas less than 80% of the English population are classified as 'white British', and non-Hispanic white Americans only make up 62% of the US population, some estimates put the percentage of ethnic Japanese in Japan at fully 99%.

Japan might still be adhering to its long-held isolationist policies now were it not for a forceful intervention in the mid-1800s. In a literal example of gunboat diplomacy, a small fleet of American warships sailed across the Pacific and demanded that they be allowed to trade with the Japanese. I am not sure that it counts as 'free trade' when conducted at gunpoint, but the easing of trade restrictions certainly influenced the course of modern Japan. As a result, alongside the beautiful temples and delicious sushi, there are Family Marts, Circle Ks and 7-Elevens, all stocking hot dogs and doughnuts.

All of which is my way of explaining why, despite travelling through a country of fascinating culture, history and traditions, my diary from our time there is filled with superlatives about ring doughnuts. I quote:

Saturday 10th May: 'Great offer on doughnuts in 7-Eleven. Five-pack for 100 yen. Amazing.'

Thursday 15th May: 'Bargain doughnuts in supermarket. Only 10p!!'

Wednesday 21st May: 'Three doughnuts for breakfast. Three more by 11am. Feel sick.'

That final, illuminating entry, from my as-yet-unpublished diary, was written shortly after leaving the chef's house. Laura had decided that doughnuts were not a breakfast food so I took it upon myself to eat the entire pack. Wishing I had more self-control when faced with baked goods, I got back on the saddle and we continued eastwards beneath a clear blue sky.

Our route took us up through tree-covered hills, past rice paddies and along winding roads, high up in the mountains. The villages we visited were quintessentially Japanese: neat rows of ornately carved, wooden houses with beautiful covered 'engawa' walkways surrounding them. The narrow, curbless streets were lined either with small, potted shrubs outside people's houses, or brightly coloured placards outside shops.

On a cool evening, we reached one such village that was set high in the hills. We cooked some noodles on our stove before walking to the local 'onsen' public baths to warm ourselves in the hot water. There were lots of families there, spanning several generations, and we got smiles and the occasional wave every time someone caught our eye. Thoroughly warmed, we wheeled our bikes back to a pagoda we had spotted on our way into town. We laid out our sleeping bags and drifted off to sleep.

After descending the hills, we continued further east, stopping regularly at the roadside to eat tofu with spring onions, ginger and soy sauce, or gorge on fresh sushi. We took a ferry to an island filled with shrines where we visited a number of temples: one high up in the hills, filled with tiny stone Buddhas, and another whose wooden walkways took us out over the high tide. The island hosted a large population of deer, which were entirely unfazed by humans and came right up to our tent to watch us making breakfast. It was such a tranquil place that, even without any understanding of Zen Buddhism, it was impossible not to leave feeling calmed.

Our time in Japan ended in Kyoto. Before Tokyo, Kyoto was the capital of Japan for over a thousand years. It remains one of the country's most historic cities, hosting no less than 17 UNESCO World Heritage Sites. Indeed, its historic significance saved it being the target of an atomic bomb: an American official involved in deciding which cities to target had honeymooned in Kyoto and could not bear the thought of wiping out so much history. As such, it is still a key tourist destination and rightly so: it is a beautiful city. We took in a few final temples and ate our last sushi before making our way to the airport for our flight to Vietnam.

PART IV

Southeast Asia

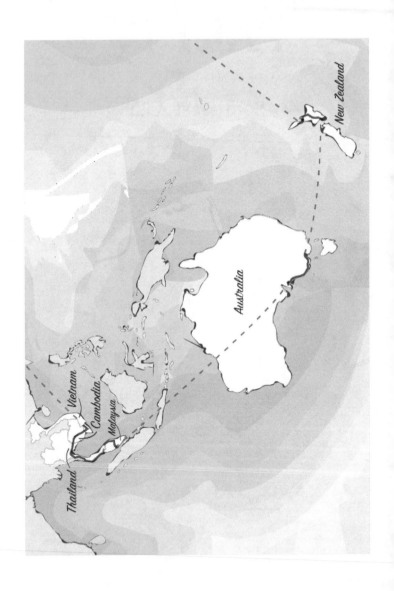

Chapter 28

'Another stressful morning spent getting bikes to an airport and fit for baggage handlers. I'm sure Ho Chi Minh City will be much more relaxing...' – Tim

'Surprisingly good to be back on the chaotic roads of the developing world. It's like an elaborate dance – no apparent rules, yet it works.'
– Laura

We landed in Ho Chi Minh City to find the heat and humidity a shock after Japan. We had arranged to stay with a cyclist for our first night in Vietnam. We arrived at her address – a huge apartment building – and made our way up to the 32nd floor after leaving our bikes in the basement.

We knocked on room number 325 as instructed but received no answer. It was 2am. After repeatedly knocking and waiting in the empty corridor for five minutes, we tested the front door and found it to be unlocked. Peering inside, the flat was in darkness except for a single illuminated room with two mattresses on the floor. Too tired to question the etiquette, we let ourselves in, dumped our panniers in a corner and promptly fell fast asleep.

We awoke, hot and sticky, with the noisy buzz of Ho Chi Minh City (better known as Saigon) rising from the streets, 300 feet below. We sat in the hot, empty room for two hours before we heard signs of life from our anonymous host. We pushed open the door to our room and offered a tentative 'good morning'.

'Oh, hi,' she said, absentmindedly. 'I'm just going out so maybe see you tonight.'

'Oh, OK,' I replied. 'Have a good day. And thanks for letting us stay!'

She left and, a few minutes later, we did the same. Outside, Saigon was hectic. The streets thronged with cars, mopeds and push bikes, all vying for space on wide, multi-laned roads. Food sellers wheeling carts shouted for attention from the pavement, offering 'banh mi' baguettes and vats of hot, steaming noodles. Shops sprawled their wares onto the street, doors wide open, customers haggling with owners for cheap clothes. The tranquillity of the Far East was gone. Down south, things were a little livelier.

We found a cycling shop and dropped our bikes off for a service. While they got sorted out, we treated ourselves to a trip around the Viet Cong tunnels then visited the War Remnants Museum. After the magnanimous impartiality of the Hiroshima Peace Museum, and the even handed treatment of all parties at the Korean War Museum, I was looking forward to an insightful account of the Vietnam War. However, I am not sure that referring to your opponents as the 'stupid capitalist invaders' and 'American pig dogs' is the best way to achieve balance. If we had known the museum's original name – the Museum of Chinese and American War Crimes – we might have guessed at its bias. It was interesting, and no doubt America did not cover itself in glory during the war, but propaganda is not informative and I learned little.

In the evening we booked onto a food tour. Along with several other tourists, we were guided between a variety of restaurants where we ate snake (chewy), mouse (tastes like chicken) and 'sticky rice' (amazing). The proper name for this latter food is xôi. It is a Vietnamese staple made from glutinous rice that comes in a variety of forms. On this occasion the rice was purple and came drenched in coconut milk, with chunks of fresh mango on top and a generous sprinkling of crunchy sugar, all wrapped in a banana leaf. The result was pure nectar, the tastiest thing we had eaten since trilece, Albania's milky sponge dessert. We vowed to eat as much of it as possible during our stay.

We licked our lips as we walked back to our mysterious host's apartment. She was nowhere to be found so we let ourselves in and went to sleep. We collected our bikes the following morning then went back to the flat to pack our panniers, ready to hit the road again. As we went to leave, the girl emerged from her room where, unbeknownst to us, she must have been all the previous evening and all morning.

'See ya,' she said.

'Bye!' we replied. 'Thanks again for letting us stay.'

It did not take long to escape the madness of the city and we were soon riding along much quieter, single lane roads through the Mekong Delta. As well as having to adapt to the style of driving in Vietnam, which was somewhat less disciplined than it had been in Japan, we also found ourselves switching which side of the road we cycled on for the fourth time in as many countries.

In Oman they drive on the right and in India they drive on the left. Korea was back to right again, but Japan was left and Vietnam was right once more. It would not be long before we switched to the left once more for Thailand and there would be more switches after that.

Outside of Saigon, the proportion of cars on the road fell dramatically, replaced almost entirely by mopeds and bicycles. It was a little chaotic, but two wheeled vehicles are far less scary than the four wheelers, and the speeds were never high. Like India, the roads were a bit mad at times but felt safer than cycling on many of Britain's busier roads.

We cruised along through the humidity of midday, with our surroundings providing a constant cinematic stream of distractions. All the way along, the roads were flanked by shops or jungle. The shops were wall-to-wall terraces of small shacks, all brightly decorated, with piles of fruit in sacks or crates of fizzy drinks stacked to chest height. The jungle was dense and impenetrable, with rows of tightly packed trees sporting huge, dark green branches and leaves.

The humidity had been building over the course of the morning and, come early afternoon, it burst. A wave of water appeared on the road ahead, blackening the grey concrete and sweeping towards us like a flood. First, flecks appeared around us, then, within seconds, clumps of water rained down on us from above.

The locals appeared entirely unperturbed by the downfall and continued about their business, which, we now noticed, was largely conducted beneath canopies. We ducked under one such shelter, which happened to be a restaurant, propped our bikes against a wall and ordered two bowls of noodle soup. When we had licked our bowls clean we asked the lady serving the soup if she had any sticky rice.

'Xôi?' I enquired, barely containing my excitement at the thought of the sweet coconut milk dribbling down my chin. She shook her head.

Dejected, we made do with some Vietnamese coffee, sweetened with condensed milk, and watched the world go by from the comfort of our plastic chairs. As we did so, a man walking past stopped in his tracks and pointed at me. His eyes were wide with surprise.

'Ho Chi Minh! Ho Chi Minh!' he shouted excitedly before snapping a photograph and giving me a thumbs up. 'Ho Chi Minh,' he added finally, before walking on.

I was used to it by now. No one had ever called me Ho Chi Minh before – I bear absolutely no resemblance to the Communist revolutionary – but I was familiar with the basis of the game. It had started back in Europe. A local would see me, clock my beard then shout the name of an historic figure from the country who also happened to have been bearded.

'Lenin! Lenin!' they cried back in the former Soviet Union, 'Khomeini!' in Iran. My favourite was the Indian group who chased me shouting 'Ali Baba!', a character who, even if he had existed, almost certainly would not have been ginger.

In Islamic countries, my beard was particularly popular and I had to disappoint a lot of Turks who had enthusiastically asked if I was

Muslim. I did not have the heart to let down the supermarket attendant we kept bumping into in Muscat though. He had taken to pointing at me across the car park and shouting 'Muslim! Brother!' whilst grinning and stroking his own beard every time we went shopping. After the third occasion I just embraced it and started shouting 'Muslim! Brother!' back at him.

Apparently, I was now Ho Chi Minh, a slight Vietnamese man with a wispy moustache and a long goatee. I set off from the cafe a new man.

Chapter 29

'Averaging three showers a day. Southeast Asia is sweaty.' – Tim

'First banh mi: pate, four kinds of meat and salad. For 45p. Very happy about this.' – Laura

The rain had stopped and the sun had returned by the time we started cycling again. We rode through the puddles to a small town called Long Tho, near Long Xuyen, where we stopped for the afternoon at a teacher's house. It was nestled off the main road, at the side of a narrow, dusty track, amidst a long row of other houses. The side of his house facing the street was entirely open: no wall, no door, just a large opening. It went straight from street to living room with no middle ground. We sat on sofas in a concrete room whose walls were painted a faded blue. Every time someone walked or cycled past, they would wave and the teacher would say hello.

The teacher did not work in a school, but instead taught English to a dozen children in his front room. The kids were due shortly so the living room was converted into a makeshift classroom: the sofas pushed to the sides and a few rows of desks unfolded in their place. The children ranged in age but were all teenagers, dressed in casual clothes. There were huddled whisperings and furtive glances in our direction, two white strangers stood with their teacher. He spoke to them in Vietnamese and, after I caught the words 'Tim' and 'Laura' in his speech, he stepped to one side and said: 'Over to you,' then disappeared into the kitchen. Laura and I exchanged a look before turning to face the class.

'We didn't exactly know that we were going to be teaching a class today, and we don't know much Vietnamese but we're English so hopefully we can be of some help.'

Silence.

190

'Can you understand me OK?' Laura continued. More silence.

'Yes, we can understand you,' came the eventual reply from one of the older girls. 'Where are you from?'

'I grew up near Manchester and Tim grew up near London.'

'Of all the places in the world, why did you decide to come to Long Tho? It's so small and boring,' asked a younger girl.

It was a good question and we did our best to answer it: 'When you're travelling by bike, you spend a lot of time in small towns and villages. It's impossible not to. It might seem boring if you've spent your whole life here. I would say the same about my hometown, but we have never been to Vietnam before, never visited a Vietnamese village and never spoken to Vietnamese schoolchildren. To us, it's fascinating.'

That seemed to break the ice and we were subsequently hit with a string of quick fire questions:

'What is your religion?'

'What do you think of Vietnam?'

'Were you in CSI?'

'How long did it take to grow that beard?'

'Were you in CSI Miami?'

Their enthusiasm kept the questions coming for the full hour of their class. Their command of the English language was excellent and needed little help from us. We had visited several schools between England and Vietnam, and the students' English was invariably far better than any of our foreign languages, but it was the thoughtfulness of the questions we were asked that was most striking. As well as questions about sore bums and CSI, we were also asked about social norms in the UK, our prior knowledge of the countries we were visiting and whether we ever questioned the purpose of spending such a long time just riding a bike. In a Turkish secondary school, we were even quizzed about LGBT rights in the UK, as compared to Turkey, and what we thought about the differences (thankfully, they strongly supported equality). We were consistently

191

impressed by the students we met and the ones in that Vietnamese living room were no exception.

When the time ran out, we helped them pack away the tables then watched them walk away down the street. The teacher was pleased to have given his students an opportunity to converse with native English speakers, and delighted to have had an hour off teaching. As a thank you, he took us to a restaurant for dinner. After we had finished our noodles, I got him to ask the waitress if they had any sticky rice for dessert. They did not so we had to make do with ice cream.

Back at his house, the teacher opened the door to a spare room in which a huge, fat man lay snoring on a bed. The teacher gave the man a kick and he spluttered in response then sleepily walked out of the room.

'You can sleep here,' he said.

I went to retrieve my toothbrush from my pannier but recoiled at the sight of a huge spider inside it. Seeing my fearful reaction, the teacher grabbed a broom and rapidly swept the spider into the corridor, through the living room and out onto the street. Nervously, we went to bed.

For the next few days, we rode along dusty tracks, through dense jungle and over wooden bridges. Every few miles we would reach one of the many waterways that divide the Mekong Delta and have to wait for a tiny ferry. Such moments provided welcome respite from the sweaty cycling and gave us the opportunity to rest in the shade. Invariably, such spots would have a stall selling lychees, mangosteen, dragon fruit or sugarcane juice, all of which were ideal on hot days.

Every afternoon at two o'clock, the heavens would open. First would come the gentle pitter-patter of rain then, within a minute, huge globs of water would drop from the sky, soaking everything in sight. On one particular day, I pulled up next to Laura during the downpour and pointed ahead to a cafe. She nodded and followed.

The cafe was little more than a shack, extended by a series of tarpaulins propped up with wooden poles. We took our place on two plastic chairs and, to our surprise, were handed a laminated menu in English. The translations however, were not much easier to understand than the original Vietnamese, but we appreciated the gesture and gamely ordered one 'fish eagle sun' and an 'egg fried erosion threat'. I am no expert on Vietnamese cuisine, but I had my suspicions that these translations may not have been entirely accurate.

The rain continued to pound the canopies and we ate our meals to the sound of a thousand tiny drums overhead. Half way through our lunch, the owner of the restaurant appeared, pushing a catering trolley with a tiny TV on. With a grin, he pushed a video cassette into a huge VCR and turned up the volume. It was a live Michael Jackson show, which opened with a performance of 'Thriller'. The owner watched us intently, waiting for us to show our approval, which we did with thumbs up and bewildered laughter. He was pleased as punch. I took the opportunity to ask if he had any sticky rice. We were not far from the Cambodian border and we still had not found any of our favourite Vietnamese dessert.

'Xôi?' I asked.

The man's face fell as he shook his head, clearly disappointed to have disappointed his customers. Feeling bad for spoiling his fun, I changed the subject back to safe territory by pointing at the TV and saying: 'Michael Jackson. Very good!' with lots more thumbs-up. The owner brightened a little and produced a microphone. For the next hour, we were not going anywhere: it was time for karaoke.

Our sights were on the Cambodian border, not far away, and we settled into a quiet rhythm of easy, mindless cycling to get there. As we passed through a town, the pavements filled with roadside vendors and I noticed a small lady in a conical hat pushing her cart along the road.

Without thinking, I slammed on my brakes.

'What the hell!?' Laura shouted. I had committed the cycling sin of bringing my bike to an abrupt stop in front of her without a hand gesture or other warning. I had just reacted on instinct and she had had to swerve at the last minute to avoid crashing into my back.

I composed myself before replying as calmly as I could. 'Two words: Sticky. Rice.' She followed my gaze to the little old lady in the hat and scanned the contents of her cart.

'Ohhh...' she replied, as the penny dropped. My erratic braking was forgiven. We propped our bikes against a sun-bleached wall, strutted up to the woman, pointed at her parcels of xôi and held up four fingers with a smile.

Chapter 30

'Shins should not sweat. #vietnam #humid' – Tim

'Contrary to popular belief, the leader of the Viet Cong was not, in fact, King Kong.' – Laura

In a state of heady ecstasy after too much sugar, we got back on our bikes. We followed tarmac out of town before taking a turning to bounce down a muddy red track. A few hundred yards after passing a tin hut with a long, drooping barrier, it became apparent that we had entered Cambodia.

Neither our exiting Vietnam nor our entering Cambodia received any acknowledgement. No passports were checked and no stamps were given. Not wanting to enter the country illegally, we went back into Vietnam to find an exit stamp.

Back at the tin hut, we found a portly man lying half-asleep in a plastic chair. He wore a white vest, stretched over his not inconsiderable belly, and an ostentatious green hat, which had all the hallmarks of officialdom. Once roused, he directed us around the corner.

Around the corner there appeared to be a boat or some kind of floating building. It was secured to the mainland by a rusty gangplank, above which was a hand painted sign reading: 'Border Customs Officials'. Clearly, this border was designed for boats ferrying their wares up the Mekong, not for overland crossings.

We boarded the boat, where we were greeted only by a sleepy looking golden retriever, but there were no people to be seen. After wandering the corridors, knocking on doors and shouting 'Hello!' we eventually reached the conclusion that the only thing defending the Vietnamese border was a dozy dog.

After waiting for an hour, the visa boat opened for business. People in uniforms arrived and we followed them inside. After several minutes sitting in a waiting room – we were the only people waiting – an official appeared, indicated that we were in the wrong place and motioned us down a corridor. Three right turns later, we knocked on a door, which was opened by the very same official. He welcomed us into the opposite side of the office we had been waiting outside just a minute before.

Vietnamese formalities completed, we returned to dry land and then back around the barrier, back past the string vest official and back into Cambodia. We now had an exit stamp for Vietnam but still no visa for Cambodia.

We stopped to ask for directions and were pointed towards a narrow muddy path through the undergrowth. It seemed far too meagre a track for an international border, but we followed it anyway. We bumped and skidded our way through the jungle and passed several wooden huts on stilts whose occupants all cried 'Hello everybody!' as we rode by. After a few hundred metres, we were pleasantly surprised to come across a large building complex. It was made of stone, surrounded by high walls and painted a light yellow colour, with the definite air of somewhere important. It seemed completely out of place at the end of a muddy track in the middle of the jungle. Yet, when we wheeled our bikes inside the compound, we were greeted by a farcically well-organised bank of numbered windows with a uniformed customs official behind each one. I had trouble imagining anyone finding their way here, let alone a surge of visitors necessitating multiple booths and a queueing system.

We presented our passports for inspection. The official looked puzzled, scratched his head, conferred with a colleague and then turned back to us and said:

'Visa?'

We nodded. He shook his head and pointed us to a man on a moped, parked outside in the jungle.

'Of course!' I thought. Why would we assume that the huge government building with a big sign saying 'Immigration' was the place to get a visa? A schoolboy error. It should have been obvious that the unshaven man straddling a leopard print scooter, with an unlit cigarette in his mouth, was the person we needed to speak to about the international boundary we were hoping to cross.

We pedalled behind the moped man through the jungle until he pulled up outside a house and disappeared inside. He came back a moment later carrying a wooden chair, into which he had apparently carved the word 'VISA' using a blunt knife. He set down the chair by a table from which he proceeded to clear a pile of rubbish. He then presented us with a crumpled bit of paper which turned out to be a visa application form and some crayons he had presumably found down the back of his sofa. I proceeded to complete his form with my usual rigour – illegible handwriting and a fictitious address. The farce was completed by the application of a rubber stamp. I half expected it to produce a picture of Mickey Mouse on a train, but it looked disappointingly official. The ritual complete, we pedalled back into the jungle, at last comforted that we had the full authority of the Cambodian government behind our presence in their country.

International borders are often drawn along arbitrary lines, but straight after crossing the border into Cambodia, the contrast was striking. Everywhere in Vietnam had felt enclosed, the roads forever flanked by shops or jungle. The only glimpses of space we got were on the ferries, when we could see up and down the wide stretches of river. Emerging from the riverside jungle across the border in Cambodia however, we were suddenly greeted with wide open spaces. The narrow road turned into a broad highway of compacted red dirt and the few buildings were set a long way back from the road with any foliage further behind them. We could even see the horizon.

The space was not the only difference. The houses were primitive, made of wood and built on stilts, and it was clear that Cambodia was a poorer country than Vietnam. The reason for the stilts soon became apparent. No sooner had I started to absorb our new surroundings than an almighty torrent was unleashed from the sky. We laughed at the suddenness with which we were drenched. Any attempt at resistance would have been futile so we embraced it, pedalling quickly until we could find shelter.

We reached a house under which two elderly men sat at a rickety table playing cards. We dismounted and wheeled our bikes towards them sheepishly, thick beads of water cascading down our faces. A small nod of approval was given and we wheeled our bikes under the canopy of the house. The men continued their game as we observed the continuing rain with awe. When it stopped, we picked a route through the mud bath that remained of the front yard, waved our thanks and continued on our way.

When we stopped that evening, we realised that we had no food left in our panniers and had not yet obtained any local riel currency. It looked like it might be a hungry evening until we managed to convince a shopkeeper to accept a stray US dollar that we found in Laura's purse. Our initial excitement at being able to buy sustenance was immediately tempered when we looked around the store. It was a breeze block warehouse with a dirt floor, sparsely stocked shelves and nothing fresh. Our dinner was two packets of instant noodles, a sandwich bag full of biscuits and a bottle of Fanta.

Phnom Penh, when we reached it the following day, was busy and dusty. The motorists did not seem to have a lot of time or respect for bicycles, so we had to crawl into the city carefully, hugging the side of the road.

'There are no social problems in Cambodia,' declared our host, after he had welcomed us into his house. 'I left the UK in the early 2000s. I couldn't stand all the lying politicians. When Blair went into Iraq, it was the final straw. I left and I've never been back.'

'Did it work?' I asked. 'Have you escaped the politics, the spin and the latest controversy from Nigel Farage?'

'Who?' he said. I took that as a yes. Rob was in his early forties and lived in Phnom Penh with his wife and two ferocious dogs. He handed us a couple of bottles of cold beer then carried on telling us about his new country.

'In Cambodia, elders are respected. Generations of the same family all live together. The kids respect their parents, and they respect their grandparents. There are no social problems.'

It was nice to hear such a positive endorsement for Cambodia, especially coming from an ex-pat. We described our experience cycling into the city and, knowing that he was a cyclist, asked if he ever rode a bike around town.

'Cars are like status symbols here. If you're on a bike, it means you're poor. And, if you get hit, the police won't do anything. There are no repercussions.'

The image of poor people being run down like skittles on the streets of Phnom Penh somewhat spoiled the picture of perfect social harmony he had been describing. However, he clearly loved his chosen country so we accepted his rose tinting and just enjoyed our beers. He gave us the keys to his house and said he was going out of town for the weekend.

'When I used to go touring,' he said, 'I dreamed about having a bit of time in a nice house, all on my own. No tent to mess about with and not having to be on best behaviour around whatever strangers were hosting me. Just some quiet time, away from the world. So that's what I do now: greet people, give them a beer, see if they need any help then let them have the place to themselves.'

Catching me eyeing his two growling canines, he added: 'Don't worry, they're coming with me.'

Our activities in Phnom Penh, over the next couple of days, largely revolved around Pol Pot and the Khmer Rouge. We visited various sites and museums, all of which detailed the horrors of the regime that ruled Cambodia after the end of the Vietnam War. The Khmer Rouge created a famine, which claimed the lives of hundreds of thousands of people, and implemented a 'social engineering' programme, which largely comprised the systematic execution of two million of its own citizens. Those would be horrific statistics in any context, but given that the population was only eight million at the time, the country's own government oversaw the death of at least one in every four people. Pol Pot's motto was: 'Better to kill an innocent than fail to kill a traitor.' He certainly seems to have lived by his word.

We spent a few more days exploring Cambodia, the highlight of which was Angkor Wat, the remarkable temple complex in the north of the country. It was a fascinating place that lifted our spirits after hearing so much about life under the Khmer Rouge. Fuelled by rice, pork and fresh fruit, on a network of bumpy, dusty dirt tracks, we crossed into our 19th country, Thailand.

Chapter 31

'Made it to Thailand. So far, been given a free night in a hotel and a large bag of rambutan. Now to pedal hard to the beach, two days away.' – Laura

'I am generally a calm man but drive your car into the side of my stationary bike in broad daylight and you will hear me shout.' – Tim

Thailand immediately seemed like a good place to cycle. The moment we crossed the border, the road quality improved markedly. Not only were all the roads sealed, but they also had huge cycle lanes for use by bikes and motorbikes. We were soon welcomed by our old friend 7-Eleven, last seen a few thousand miles north in Japan. The doughnuts were gone, replaced with some half-boiled eggs and a wide range of soya-based drinks, but the shop was generally well stocked, which was more than could be said for anywhere we had found in Cambodia. Importantly, it offered ice cold drinks and air conditioning, both of which were very welcome in the heat.

The only fly in the ointment was that, shortly before we arrived in Thailand, the country had undergone a coup. It had ousted its democratically elected government and replaced it with military leadership. This was by no means the first time such an event had occurred there (Thailand has had about a dozen coups in the last century), but it was the first time we would be cycling in the immediate aftermath of one.

The recurring problem seems to be that the Royal Thai Army rule the country until they think it is safe to let the population have a say, then they call an election. The people cast their votes and invariably elect a government that is not the army. This eventually becomes intolerable to the military, who stage a coup and restart the process.

The government's machinations did not actually affect our daily cycling routine until, a few days into our visit, we were flagged down by armed militia. We had just got back on our bikes after lingering beneath a 7-Eleven air conditioning unit, when a man wearing body armour and carrying a gun signalled for our attention. We slowed to a halt and offered a tentative 'sawasdee' hello.

The man kept one hand on his automatic weapon while holding out the other, indicating that we should not move. It was impossible to read his expression behind the balaclava he wore, but I imagined it to be an angry scowl. We had passed many police checkpoints since arriving in the country, and seen a strikingly heavy military presence for a country at peace, but this was our first direct encounter and we were a little nervous. The masked gunman reached into the truck next to which we stood and removed an object that I hoped was neither handcuffs nor another weapon. He waved it in front of us and I was relieved to see that it was not a gun but a stack of electrolyte sport drinks. He thrust them at us, pointed to the sun and said 'Very hot!'

He gave us a double thumbs-up and waved us on our way. We made to pedal off, relieved not to have been shot but still not too keen to hang around with the machine guns, when we heard a call from behind: 'Wait!' We turned around to see that three more armed men in black fatigues were staring at us. The first man pulled his mask down, gave us a grin and said: 'Photo?' They lined up next to us and got a colleague to snap a picture. Relieved to have avoided any military conflict, we continued riding but soon managed to create our own conflict through a combination of being hot and hungry.

Since getting home, we have often remarked upon the amount of time we spent together on this trip. Although it may be obvious, it is nonetheless worth noting: for 16 months, Laura and I were rarely out of each other's sight.

On our bikes, we would never be more than a couple of hundred yards apart. That is partly because Laura had – and still has – an overriding fear that something catastrophic might happen to her if we got separated. Even without that fear, there was no reason to cycle apart from one another and it made perfect sense to remain within eyesight.

Meals were bought, cooked and eaten together. We slept next to each other, zipped into the same tent or side-by-side under the stars. On rest days we would treat ourselves to cafe trips (together), go shopping (together), or hang out with whoever was hosting us (together). We were told by another cyclist that every year spent together on a bike tour was like six years of normal life and I can believe it. A normal week at home may only include a few hours in each other's company, but on the trip we were with each other 24 hours a day, seven days a week.

Having now been back in the UK for longer than we were away on our bikes, I am able to reflect on the density of experiences that we went through as a couple. There is no doubt that this journey around the world brought us closer together, but it also led to a couple of arguments.

On that hot day in Thailand, conditions were ripe for a falling out. We had each become quite skilled in identifying when the other was in a bad mood and had developed techniques for dealing with it. This almost invariably meant avoiding conversations when hungry. Can't decide which road we need to take and starting to get a bit shirty? Have a sandwich then go back to the map. Arguing over whether we need to stop now or can push on for another hour? Hold that thought and have a block of chocolate. This magic method – eat first, ask questions later – worked wonders. Arguments almost never went further than:

'I think we should go this way.'

'No! Let's go this way.'

'Actually, let's just have a sugary drink.'

Despite spending an intense year and a half together in circumstances that were frequently trying, we rarely said more than a single agitated word to one another before pausing to ingest some sugar, then laughing about whatever was winding us up moments before. That day in Thailand however, we forgot the cardinal rule and got into a heated debate on an empty stomach.

The topic, as I recall, was UK asylum policy. Not, perhaps, the most obviously divisive issue when holidaying in Southeast Asia, but I can only blame whatever political podcast I had been listening to that day. Even if I could remember them, the details were hardly important. The problem was just that we needed to eat. Nonetheless, in the heat of the argument, Laura slammed on her brakes and I crashed into the back of her, breaking a spoke in the process.

Two large iced coffees later, the whole thing was forgotten and Laura admitted that I was right[1]. We continued on our merry way, vowing to ensure any further disputes were conducted at lower speeds and higher blood sugar levels.

As if to remind us of the need for calm, we stopped that night at a Buddhist monastery. Religious institutions had proved generous hosts in most other countries so a monastery seemed like a safe bet, especially when the alternative was camping on the outskirts of a busy town.

However, whilst I was quite familiar with the customs of Christian churches in Europe and to a lesser extent, of Islamic mosques in Turkey and Iran, Buddhism was an unfamiliar religion to me. We had visited temples in Japan but only as tourists, so Buddhism still felt like something strange and mystical. We knew we should wear long trousers and take our hats off when entering a church, and Laura knew to cover her head when visiting a mosque, but what rules did

[1] I made this bit up.

the Buddhists have for visitors? I had no idea so just had to hope that we were not doing or wearing anything offensive as we approached the temple, wheeling our bikes and trying our best to look friendly.

Three young monks sat on a bench in front of us, each sporting a shaved head and bright orange robes. We approached tentatively, clutching our Thai Magic Letter like a shield, unsure of the etiquette of communicating with Buddhist monks. At first, they appeared to be ignoring us and I wondered if we had made some kind of faux pas. Once we got closer however, I realised that they were just engrossed with their smartphones and I recognised the familiar colour scheme of Facebook on their screens. I proffered a 'sawasdee' in greeting, and moments later, they were asking us to pose for selfies with them.

They directed us to an older monk who welcomed us into the monastery. Inside it was surprisingly modern, with freshly painted walls and carpeted floors. He showed us to a small library, walled on one side with bookshelves and on the other by glass. There was a young monk inside, sat at a desk browsing the internet, but he was kicked out to make room for our camping mats. Our guide handed us a remote control for the air conditioning and wrote down the password for the monastery's wifi. Perhaps Buddhists were not that different after all.

We lay down in our private library, adjusted the air conditioning and turned off the lights. I relaxed in the cooled air, finding my heart warmed by the kindness of strangers one more time. The relaxation did not last long however, before I heard the familiar buzz of a mosquito. However, given where we were staying, I thought better than to try squashing it on this occasion.

Chapter 32

'There is no such thing as mild chafing, only that which is bad and that which is about to be.' – Tim

'Defeated by tiredness and the heat, stopped at lunchtime today. Staying in a cheap hotel, watching films. BLISS.' – Laura

We continued pedalling south for the next few weeks, seeking regular sanctuary beneath the straw umbrellas of roadside cafes, eating from their huge piles of noodles and drinking from freshly cut coconuts. We followed the coast for much of the way, swimming in the sea to cool off after a hot, sweaty day's riding before sleeping on the beach. Being on the coast meant that we were regularly treated to the site of stunning karst formations, huge pillars of limestone that rise out of the ocean, hundreds of feet high.

Another treat in Thailand was the proliferation of 'spirit houses': miniature wooden houses that are placed on plinths outside homes and businesses for protection. Invariably these were decorated with brightly coloured paints and gold trimmings, and bedecked with offerings to the spirits. Even petrol stations had technicolour spirit houses outside and we enjoyed keeping our eyes peeled for the brightest and boldest.

Our route eventually took us back inland as we aimed for our border crossing into Malaysia. Deprived of a beach on which to sleep one evening, we looked around for an alternative and eventually settled on a police station.

'Hello, we are Tim and Laura. We have cycled 8,000 miles from the UK. Is there somewhere safe we can sleep?'

The magic letter prompted much debate amongst the officers, who eventually pointed us towards a restaurant on the other side of a busy road and indicated that we should get ourselves some dinner while they found us somewhere we could camp for the night.

After a large portion of pad thai, we returned to the police station and were shown to a nearby building where we could sleep. The building was in a state of disrepair and appeared to be either derelict or not yet finished. It was entirely made of bare concrete, with no windows or fittings inside. We thought that it would be fine for sleeping in, however.

We thanked them for their help and lay our camping mats down on the floor, ready for another sticky night in the heat. Wanting to make the most of sleeping indoors, I went in search of a plug socket to charge my e-reader. The building had no lights so the only light came from my small torch. I turned down a corridor, in search of a plug socket, but stopped in my tracks when I found a pair of eyes staring up at me from the floor. The owner of those eyes nodded at me, from behind the bars of his cell. I nodded in reply before quietly retracing my steps and lying down next to Laura with my uncharged Kindle.

'No sockets?' she said.

'No,' I replied, pausing for a moment, 'and I think we're in a jail. An inmate just waved at me from behind bars.'

After lying awake for some time on the jail floor, nervously listening for signs of a prisoners' revolt, fatigue gradually overcame fear. We slept until sunrise then made a swift exit.

As we approached the Malaysian border, we entered dense jungle on the slopes of a mountain. During the ascent, the unmistakable black form of a scorpion raced across the road in front of us. The size of a large crab, it was easily the biggest such creature I had ever seen. At a distance of some 20 yards and separated from us by seven hundred millimetres of bicycle wheel, there was no real danger, but it still sent a shudder down my spine.

We had already seen several snakes that morning, which was a daily occurrence in Southeast Asia. Usually glimpsed fleetingly as they shot away from our wheels, we would occasionally ride past one sunning itself on the black tarmac or making a leisurely crossing in front of us. They came in all colours and sizes and I had no idea which were dangerous and which were not. The biggest we saw was at least eight feet long and as thick as my calf.

Not long after seeing the scorpion, we passed a huge monitor lizard. Bright green and the size of a large dog, it stood perfectly still at the side of a dual carriageway. It felt like something from another world, something that should have gone extinct around the time man invented fire. If you ignored the big claws, the miniature dragon looked quite innocuous. Its stillness made it a tempting target for a close up with the camera, but prudence and horror stories got the better of us. We kept on riding with one more reminder that the world still had the capacity to surprise.

The road grew quieter as we ascended the mountain towards Malaysia. People and cars disappeared, snakes, scorpions and dragon lizards taking their place. We had chosen this quiet border crossing because the south-eastern part of Thailand was off limits with political trouble and we wanted to avoid the crowds and busy roads of Malaysia's west coast. That led us to an obscure crossing halfway up a mountain. It was an eerie place to be, surrounded by jungle vines, animals and few signs of human life.

The border would be closed by the time we arrived so we stopped a few miles beforehand at a cafe. It too had closed for the night, but the owner made us some rice anyway and swept out a shed for us to sleep in. Lying awake for several hours that night, struggling to sleep in the heat, I watched the shadows of huge spiders crawling across webs on the ceiling above me. I prayed that they were neither poisonous nor territorial.

First in line at the border the next morning, the official at the desk refused to charge us anything to enter his country and instead tried to give us money, pressing fists full of ringgit into our hands. He was blown away that we had cycled all the way up that hill to enter Malaysia and came out of his office to pose for a photo with us. We often found that people would offer little reaction to hearing that we had cycled across Europe and travelled many thousand miles, but would be astounded when we told them the name of the last town from which we had cycled. Perhaps 'cycling around the world' was too abstract a concept to process, whereas cycling 100 miles from a nearby city was both easily relatable and sufficiently outlandish to impress. We declined the official's money but happily accepted two bottles of pop and a packet of crisps before pushing off for the descent into Malaysia.

Chapter 33

'Three weeks since our clothes last saw a washing machine. We hand wash them most days but, frankly, they're disgusting.' – Tim

'Back in a Muslim country; back to absurd levels of generosity.' – Laura

My handlebar bag packed full of crisps and fizzy drinks, compliments of our new favourite border guard, we freewheeled away from the spiders, snakes and scorpions and rolled down the far side of the mountain we had climbed the day before.

By the time we reached the first town in Malaysia, Kuala Perlis, we were long overdue for some breakfast, but despite it being mid-morning, everywhere was shut. Not just the cafes and restaurants, but the supermarkets too. Nothing was open, because it was Ramadan.

The official religion of Malaysia is Islam, which means that for one month each year, no one eats or drinks while the sun is up. Shops stay closed all day and restaurants only open at sunset. That year, Ramadan ran through August: the middle of summer, when the sun was at its hottest. That same year, two hungry foreigners chose the month of August to cycle the country's length.

This might be considered poor planning on our part, but the timings of our journey were largely set from the moment we left home. Our summer departure was fixed by the need to finish teaching a school year and attend a friend's wedding. That meant a blissful European summer and a frigid Turkey. Had it not been winter when we reached Iran, we might have opted to head north through Central Asia, but instead, we chose the warmth of the Arabian Peninsula and India. And now we had arrived in Malaysia during the height of summer, in a month when nowhere sold food or drink during daylight hours.

The issue was exacerbated shortly after our arrival when we crossed over to the east coast, which is the less populated and more Muslim side. We got the quieter roads we wanted, but with the local population more devout than their neighbours on the west, it also meant that everywhere was shut.

'Everywhere's shut,' I declared glumly.

'Not everywhere,' Laura said with a glint in her eye. 'Look.'

She pointed at a familiar plastic façade in the distance with the unmistakable red and white logo of Kentucky Fried Chicken.

We had heard so many great things about Malaysian food, but its purveyors had all closed up shop, leaving us outside in the heat with KFC as the only option. We wheeled our bikes to the entrance and leaned them against the window. There was a sign on the door warning that it was illegal to sell food to Muslims during Ramadan, but even with my big beard, we figured it was pretty obvious that we were from out of town.

It was deserted inside and pleasantly cool. We walked to the counter, me huffing that we were in Southeast Asia and forced to eat fast food, Laura grinning like a Cheshire cat. KFC is her secret vice and she is always pestering me to go. I rolled my eyes and ordered whatever daftly named product on the menu sounded least unappetising.

The next day we found ourselves in the exact same situation: everywhere closed but KFC. With a little less reluctance this time, we cycled straight over, parked our bikes and placed our orders.

'I can't believe we're in Malaysia, with all of its amazing food, and we have to eat KFC every day,' I said, half-heartedly.

'Yeah, bummer,' Laura replied with a piece of chicken in her mouth. 'Will you get me another drink if you're going up?'

We ended up eating in KFC, or somewhere similar, nearly every day. After initially going through the motions of right-on, middle class Westerners – convincing ourselves that we were only there because we had to be and did not really like the food – we soon forgot our pretences. In fact, open restaurants and food stores were so rare during the coming weeks that we would punch the air when we saw a KFC sign, knowing that high fat, high salt, high sugar food was just moments away.

I ate more fast food during our month in Malaysia than I had done in the thirty years of my life that preceded it. Like Lidl in Europe, KFC provided an easy consistency in an ever-changing world. Circumstances had forced it upon us, but KFC turned out to be a welcome, air-conditioned sanctuary.

Once we had accepted that fast food was our only option, we developed a routine for cycling in Malaysia. We would wake early before the day was at its hottest and cycle non-stop until we found a fast food joint. Sometimes it would get to the middle of the afternoon and we still would not have found anywhere that was open. In those instances, hot, hungry and thirsty, all communication between the two of us would have long since ceased. We would pedal blindly onwards, repeatedly squeezing our empty bike bottles over our mouths in the hope that we might have missed a bit last time, and trying not to think too hard about what might happen if we never found another open restaurant. On other occasions however, we would stumble across a McDonald's first thing in the morning and feel obliged to make the most of it since we would not know how far off the next one would be. That is what happened on the day of the World Cup semi-final.

Despite not watching a single game until that morning, I had been following the World Cup more closely than any other football tournament in my life. I had been listening to a daily podcast (downloaded on KFC wifi) which discussed all the action from the previous day's matches in Brazil. I had only seen sixty seconds of

212

actual play, glimpsed in a late night petrol station, but I knew every little detail of what had happened from my radio show.

Having set off at some ungodly hour that morning due to my recurring inability to sleep in the humidity, we had passed a McDonald's outside, which a crowd of young Malaysians had gathered around a TV screen showing Netherlands vs Argentina. It was only 5am, but we each ordered a Big Mac Meal and settled down to watch the game.

I am not a football fan and, under normal circumstances, would not follow it at all, but keeping up with the World Cup somehow felt like a small connection to home. Despite being on the other side of the world, I could live the same drama along with the rest of my country and share its pain at our inevitable early demise. I could email my dad to get his prediction of when England would crash out and ask if he had seen Germany thrash Brazil. It meant that I could be a part of something that was more than just riding a bike, even if in this case, it was just kicking a ball instead.

We hung around for the end of the match, preloading on drinks ahead of another hot day's riding, and set off with burgers in our bellies shortly after sunrise. We spent the day riding through mile after mile of oil palm trees, which grew in neat rows that stretched as far as we could see. Palm oil is big business in Malaysia. It is the world's second largest producer, accounting for four out of every ten litres made globally. The plantations required to produce such large quantities are vast, as we were discovering the hard way on our bikes, and it has been estimated that a sixth of Malaysia's entire surface area is dedicated to them.

Palm oil goes into all sorts of everyday items, from cosmetics to cookies, and some claim that it can be found in half of all packaged products sold in supermarkets. Its use in such volumes is controversial as plantations are often developed at the expense of native forests, destroying animal habitats and ecosystems in the process.

Cycling through the plantations was interesting, but after ten hours of it I think we would have preferred somewhere selling cold beverages. Stopping in the shade to drink the remnants of warm water from our bike bottles, we spotted a group of teenagers crouching amongst the palms. They were surreptitiously scoffing takeaway meals, in breach of their fast. They jumped when we arrived, but realising we were just tourists they quickly returned to their food.

We eventually escaped the plantations and reached a quiet village as the sun was beginning to set, just before the locals were allowed to break their fast. The few people out on the street were all heading towards a huge, open-air market. There were rows of stalls, each with a huge steaming pot of curry or frying something fragrant, while scores of Malaysians queued dutifully, waiting for sundown. There was no real need for us to wait for the sun to set before eating, but we joined a queue like everyone else and took part in the 'iftar', breaking of the fast, when the time came.

Malaysian food is unique. That is partly because Malaysia has three distinct ethnic groups – Indian, Chinese and Malay – and each of them brings a different cuisine to the table. It was also a British colony until 1957 so has some western influences in its food too. The results are excellent. We may have lived off junk food during the day, but when the sun set we ate like kings.

In the market that night, we filled two styrofoam tubs with steaming piles of rice and curry, then perched ourselves on a bench to people watch while we ate our dinner. As soon as we finished our mains, I went straight to the guy making 'roti' pancakes. Soaked in condensed milk and covered in sugar, roti filled the void left by Vietnam's sticky rice dessert. Finally sated, we wheeled our bikes down to the beach to camp.

We pitched our tent on the sand and I climbed inside reluctantly, knowing that I would struggle to sleep, as I did every night in Southeast Asia. It was too hot and too sticky. I could cope with the dry heat of the Middle East and India but could not handle Southeast Asia's humidity. In particular, I found the tent unbearable. Even just pitching the inside mesh and sleeping with nothing but a silk sleeping bag liner underneath me, the heat would drive me to distraction. Sleeping outside, on the other hand, meant dealing with mosquitoes, which was just as bad.

Unfortunately, I am not very good at operating without eight hours of sleep. It is not getting up that I find hard. I hate the snooze button and prefer to spring out of bed immediately when the alarm goes, but I feel the consequences of even the slightest reduction in sleep, with the inevitable result of making me bad company.

As a result – and as Laura will happily attest – I spent most of our three months on the Indochinese peninsula in a bad mood, complaining about how hard my life was. Laura also found it hot, but she slept better than me and shrugged off any deprivation. She has always considered my need for more sleep than her to be a severe character weakness that she has never quite been able to reconcile. As such, my grumbling was rarely rewarded with the sympathy it did not deserve.

That night on the beach, I spent an hour huffing and puffing inside the tent, lying on my back in a pair of shorts, sweating into my camping mat and feeling sorry for myself. It felt like it took all of my self-control not to scream in frustration. I would try anything to cool down including, at one point, adopting the 'downward dog' yoga position, thinking that minimising contact with the floor might minimise stickiness. Needless to say, it did not help. My diary entry for that night reads, with no sense of drama: 'Too hot to exist.'

Unable to stand it any longer, I unzipped the door and vowed never to sleep in the tent again. I paced the beach before setting my mat down a hundred yards from the tent. I dressed myself head to toe in thermal clothing and woolly socks then topped off the outfit with a mosquito head-net so I was fully protected from pesky bites. I am not sure that this could really have been any cooler than inside the tent, but it made me feel better and, eventually, I dozed off.

After an unknown period of time passed, I woke with a start at the sound of Laura's voice, which had a clear sense of fear in it: 'Hello? Who's there!?'

I jumped up and ran across the beach towards her tent in darkness. 'What's going on? You alright?'

'I woke up,' she said 'and there was a man there. Just watching me.'

On one of the only occasions, during the previous twelve months on the road, that I had slept more than two feet from my wife, someone had crept up to her tent in the middle of the night and watched her sleep. She had no idea how long he was there: a few seconds? Half an hour? Was he just a curious passer-by or something more sinister? She woke to see his silhouette turn and disappear into the trees as I ran across the sand. I climbed back into the tent and stayed there until sunrise.

Chapter 34

'Camped on a beach beneath a full moon with phosphorescence glowing in the waves. Still can't sleep in this bloody heat though. I'd prefer AC.' – Tim

'As time goes by on this trip, I spend more and more time sewing our clothes together. It's all about reuse, recycle on this journey.' – Laura

There was no further disturbance that night although I am not sure how much either of us slept. We packed our tent away in the cooler morning air and wheeled our bikes back to the road.

I was feeling particularly sorry for myself that morning. Deprived of another night's sleep, the heat soon returned and we experienced a particularly long drought in places selling food and drink. My frustration was compounded by a seemingly never-ending supply of dogs with nothing better to do than ambush cyclists. Every fifty metres, another canine assailant would dart out of the bushes and bark its head off at us, continually interrupting any attempt at settling into a rhythm and letting my mind wander.

As we slogged up one particular hill, a lean white mongrel hurled itself towards me with a rapid series of barks. I lost my stride and, with it, the momentum I had fought so hard to build on the steep gradient. I stumbled to one side and cracked my shin on the pedal.

The dog, of course, immediately stopped running and, instead, just stood beside me barking. Low on blood sugar and having a bad day already, I was so infuriated by this futile gesture that I screamed: 'F*** OFF!' at the top of my lungs.

The dog was momentarily taken aback but soon resumed its vocal protest, albeit from a safer distance. The violence of my reaction had come as a complete surprise to me, but it must have been even more surprising for the poor old woman sitting next to me. I had not noticed her before I let rip. I am sure she did not speak English so I was at least spared the full scale of the embarrassment one might feel at having screamed an expletive in front of an old lady. Although a little ashamed, another part of me still resented the fact that she did not bat an eyelid when her dog ran into the road and attacked a member of the public. I had shamed myself, but did she not feel some shame too, having watched her dog nearly cause an accident?

We continued our journey on a long straight road through dense jungle. Rows of huge trees flanked us on either side, without a settlement in sight.

The flat tyre came during a downpour somewhere around midday. We stopped at the side of the road and flipped my bike upside down to start our repairs. The rain was sufficiently heavy to cause the branches of surrounding trees to fall to the ground around us, but it was a welcome relief from the heat. Monkeys gathered in the branches above us.

Whilst pumping up the tyre, I felt an itch through my glove. Upon inspection, the source was identified as a large ant that was burrowing its mandibles into my hand. I brushed it away as Laura put the tyre back on my bike. The rain stopped and the monkeys crept closer.

Tyre repaired, Laura pulled two bottles of chocolate soya milk from her handlebar bag and we sat down to glug some calories before continuing on our way. From the corner of my eye, I saw a flash of grey fur.

'Hey!' Laura shouted, as she sprang to her feet, but she was too late. The monkeys had made their move and the contents of her handlebar bag lay strewn across the road. As they retreated, I saw that one of them had her sunglasses and another her phone.

Our initial response was to treat them in the same way that we treated the angry dogs we encountered: by shouting and waving our arms. Instead of backing off, the monkey with the sunglasses just hissed and lashed out. He was not big, but I had no particular desire to test the efficacy of my rabies vaccine so we stopped the aggression.

The monkey took the opportunity to clamber up a tree, where he held the sunglasses at arm's length, marvelling at his own reflection. The other one retreated to a safe distance before holding up the phone in one hand and reaching out to touch it with the other. For a terrifying moment, I thought that we were about to witness the evolutionary leap of a monkey operating a smartphone, but the veneer of intelligence vanished when he turned it upside down and tried to eat it.

We didn't know whether to laugh or cry. It was absurd. We were alone in the jungle, shouting obscenities at a monkey carrying sunglasses. Laura grabbed a stick and tried to frighten the primate phone operator when, without warning, both monkeys grew bored of their toys, tossed them to the floor and scarpered. Laura retrieved her belongings and stowed them safely back in her handlebar bag.

Still wet from the rain and now covered in mud from our roadside repairs and tussle with the monkeys, I realised what a state we looked. Our general dishevelment had recently been enhanced by the gradual disintegration of our shirts. The fabric had simply given up after being worn every day for a year and repeatedly hand washed. They were ripped to shreds at the back and it looked as though we had both received fifty lashes for some heinous sin. It also meant that we were getting weird, suntanned stripes on our backs where the shirts no longer offered any protection. We vowed to spend some money from the luxury pot on new shirts at the next opportunity.

Reaching a town that evening, we treated ourselves to a hotel for the night. It was just a tiny, windowless room that cost a few pounds, but it had air conditioning, which guaranteed a better night's sleep than the tent. It also meant showers and a chance to wash our clothes in the sink.

Stepping into the shower cubicle once Laura was finished, I noticed an unusually large amount of her hair clogging up the drain. When I stepped out of the shower, I saw Laura holding a brush in one hand and a clump of hair in the other.

'Gross,' I said, helpfully.

'It's been doing this for a couple of weeks, but it's not normally this bad.'

'Perhaps your body's evolving to the heat,' I said, slapping my head. 'Like mine.'

Further down the peninsular, we had arranged to stay with another cyclist. He ran a bike shop and, minutes after we arrived, he had our bikes on stands, giving them a service.

'What do you think about MH370?' he asked, while oiling my chain.

He was referring to a Malaysian Airlines flight that had recently disappeared in mysterious circumstances. We were often out of touch with current events while on our bikes, but given that we were in Malaysia at the time, even we had heard about this.

'It must have been the government,' he continued. 'There's no way it could go missing like that within an hour of take-off.'

We had not read anything about the government being implicated.

'Of course you haven't. That stuff never gets in the media. Like Diana.'

I looked at Laura for clarification, but she just shrugged.

'You know: the Princess Di cover-up. I've checked the route on Google Street View. There's no way it should have taken the ambulance 40 minutes to get her to the hospital.'

Unsure how to respond, I changed the subject and asked if he had done much cycle touring.

'Yeah, I went up to Thailand once. I took a tazer with me because I was worried the girls up there might hug me, then their boyfriends would get jealous and try to shoot me. It was worth it though, because I got all of this marijuana.'

He produced a sandwich bag with a large brown slab inside. 'I got bone cancer a few years ago but the marijuana keeps it at bay,' he said. 'Anyway, it's getting late. You guys probably want to get some sleep.'

We had no idea what he was talking about, but we had become used to quirky characters and, besides, he seemed friendly enough. We helped him pull down the shutters at the front of his shop and move some bikes around to make space for our camping mats. Despite our insistence that it was not necessary, he stayed awake adjusting the spokes on our bikes while we went to sleep surrounded by display bikes, listening to the gentle whir of our wheels being spun. When I went to use the loo at 4am, he was still tinkering with our wheels.

When we woke, we decided to treat ourselves to a day off the bikes. Agreeing how to use our spare days was a matter of some debate. I branded such occasions as 'rest days' and suggested that we do just that. Laura rarely felt any need to rest and considered such days an opportunity to explore a place that we might never visit again. For me, rest is the natural corollary of a hard day's cycling. For Laura, it is something to do when you are dead. And, to be honest, I am not convinced she could bring herself to do it even then.

In the name of democracy and good marital relations, we had come up with a system of alternating our rest day activities. Sometimes we would take it easy, read our books, write blog posts and watch films. Other times, we would head out first thing and see the sights.

Sadly, on this occasion, it was Laura's turn to plan the rest day, which she did while I got on with the some reading. Half an hour later, she told me that she had found a waterfall on the map that was a great swimming spot and, apparently, 'unmissable'.

'Yeah, looks great love,' I replied without looking up from my book.

'I've done a bit of research, though,' she continued hesitantly, 'and I think the easiest way to get there is by bike.'

'Really?' I said, putting my book down and starting to pay attention. 'Cycling on a rest day? How far?'

'25 miles.'

'We're not cycling 25 miles on a bloody rest day!' I spluttered.

'No, you're right,' she grinned. 'We've got to get back again so it'll be more like 50.'

We went and I complained all the way there. It was brilliant and I complained all the way back. I can only hope that whenever Laura grumbled about me enforcing a DVD day, she too secretly enjoyed them. After another night in the bike shop, our host joined us for breakfast and suggested a good route for our last few days into Kuala Lumpur.

During the ride to the capital, more and more of Laura's hair fell out. Every time she ran her fingers through it, large clumps would come away. Her usually thick hair became visibly thinner and we started to worry that something was up. When we reached Kuala Lumpur, Laura went to see a doctor. He said that hair loss often occurred a few months after a trauma or particular hardship. The doctor looked at her fingernails and commented on a ridge that ran across them all, about halfway up. That, apparently, was another indicator of the body recently being under stress.

'Did anything happen to you in the last two or three months?' he asked.

We paused for a moment and thought back through what we had done in recent months and where we had been: Thailand, Vietnam, Japan, South Korea and…

'India,' Laura replied with a sudden realisation. 'We went to India.'

After our escape from the country, we had not given much thought to our illnesses in India. 'Delhi belly' is almost a rite of passage for travellers to the subcontinent so we did not feel like it was anything unusual. But those repeated bouts of illness, the days lying in bed unable to take in food or water, had clearly taken a toll on Laura's body and now it was shedding its hair.

The doctor prescribed an ointment: 'If you use this twice a day then the hair loss should stop before…' he gestured towards my bald head. 'You know.'

After a few days exploring Kuala Lumpur, we cycled to the airport to catch a flight to Australia. Upon arrival, we dismounted and wheeled our bikes inside. Unfortunately, taking bicycles into the terminal was not acceptable to airport security. Two skinny little men approached us, each wearing a large black hat and a uniform two sizes too big. They pointed at our bikes, shook their heads and said 'No.'

'Don't worry, we won't ride them,' I said with a smile. 'We'll just get them to the check-in desks then pack them up there.' The heads shook again.

'It's no different from pushing a trolley around,' Laura added.

It really wasn't. If they had their way, all we would have done is pay money to put one wheeled object onto another wheeled object that didn't do its job quite as well.

'No,' came the response.

'We've done it in loads of other airports. Why don't you check with your boss?' Laura said, pointing to their radio. The two conferred with one another in whispers (somewhat unnecessarily given that neither of us spoke Malaysian) then turned away to talk into their radio.

Laura and I exchanged a glance then ran for it. We pushed the bikes as fast as we could towards a nearby lift. We sprinted through crowds of tourists, looking over our shoulders to see if Malaysia's answer to the Blues Brothers had noticed our escape.

'Hey!' they shouted, but we had gained fifty yards by that point. I waved a smile in response and gave them a thumbs-up. Always act innocent.

Laura pressed the 'up' button for the elevator and did not stop hitting it until the doors opened and we squeezed our bikes into a crowd of bewildered Malaysians. Through the glass walls I could see Chaz and Dave running towards us and I held my finger on the 'close doors' button, bouncing nervously.

With slapstick timing, the guards appeared in front of the lift's double doors at the exact moment they were secured. One of the guards banged his palm against the glass while the other shouted into his walkie-talkie. I continued smiling and gave them an innocent wave.

Running along the mezzanine two storeys up, we heard a cry from the floor below and saw our pursuers pointing at us as they charged back towards the stairs. We hurried out of the nearest doors, crossed the road and entered the next terminal where we collapsed on the floor, gasping for breath and unable to stop laughing. We eventually settled in a quiet corner and set about preparing our bikes for transit. The guards never found us.

During our dash, I had noticed a man offering to wrap any item of luggage for a dollar. 'Any item: $1,' said his sign. Many airports have something similar. People queue up with their suitcases, hand over their money and watch as their belongings are sealed in industrial strength cling film. Fresh from our comic brush with the law, I approached the man to confirm the price:

'One dollar,' he said.

'For *any* item?'

'Yes. One dollar, any item.'

I returned to Laura with confirmation of our suspicion and she cracked a smile. We pushed our bikes over to the baggage man and asked one last time: 'Any item, one dollar. Right?'

It took all three of us plus two other members of airport staff, but we managed it. We held the bikes upright, one at a time, with the back wheel sticking in the air. The man in charge gingerly pressed the button to make the whole machine spin like a giant potter's wheel, cocooning our bikes in a transparent web, ready for their flight. We carried them to the check-in desks, handed over our passports and got ready to fly to Australia.

Chapter 35

*'There is something deeply satisfying about assembling your bike in
Arrivals and cycling out of an airport. P.S. WE ARE IN AUSTRALIA!'*
– Tim

*'I love that after almost a year on the road, I still have days which
make me stop and say WOW.' – Laura*

In the unlikely event of being asked, with a gun to my head, to name
my favourite airport, I would be sorely tempted to plump for
Adelaide. I liked it immediately because, unlike in Southeast Asia,
the air was cool and the humidity was not 100%. More importantly,
it has a shed full of bicycle tools just outside the terminal. It is free
to use and installed for the sole purpose of helping cyclists dismantle
their bikes for a flight and reassemble them after arrival. The Allen
keys, pedal wrenches and pump got us back on the road in no time
and we cycled away from the airport in high spirits.

Another reason for feeling cheerful was that our arrival into
Adelaide confirmed our proximity to my big brother, who lives with
my sister-in-law in Melbourne, only a few weeks' cycling away.
Reaching their house was ostensibly the goal of our entire trip and I
was excited to see them.

From Adelaide, our plan was to follow the south coast and take
the Great Ocean Road to Melbourne. Originally, we had planned to
fly into Perth and ride across the legendary Nullarbor, the long,
bleak, desert-like plain that makes for notoriously tough cycling.
However, time was against us. If we wanted to get home in time for
Christmas, we had to choose between crossing either the Nullarbor
or America. As such, we opted for a shorter route in Australia in
exchange for being able to cross the United States, coast to coast.

When we booked our flights to Australia, we also booked our onward flights to New Zealand, America and back home to the UK. Our timeline was fixed and our journey had a definite end: 14th December. It felt strange, and a little sad, to be thinking about the end of our trip, but we still had four months of cycling ahead of us, which would be longer than any other holiday we had been on before. Our timeline gave us a renewed sense of purpose: no dilly-dallying, we had flights to catch and family to see. The deadline also gave us a new appreciation for the preciousness of our time on the road: we began to recognise that the journey, which had seemed unfathomably large a year ago when we left Hampton Court, would eventually end.

Australia did not allow to us to indulge such pontifications for long, however. Riding away from the airport, two abreast in a bike lane, a Mamil (Middle aged man in lycra) flew around a corner, heading straight for me. Clearly annoyed at finding me cycling on the wrong side of the lane, I pulled behind Laura just in time for him to shout: 'Ya bloody twit!'

'Australian charm,' I commented to Laura. However, she insisted that I had misheard him and he was not shouting abuse at all. Instead, he had simply seen the state of us – dishevelled and, in my case, bearded – and been a Roald Dahl fan: 'It's the bloody Twits!'

We continued along the bike lane, riding out of town, and were treated to our first animal encounter within an hour of landing in the country, when a kangaroo hopped right across our path. A little further up the trail, we re-joined roads and soon found our path blocked by roadworks, so stopped to check our map to find an alternative route. As we did so, I noticed two workmen glance over at us. It took me a minute to realise that I could ask them for directions because, of course, they would speak English.

Not since leaving home 12 months ago had we travelled through an English speaking country. We had passed through 20 different countries on our trip so far, with almost as many different languages, none of which was English. In fact, only three countries since Europe even had recognisable alphabets: Turkey, Vietnam and Malaysia. The rest used scripts and characters that I could not recognise, let alone read. To once more find ourselves amongst English speakers was a novelty. It came with both relief and sadness.

Relief because directions would be more easily obtained and routes more easily followed. Relief because the long evenings staying with hosts would be made infinitely easier now that we could communicate with clarity rather than clumsiness. And relief because we could have proper conversations with people on deeper topics and with more nuance than stilted translations allowed, putting an end to months of interactions that rarely went beneath the surface of an issue. But there was sadness too because the familiar language marked an end to our exotic travels. We knew that Australia, New Zealand and America would each have plenty to offer the travelling cyclist, but with a common language and similar cultures, there would be more that was familiar to us and less to expand our minds.

This all went through my head as I approached the Australian workmen and I tried to stifle a grin. This would be my first opportunity in many months to request specific directions and understand the response.

'Hi guys, we were hoping to follow the veloway out of town towards Willunga, but I can see it's closed at the moment. What's the best way around?'

'Right mate, you wanna follow that path up there...' one of them said, putting his tools down and pointing into the distance with a gloved finger before detailing the best route out of town on a bike.

Delighted to have received intricate directions rather than just some hand gestures and a few indecipherable vowel sounds, we followed his guidance and cycled out of Adelaide.

Having been mentally prepared for the bleak Australian outback, I was pleasantly surprised at how green and fertile the land was. I found it much cooler than I had expected too, having lazily assumed that all of Australia was always hot, all of the time. It probably felt cool, in part, because we had just emerged from three months of permanent warmth in Southeast Asia. The roads were quiet and we enjoyed winding our way through vineyards and small, old-fashioned towns.

As the sun sank, drawing a close to our first day in Australia, we thought we had found a quiet spot to camp for the night, hidden away amongst some trees. When the family living in a nearby house stepped into their back garden for a barbecue however, it soon became apparent that we were in clear view.

Although I enjoyed the idea of producing an Australian edition of our magic letter ('G'day mate, this is my Sheila and we've cycled a bloody long way...'), for once, we were left to explain ourselves verbally rather than just handing over a piece of paper. Our story given, the family filled up our water bottles and reassured us that we would have no problems camping where we were.

They did, however, warn us that it might get pretty cold overnight. When we packed off our winter kit with my younger brother in Dubai, six months earlier, it had never occurred to us that we might need it again in Australia. India, Japan and Southeast Asia had been either been warm or hot and we had never missed our extra layers, but we felt their absence that night.

We put on all our clothes and buried ourselves inside our summer sleeping bags with the draw cords tied tightly around our faces. I woke up shivering to find the tent covered in frost. For the last six months, we had cycled exclusively in sandals and thought nothing of it, but with frozen grass crunching under our feet as we packed up our tent that morning, I sorely missed having a proper pair of shoes.

With the sun obscured by clouds, we were little warmer by lunchtime so sought refuge in a pie shop. A tiny television mounted on the wall beamed live footage from home courtesy of the Glasgow Commonwealth Games. Despite us being hungry enough to eat two pies each, Australia was proving itself to be one of the most expensive countries we had visited, so we settled for sharing one. We eked out a cup of tea for as long as was polite whilst debating whether it was acceptable to ask to get our thermos filled on the way out (it was and they did).

That night we stopped in a layby on a long stretch of empty road. There were no buildings for miles around and not a single vehicle passed us all evening. It was bliss. We had had two months of hustle and bustle in Southeast Asia, with quiet moments few and far between. To lean our bikes against a park bench at the end of a day's riding without a soul in sight was a real treat. We pitched beneath a clear, star-filled sky and set about cooking dinner.

Dinner in Australia was rice and dahl. Every day. It was an expensive place to travel, but like all expensive places, its supermarkets had budget options so we were still able to stick to our daily budget. We had a couple of weeks' cycling before reaching Melbourne so forked out for a huge bag of rice and an equally large sized one of lentils. Coupled with some herbs and spices, plus whatever vegetables we came across, this made for a cheap and tasty tea.

Following on from the success of her stove-top bread making in Korea, Laura turned her hand to hay box cooking. She would bring a pan of rice to the boil, clamp a lid on then bury it in either a sleeping bag or twigs and leaves. We could then leave that to cook itself whilst repeating the process with the lentils. It saved time using the noisy stove and money burning gas. It was also just fun to experiment. It worked well and the only issue we had with the method that night was the curiosity it sparked in a passing possum.

As well as enjoying the ability to camp somewhere quiet, it was also nice to be using the stove again, buying food from supermarkets and cooking for ourselves. We had been spoiled in Southeast Asia, where it had been far easier to eat in a restaurant than it was to find shops and buy our own ingredients. Alongside India, it was also one of the few places where we could afford to do so. Huge bowls of Vietnamese noodle-filled broth, sticky rice and pork in Cambodia or a KFC Bargain Bucket in Malaysia, all fell easily within our daily allowance. For the most part, it made our lives easy and meant that we got to eat delicious food every day, but a part of me craved simple, home-cooked food, even if that meant plain rice and lentils, prepared outside in the cold.

Chapter 36

'Snakes? Spiders? Crocodiles? Forget 'em. It's the magpies you gotta watch out for. Getting dive bombed is genuinely quite scary.'
– Tim

'Tonight's challenge: possum-proof our food bags. One persistent critter is hanging about. Have we done enough? Let's see what happens.' – Laura

Cooking breakfast the following morning – porridge made from a big bag of oats and a big bag of milk powder – we were joined in our layby by a dilapidated van. The driver's door swung open and out sprang a sprightly, grey haired man with an eye patch. He was immediately followed by a Jack Russell that hopped off the driver's seat and trundled towards the bushes.

'Dixie!' shouted the man. 'Dixie Flash, you get back here right now!'

The chubby little dog kept waddling away. The man slammed the van door closed and began rummaging through a nearby bin before catching our eye.

'Good morning!' he cried, extending a hand. 'I'm Jake and that's my dog: Dixie Flash. She's the fastest dog you'll ever see.'

As the portly pooch inched into the distance, I concluded that this claim might be true if I never saw another dog.

'What brings you all the way out here then?' he continued.

'We're cycling to Melbourne. How about you?'

'Treasure,' he said. 'I've got a map. Do ya wonna see it?'

First an eye patch and now a treasure map. Captain Jake leaned through the passenger window of his van and extracted a folded sheet from the glove compartment. He spread it out carefully over the picnic bench upon which we had been breakfasting. It was a crumpled topographic map of the local area, with a circled 'x' in the middle, presumably marking the location of the treasure.

'My brother got it. He won the double trap in the 1982 Commonwealth Games then he bought this map off a guy who told him, for sure, that there was a stash of treasure buried out here.'

'Nice,' I replied. 'How come your brother's given it you?'

'Dunno. Said he didn't want it any more. Daft bugger.'

Jake gave Laura a sideways glance then, perhaps concerned that she would commit his map to memory, swiped the sheet away quickly and folded it back into his pocket.

'Listen, are you guys into art? Because this might just be your lucky day.'

He returned to the back of the van and pulled out a huge canvas. On it was a large, childlike painting of two gorillas. 'I painted this a couple of years ago. The art gallery in Adelaide said I'd got the colour of the gorillas just right,' he said with some pride. The gorillas were black. 'I'll do you a good price if you want it?'

'That's very kind,' I replied, 'but I think we might struggle to carry it on our bikes. You should keep it. I'm sure it must have sentimental value.'

'Fair enough,' he said, and tossed the picture into the back of his van, just as Dixie Flash waddled back over the horizon and hopped onto the front seat.

'Right, I guess we're off then!' He pulled the door closed, revved the engine and pulled out of the layby shouting: 'The next time you guys see me, I'll be rich!'

We bid him farewell then returned to our porridge. This was just one of many brief and baffling encounters we had on our way around the world and, however far-fetched it might have been, I hope he found his treasure. Breakfast finished and pots washed, we packed away our tent and set off east.

Over the coming days, the landscape turned from vineyards and greenery to dry, dusty desert. Following a morning's ride through sandy scrubland, we stopped for lunch in a tiny town at the intersection of a railway line and parked ourselves on a lone picnic bench. Lunches in Australia were primarily bread, butter and jam. The bread was cheap and the temperature never got high enough to melt the butter. I got through 12 slices that lunchtime.

Thirsty from consuming the best part of a loaf of bread and a jar of jam, we attempted to find some water with which to fill our bottles. It was on sale in tiny glass bottles at a nearby bar, but it took conversations with six different people before someone was able to find us a cheaper solution. It involved going around the back of the local museum, climbing over a fence and wedging our bottles under a room-sized water container with a tiny tap. Apparently, drinking water was not easy to find out here.

'You'll not get any more for thirty miles,' we were warned as we cycled out of town. Thirty miles later and a couple of hours before sun down, we reached a roadhouse. Arriving there felt as though we had stepped back in time. It was a simple, wooden building with a corrugated iron roof and an old-fashioned petrol pump out front. Aside from a couple of barns visible in the distance, there was very little around besides scrub and dirt.

It may have been a place with an interesting history, but it was distinctly lacking in life by the time we arrived. As a result, it was something of a surprise to step through the front door and be greeted by two six-foot, blonde girls.

'Hi! We are from Sweden!' explained the young girls in unison.

'What brings you out here?' Laura asked. They looked completely out of place, youthful and glamorous in an ageing, dilapidated roadhouse.

'We're on our gap year!' they replied cheerfully.

I thought gap years were usually spent travelling the world or volunteering in some needy country. Manning the tills at a deserted petrol station seemed like an unusual choice.

'Do many people do this on their gap year?' I asked.

'Yes! Bob, the owner, needs help running the shop so, every year, he puts an advert online. This year, apparently, he got over 2,000 applications!'

An ageing Bob wandered past in the background carrying some boxes. He glanced across at his long-haired, long-legged Swedish volunteers and gave us a grin.

'I wonder what made him pick you two?' Laura asked.

'We don't know!' they grinned in response, showing their perfect white teeth, 'But it's nice. We can work in shifts then go out and explore in our downtime. We go out running every morning and almost always see emus.'

In fairness, I could see the attraction. There is a certain appeal in being cut off from the world, isolated in the wilderness.

We took our leave of the gap year girls and looked around their shop. Even for Australia, the prices were eye wateringly high and there was a high fee for camping in the back garden. We had enough food in our panniers for another day's riding and there were hundreds of miles of uninhabited land on which we could have pitched our tent. It was clearly a struggling business though (a sign in the toilet asked for donations to help with maintenance costs) that offered a useful service to passers-by. If we were using their toilet and water then it seemed only fair to reciprocate. We paid our pitching fees and erected our tent round the back of the shop. The decision was justified when Laura's camping mat exploded after inflation. It would have meant an even colder night than usual, but the roadhouse donated a duvet for her to sleep on.

We awoke to a tranquil blue-grey sky with the sun bathing us in gentle orange. We packed away our tent while letting our porridge cool, then ate it sitting on some steps outside the roadhouse, wrapped in all of our warm layers. With the warming breakfast inside us and our panniers back on our bikes, we remounted and continued heading east.

As we inched towards Melbourne, Australia became more populated. Gone were the long, empty stretches of road. In their place came towns, shops and people. The cold, dry weather gradually gave way to cool and drizzly and, by the time we reached the Great Ocean Road, the freezing nights were behind us.

We arranged to spend a night with a retired couple who had built their dream house a stone's throw from the ocean road. It was a beautiful structure of wood and glass with a huge, open-plan top floor and wall-to-wall windows looking out to sea.

Over a three-course meal and red wine (which made a nice change from dahl and tap water), they told us about the first thing they did upon reaching retirement age: quit their jobs and mountain bike across the Australian interior. Baked in the heat, their bikes would constantly clog with thick, red mud and they would have to push their bikes for miles. Their daughters drove a support car and set up camp for them every night, baffled at their parents' choice of how to spend their retirement.

The couple had been on several other short cycle tours in different countries around the world since then. They dreamed of undertaking a longer trip, but after missing the birth of their first grandchild whilst cycling across Sweden, they were under strict orders from their kids that they were not to disappear for more than a month at a time.

They talked about the solitude they found in the outback and the feeling of pushing oneself. After a few more glasses of wine, the wife shared an idea she had been mulling over for some time: she wanted to get on her bike and just keep riding until she could not ride a single metre more. Like us, she had frequently experienced exhaustion on a cycling trip but never felt that she had reached her limit. She was curious about where that limit lay and was hungry to find out. Her plan was simply to start cycling and keep going, on and on, with food, drink and moral support from her husband in a car, and see how far she could get before she collapsed and could not go a single stroke further.

'What do your kids think of that idea?' Laura asked.

'Ha!' she replied. 'I wouldn't even tell them after I'd done it!'

Not long after our stay with the "retired" couple, the ocean road came to an end. That meant we were close to reaching our destination. We had set off from England a year before with the audacity to believe that we could cycle to Australia (even if we did not have the confidence to tell that to the people we met along the way). We had crossed the Alps and enjoyed it. We had survived the long, cold winter of Turkey, Georgia and Iran, and been rewarded with some of the most heart-warming experiences of our trip. We had been through the madness and splendour of India and learned when to admit defeat. We had treated ourselves to a holiday within a holiday in Korea and Japan where we travelled in a constant state of happy bewilderment. We had pedalled the length of Southeast Asia whose heat and humidity had tested me more than any other environment. And, finally, we had reached Australia for what we thought would be a perfunctory lap of honour but turned out to be much colder than expected. Nonetheless, our journey to Melbourne was almost complete.

The last time I had seen my big brother was the day of our wedding, three years before. He and his wife had moved to Australia some years earlier and opportunities to see them were few and far between. I would be lying if I said the only reason we had got on our bikes was to visit them (there are faster and easier ways of doing that), but reaching their house on the other side of the world had been our focus since day one, and now we were within striking distance.

I had never been to visit them in Australia, never borne witness to their new lives. As Laura and I rolled along the waterfront cycle path into St Kilda, Melbourne, where he and my sister-in-law lived, I thought about how far we had come. I thought about all of the places we had been and all of the people we had met, as well as the two we were about to. I felt a wave of well-being flush through my body.

My reverie did not last for long, though. Our cycling in Australia was destined to end in the same way that it had begun: with a high speed Mamil shouting expletives at me for being on the wrong side of a cycle lane:

'Out! Out! Get out!' he screamed. 'What are you doing, you bloody idiot!?'

Roused from my daydreaming, I swerved out of his path and regained my composure just in time to see two figures running across the road with grins on their faces and arms in the air. As we pulled to a stop those same arms embraced us. We had cycled to Melbourne.

'On a warm winter afternoon beneath a brilliant blue sky, after 9,698 miles, Laura and I arrived in Melbourne.' – Tim

'We reached Melbourne this afternoon, having cycled just under 10,000 miles in just under a year. Boom.' – Laura

Chapter 37

'Gave a school talk this morning, then overheard one girl tell her friend "We should totally do that". Mission accomplished.' – Laura

'Such an honour to be part of the cycle touring community. As tonight's host said: "We cyclists help each other out".' – Laura

We woke to the unmistakable signs of a tent buckling under the weight of snow.

We had arrived in Wellington a few days earlier, following a delightful month off the bikes in Melbourne. We had explored the city; swum in the sea; been out to restaurants, pubs, bars and cafes; been running on the beach; watched films; played computer games; celebrated my birthday; celebrated my brother's birthday and generally lazed around the apartment, revelling in the lassitude.

Eventually, we had to say a sad farewell because our journey was not yet over: we still had to cross the United States. But first, we had a short stop in New Zealand.

Since arriving there, we had become used to the wet weather. So, when we heard precipitation falling on our tent that night, we had assumed it was rain. When we roused from our slumber however, everything was silent. No rain falling, not even the sound of water dripping from trees. Just silence. Laura peered out of the tent, then said: 'You're not going to believe this.'

Our sandals had not been the ideal footwear for the frosty mornings in Australia, but they were categorically inappropriate for the foot of snow that greeted us on the North Island that morning.

Having arrived in town the previous evening, we had enquired at a hotel about places to pitch a tent. The owner, whose memories of growing up in Lancashire provided lengthy distractions for both him and Laura, set about ringing around to find us somewhere to camp.

Two phone books and five phone calls later, he found a willing participant.

'Jim'll let you pitch in his garden.'

Aware that Jim was the fifth person the hotel owner had tried, I wondered if Jim might live some distance away, so I asked for directions.

'Jim's house?' he laughed. 'It's just there.'

He pointed out of the window to a house less than 20 yards away, where a man beamed back at us and waved. We pitched in his garden amongst the ducks and chickens then enjoyed the day's third meal of cheese sandwiches, the local shop having closed before we arrived, depriving us of an alternative. After that, Jim invited us in for a cup of tea.

As a young man, Jim had contracted New Zealand's last case of polio. He had been paraplegic ever since, but that had not stopped him living a life of adventure.

'I paddled the English Channel once,' he said with real pride as his wife leafed through a photo album to prove it. 'Took us four hours. The Cook Strait was half as far but that took 14 hours.'

It transpired that he had subsequently paddled across Lake Titicaca in Bolivia and travelled the length of the Nile. He had also represented his country in shotput at the 1972 Paralympic Games in Germany and those were just a few examples in a long line of achievements. He did it all, he said, to promote what disabled people can do and encourage others to stay active.

His efforts had been rewarded with the receipt of a British Order of Merit from the Queen. In his 80s by this point, he lived with his wife and daughter who had recently moved home after losing an eye to cancer. She had a bachelor's degree in wine (who knew?) and worked as a chef but had been forced to move home whilst undergoing chemotherapy for the cancer that had now been found in her liver. Both his daughter and wife clearly enjoyed the opportunity to share Jim's story once more and we were only too happy to listen to it.

We crept back to our tent after nightfall and went to sleep beneath an ominous sky. When we woke to a blizzard we immediately wondered about the state of the road that lay ahead of us. There was only one route through the Rangipo Desert, but it was liable to closure in bad weather. As the weather at the time suggested, the Rangipo Desert is not a true desert. Its particular poor soil keeps it barren and looking like a desert, but it actually gets more rain than London. It is not unusual for the 'Desert Road' to close during winter months, but this was September. We cycled to the snow patrol hut at the start of the road in soggy socks and sandals. A barrier blocked our path and a sign at the side of the read:

'#1: Do not ask if the road is open or closed. #2: Do not ask when it is going to snow or stop snowing.'

With little else to do but wait, we hid under the hut's canopy and jumped around to stay warm in the hope that the road would re-open soon. Apparently, the weather was as much of a surprise to locals as it was to us. So much so, in fact, that a film crew arrived to capture footage of the unseasonal snowfall. They were delighted to find two stupid Brits who wanted to ride their bikes over the pass in a pair of sandals and immediately pointed their cameras at us.

The road did eventually open and we were able to continue on our way to Auckland. The only difference now was that whenever we met someone in a petrol station or outside a shop, they would say: 'Hey, are you those Brits from the TV that tried to cycle through a blizzard in your sandals?' Apparently, we had made the national news.

Some warmer, drier cycling days followed as we moved further north, through the lush green hills of the North Island. Fittingly for New Zealand, we spent one night with a rugby-obsessed couple sporting matching mullets, another night camped outside a Lemon & Paeroa shop and one more in a sheep shearing shed. We crept into the suburbs of Auckland on a quiet Monday morning. Our arrival there meant that we had only one country left on our journey: America. It would be our biggest yet.

PART V

USA

Chapter 38

'Tomorrow begins the ride east and the final leg of our journey. Day 1 is a climb from sea level to 4,000ft. Crikey.' – Laura

'Celebrating my first day's cycling in the US with a 12-pack of doughnuts.' – Tim

We were met at San Francisco airport by Laura's aunt and uncle. They lived nearby and we were looking forward to spending some time with them before cycling to the east coast. As we exchanged hugs in the airport arrivals lounge, Laura felt a tap on her shoulder. She turned around to see her mum and dad beaming back at her. Unbeknownst to us, they had flown over from the UK as a surprise. The deception was exceptional. Not only had their plans been kept entirely secret, they had even gone to the length of telling us about a fictional parcel of supplies they had posted to San Francisco for us. The last time we had seen them was in Istanbul, one year and seven thousand miles ago so it was an excellent surprise.

After New Zealand's snow, we basked in the Californian sunshine and spent a happy week out of the saddle, enjoying home-cooked food and lounging by the pool. Laura caught up with her 'American family', many of whom I met for the first time, and I devoured her uncle's back catalogue of Economist magazines.

The week soon slipped away from us and we found ourselves saying goodbye to family once more. It would be a long time before we saw the American contingent again, but all going well, only a couple of months before we re-joined Laura's parents and the rest of our families back home.

San Francisco was too far north for our plans so we drove a hire car southward along the coast towards Los Angeles. We pulled our bikes out the back of the car upon arrival, reloaded our panniers and cycled across South LA.

We pedalled through block after block of low rise buildings, with people sitting out on their porches and kids hanging out on the corners. It looked exactly as I had expected from watching Boyz n the Hood and White Men Can't Jump. There were a lot of homeless people roaming the streets and we had to make a detour because the road we wanted to take was taped off by police to preserve a crime scene. South Los Angeles has a reputation as a dangerous place, but it did not feel in the least bit threatening as a cyclist. Most people paid us no attention, a few waved from their porches. Even those without homes maintained a sense of humour. One guy holding a hat out for money carried a sign that read 'Why lie? Need money for weed.' Another, urinating against a lamppost as Laura cycled past, shouted cheerily: 'You have a great day now ma'am,' before resuming his business, adding 'You too sir!' when I followed a moment later. The sun was blazing and it was as fascinating a place to cycle through as anywhere on our trip.

We made our way south out of LA to begin our journey east. The following morning, we left from the town of Oceanside, just north of San Diego. It was a fitting name for the starting point of a trip from the Pacific to the Atlantic, from sea to shining sea.

The sky was a brilliant blue throughout the day we began our ride east across the United States. The sun beat down on us from the moment we started cycling until the moment we got into our tent at night. California was going through a drought and the orchards of almond trees we passed were clearly suffering.

To reach the flat desert plains of eastern California, we first had to cross a small chain of hills. The towns slowly thinned out and the roads quietened as we inched upwards, away from the coast. We were surrounded by an unfamiliar landscape of barren, sun-bleached rock.

Every turn in the road brought into sight a new hillside, each emblazoned with huge, white numbers, crudely painted onto the rock faces of the summits. We later discovered that they were the years in which their authors graduated, each cohort trying to outdo the last in the size and ambition of their graffiti. They were a welcome distraction from a long, slow ascent in the heat.

The top of the pass arrived without announcement. We paused for some water and to take in the view before beginning our descent. And what a descent it was. The road swept this way and that, curling around the mountainside like a snake. The gradient was such that we could fly downhill without touching our pedals but not so steep that we had to ride our brakes in fear. The heat that had been so stifling on the ascent was tempered by the cool rush of air and, through it all, we could see what lay ahead of us: a huge expanse of wild, open desert.

The pull of gravity catapulted us into the desert and passed us to a tailwind as we reached level ground. The sun hung low above the mountain behind us and we cycled side by side, each beaming at the empty, pristine wilderness that surrounded us. To cap off the good feeling we had about the place, we passed a sign that read: 'Wild camping allowed'.

A solitary building came into view in the distance. It was a half-built truck stop and petrol station, currently just a huge concrete shelter with tables, chairs and water fountains. Brand new, with running water and in pristine condition, it was perfect for bivvying.

We had not seen anyone for some time and assumed that we were alone, but as we pulled off the road and came to a stop, the roar of an engine became audible. It was not coming from the road behind us though; it was coming from the dunes ahead. A plume of sand appeared, followed by the black silhouette of a buggy. It careered towards us at speed and screeched to a stop a few yards away.

I pulled my sunglasses off to get a better look. A man with wild, sand-filled hair sat behind the steering wheel of a dune buggy. It looked like something out of Mad Max: a crude, metal frame of a vehicle that left its driver exposed to the elements, shuddering constantly above the loud, rumbling noise of its engine. I watched the driver, motionless at the wheel, and struggled to comprehend where he had come from and what he was doing.

As I stared at him, the driver tugged his goggles off to stare back. In front of him were a young couple in the middle of a desert, standing next to a pair of bicycles loaded with baggage. Their clothes were grubby, their bikes showing clear signs of wear and tear. He was probably wondering where we had come from and what we were doing.

We stayed that way for perhaps a minute before I eventually gave him a nod. He did not react immediately but remained perfectly still and let a moment pass before nodding back. Still holding my gaze, he pulled his goggles back on, revved his engine and tore off into the desert.

That evening we washed ourselves in the warm evening sun and ate our dinner with an overwhelming sense of tranquillity. We had developed a love of deserts after our time in Oman, when we spent several days walking across the Wahiba Sands. Deserts can feel so alien and inhospitable, but there is a stark beauty to them too. There is something about their sterile purity, unchanged for centuries, that nourishes the soul and they are one of the few places that we both feel at peace.

We lay down beneath an open sky thinking about how lucky we were as the moon rose above us. We did not see another soul until we were back on the road the following morning.

From the desert basin, we wound our way towards Yuma, Arizona and the Continental Divide: the great line that that runs down the spine of the Americas and separates its two watersheds. On one side, water flows west towards the Pacific and, on the other, it runs east to the Atlantic. Since leaving the Pacific Coast, the Great Divide had been our focal point, the first hurdle on our run to the Atlantic.

Despite arriving into Yuma shortly after 3pm, it took us so long to cross the city that, as we struggled to navigate our way out the other side, it got dark. We trudged through endless suburbs and crossed multiple dual carriageways, but try as we might, we just could not get back out to the desert to find somewhere quiet to put up a tent. Our will broke halfway across a huge industrial park at about nine o'clock. It was late, it was dark and we were tired so we just stopped where we were: a big, empty car park.

We checked around for security guards then put our tent up on the tarmac with a large RV between us and the road. We took turns to keep watch while the other strip washed after another hot, dusty day, no doubt contributing some new shots to the library of incriminating footage accumulating on the world's CCTV cameras. We bedded down for the night, the RV concealing us from the road, and set an early alarm so that we could strike camp before anyone arrived for work.

Returning to the map in the morning, we realised why we had struggled to find our way out of town the night before: the only route east was on an Interstate Highway. Those highways criss-cross the United States like a giant dot to dot, connecting every town, city and port with a ribbon of concrete. They are what makes America so great for road trips and travelling by car, but they are not designed for cyclists. However, it is actually legal to ride a bike on a highway if there is no alternative and, since we could not see one, we decided to take the plunge.

We approached the Interstate with some trepidation but found it surprisingly quiet. It also had a broad shoulder, which was wider than the car lanes and effectively meant that we had a huge bike path, all to ourselves. In some ways, we actually felt safer than we did on many other occasions when we had had to share a road with traffic. The drivers in America were by far the most aggressive and least friendly towards cyclists (or certainly towards us) of any country we visited. On roads without shoulders – and even some with – drivers would frequently come within inches of us at high speed, sometimes deliberately, and honk their horns or shout out of their windows, simply because we had the audacity to use a bike on a road. Mercifully, even in the US, it was only a tiny minority of drivers who behaved like that.

After a few hours riding on Interstate 8, we pulled into a service station where we picked up a quarter-gallon cup of PowerAde for fifty cents. Such cheap soft drinks are probably not ideal for drivers, but water, sugar and electrolytes were ideal after a morning's sweaty cycling. We topped them off with two hot dogs, which were fifty cents and came with unlimited toppings. Obviously, Laura saw this as a means of maximising value so drowned her frankfurter in a tricolour of red, white and yellow, after which she spent the afternoon feeling sick.

The town we reached the next evening was not big enough to have a campsite but too big to discreetly wild camp. We asked for recommendations at the local police station and the Sheriff's Deputy said we could pitch in his yard. It was a patch of dirt on the edge of the desert, marked out with a chain-link fence and filled to the brim with junk. He was a hoarder and had all sorts in there: the upturned hull of an old wooden boat, a collection of unused toilet bowls, a large box of tennis balls split in half, several derelict vehicles and a range of pick axes.

While we were reading our books beneath a starry sky that night, I was startled by a loud whistling noise. The deputy's yard backed straight onto a railway line and, apparently, the trains ran all night. Although better known as the home of the automobile, America has a strong railroad history too and, as it happened, our route would be following a little bit of it for several weeks.

We rode out of town and up into a barren, rocky hillside the following morning. Beneath us on the desert floor, we saw a steam engine crawling along, billowing smoke. I imagined myself a Native American, riding on horseback, and pictured cowboys appearing, silhouetted on the skyline above me. We dropped back down, closer to the track some days later and raced the train as it passed. It was far too fast for us so, when the next one came, we switched to counting its carriages to work out how long it was. By my reckoning, the longest we ever saw was over 100 carriages and two kilometres long.

That night I fell asleep to the now comforting sound of a train's chugging engines. We had pitched outside some kind of hostel full of young men after a Mexican guy led us there when he saw us hunting around for camping spots.

'There's a shower inside. Just warn the guys before you go in,' he added, looking at Laura.

'What is this place?' she asked.

'Rehab centre. These guys are fresh out of jail. We give them a place to stay while they sort themselves out.' Ex-cons or not, they were just about as friendly as anyone else we met.

Waking with the sun, we resumed our course alongside the railway tracks and followed them into Tucson. Over the coming days, we climbed our way towards the Continental Divide and felt the familiar satisfaction of having conquered another milestone, as we finally crossed the watershed. At the top, we pointed our bikes towards the Mexican border and set sail.

Chapter 39

'Stupendous scenery and the best skies of the whole trip, but America, some of your road surfaces are among the worst in the world.' – Tim

'Listened to three men in Stetsons discussing the best place to buy customised boots. The Wild West: where cowboy gear is entirely unironic.' – Laura

'Following the border, eh? You got a gun?'

It was a pretty direct question for someone we had just met in a car park, but perhaps that is the American way.

'Er, no. We've not got a gun, I replied.

'You got pepper spray at least?'

'No pepper spray either.'

'No gun? No pepper spray?' he shook his head in disbelief and leaned against the window of his pickup truck to give this some thought before adding: 'Well, I guess you've just got God then.'

He reversed his car out of its parking place and, before driving off, paused to shout: 'Good luck!'

Our decision to stick to the United States' southern border for our crossing of the country was driven by two things: temperature and time.

It was late autumn when we arrived and would be winter by the time we left. Cycling in the north of the country would have meant snow and ice and we had had enough of that earlier in the trip. Down south, it was much milder. America is also narrower at the bottom than at the top, which meant it would be quicker to cycle across. That was important because we only had a couple of months until Christmas and our flights back home. As such, staying south made sense for us. However, that meant following the Mexican border, which caused consternation for some. Following the talk of guns, God and pepper spray in the parking lot, we set off towards the border with a little trepidation.

Crossing the Continental Divide had brought us into New Mexico. The landscape in our new state remained barren and rocky, and the temperature stayed high. The choo-chooing of the steam trains continued, too. Despite being within inches of the border on our map, it was several days before the road ever strayed close enough that we could actually see a fence. Most of the time, we just knew that it was out there in the desert, somewhere to our right. The primary indicator of our proximity was the proliferation of white Border Patrol vehicles.

'We catch about 40 people a day trying to make the crossing into the United States,' John from Border Patrol told us. 'And New Mexico's not even got a big stretch of border. Over in Texas they get more like 300.'

40 people a day meant 280 a week and well over a thousand a month and that sounded unfeasibly high to me. I figured that he was probably exaggerating a bit so I Googled it to find out the real figures as soon as we had left his company. The first article I read referred to 5,000 people getting caught attempting the crossing in a single month, even more than he suggested. The problems it causes and the solutions to them may be a matter of some controversy, but one thing quickly became clear: a lot of people try to cross that southern border.

'99% of border incursions are drug smugglers,' John continued.

'Cartels?' I proffered in the hope that those hours spent watching Breaking Bad might at least have equipped me with the correct vernacular for this conversation.

'Sort of, but they're not the ones out there in the desert. Those are just your average Joes who've had a gun held to their head and been told that if they don't carry a bag of drugs into America then their family is going to die.'

Walkers, they call them. They are given a bag full of drugs, dropped in the desert on the Mexican side of the border and pointed in the right direction. If they are lucky, they will get some water and salt to carry too.

'We probably only catch ten to fifteen percent.'

This astounded me almost as much as the 300 a day stat. We had seen dozens of white border cars driving up and down the roads, passed loads of border checkpoints and seen signs up everywhere. How hard can it be to stop someone getting across a border?

'Can't you just put a fence up or something?'

'There's 2,000 miles of border out there,' he replied. 'But we did try it actually. At least for the narrow border in New Mexico. We used some old World War II anti-tank barriers. We reckoned nothing was going to get through that, but they did. Cut right through them with plasma torches.'[1]

'Plasma torches? How the hell did the cartel get their hands on plasma torches?' I don't really know what a plasma torch is, but it doesn't sound like the kind of thing your regular drug dealer carries.

'Oh, they've got all kinds of stuff. Plasma torches, rocket-propelled grenades, drones, helicopters, submarines, aeroplanes...'

Drug dealers with submarines? That I could not believe. So, again, I Googled it and, again, it is absolutely true. Drug smuggling by submarine happens. As it does by plane. Some estimates put the number of planes owned by the cartels in Mexico as greater than those owned by the national airlines. That might be a bit far-fetched, but it does not really matter because the cartels have long since switched to using drones.

'But I don't usually see that sort of stuff: planes, subs and all that. My job's tracking the walkers.'

'Don't you have drones that can do that for you?'

---

[1]This was before Donald Trump had stood for president and announced plans to build a wall along the Mexican border. Apparently, it has been tried before.

'They've got the drones. Not us. We can't afford that kind of thing. We've got some balloons though.'

'Balloons?'

'Yeah, hot air balloons with cameras in, but that's nothing to do with me. I'm on the ground, looking for footprints and unusual disturbances in the foliage.'

I loved this. Whilst the drug barons of Mexico dispatched unmanned drones across the border, cut through anti-tank barriers with plasma torches and smuggled drugs using submarines, John was out in the sand with a magnifying glass trying to determine whether the size nine prints he found looked Mexican or American.

In truth, despite the stories, while others may have been worried about us spending two months following the Mexican border on a bicycle, we were not. Thousands of people, if not millions, live along America's southern borders and life there is lived just as normally as it is anywhere else.

After our conversation with John, we rode off on another hot and sunny morning, following a long, flat road through the desert. After stopping for lunch at a little Mexican place selling fish tacos, we spent the afternoon riding immediately parallel to the train tracks. Settlements were few and far between on this stretch of our route, but we had managed to find a willing host just over the border in New Mexico.

By the time we reached his town, we were parched so stopped off at a convenience store before finding our host's house. We frequently found ourselves craving milk at the end of a day's cycling so, inside the shop, I went straight to the refrigerated section. In America, it is often cheaper to buy an entire gallon of milk than it is to buy a single pint. I do not mean that it works out cheaper per millilitre, I mean it actually costs less to buy a big bottle than it does to buy a small one.

I emerged from the store with a 3.7-litre bottle of milk. We drank as much as we could, but not for the first time we had to strap a huge, half-filled plastic milk bottle to the back of my bike.

We pedalled half a mile through town and pulled up to the address we had been given. It was a small, wooden, corner house with a rickety picket fence and a petite, unkempt garden. The door opened and Sam appeared with two friendly dogs in tow.

'Come on in,' he said, and I bumbled through the front door carrying two panniers in each hand and a one-gallon plastic bottle, still half-filled with milk.

We sat down in his living room and were stunned to see an armoury of guns laid out on his coffee table. Sam disappeared into the kitchen to fetch some drinks then called back: 'How was the ride? Pretty hot out there.'

'Yeah, pretty good. Another long, flat desert road. Tough in that heat,' I shouted back to Sam, distracted by what was in front of me.

'You guys want spaghetti squash or tartiflette for dinner?'

I was struggling to concentrate. We were in the living room surrounded by all these terrible things and he was offering us a range of gourmet meals.

'Er, squash? Yeah, the squash. Sounds great. Thanks,' I replied eventually.

'Here,' he said, coming back into the room. 'I made you a couple of ice teas.'

It all seemed so civilised. He seemed so normal. Tea, dinner, nice conversation. But that did not change what was before our eyes. Laura couldn't take it. She had to bring it up. 'Sam,' she began, tentatively. 'Sam... why is there a machine gun on the table?'

'A what?'

'A gun. Lots of guns, in fact.'

Sam told us he was a Federal Agent. Like so many people around here, his job was working on the border and working on the border meant carrying firearms for protection. That, apparently, was part of the reason his lounge looked like the props room for Rambo III.

'But mostly I just like guns.'

He proceeded to show us his gun locker, not that we could have missed it. The room in which we sat was tiny and half of it was taken up with the huge black edifice that was Sam's gun locker. Size wise, it was somewhere between a large American fridge and a walk-in wardrobe. He punched in a code, hauled open the thick metal door and started extracting weapons of war from its many shelves.

'This one has a telescopic sight and automatic magazine. Oh, and by the way, I don't have any 'machine guns'. Fully automatic weapons are against the law, even in New Mexico. Have a go!' he said, dropping a large weapon into my lap.

I am British. The only time we use guns is for shooting clay pigeons on stag dos. I was immensely uncomfortable with even the concept of gun ownership let alone the possession of an entire arsenal of semi-automatic weapons. I was scared and I did not want to touch the guns.

Sam came back with a pistol: 'Check out the sight on this one. I built it myself.'

It did not feel right. Skip forward 12 hours however, and... BAM! BAM! BAM!

'Nice!' I shouted, as Laura lowered a long black shotgun to survey her work. 'Can I have a go?'

Sam had badgered us to go shooting with him all through the previous evening after opening up his gun cabinet. Our queasiness about guns had gradually melted away as the night wore on and was soon overtaken by total and utter fascination. We felt the weights of the different weapons, compared the sights, checked out the loading mechanisms and looked at the varieties of bullet. We asked about the differences between each weapon, why he had chosen them and in what situations he would use each one:

'This one's standard issue at work. This one I'm building for my friend who wants something light and easy to use if there's a break-in. And this one's my personal favourite and just flashing it got me out of some trouble in Florida last year.'

We asked about the gun laws. In most states, you are required to conceal your gun. However, some states have an 'open carry' law, which means it is legal to have weapons on full display. Some real enthusiasts show their support for the law by meeting up in cafes with all manner of weapons hanging off their person in an ostentatious display of their right to openly carry arms.

In the morning, he had finally twisted our arms and we agreed that we would join him at the shooting range before heading off. As he loaded gun after gun into the back of his car and drove us out into the desert alone, I think we were both starting to question our judgment. He screeched around corners at speed and skidded along a sandy trail before circling to a stop in an empty car park in the middle of nowhere. We had not seen anyone for half an hour and now we were in a deserted parking lot with a complete stranger carrying an assortment of large guns.

'This is it,' he said before jumping out and loading a weapon. He didn't point it at us so we relaxed a little. 'Want me to show you a drill?'

He flung half a dozen clay pigeons onto a sandy embankment then walked back to the car. He had an automatic rifle slung over his shoulder. 'Ready?'

He spun around, pulled the rifle up to his face and let loose a volley of deafening shots, with pieces of clay pigeon scattering everywhere as he strode towards the sandbank. Magazine empty, he continued moving forward without a pause as he whipped a pistol from a harness on his belt and emptied eight more rounds into the remains of the targets. It was an impressive display of extreme violence.

'That's just a little routine we do at work. In case we meet some really bad guys.'

We stood stunned for a minute. He eventually coaxed me into having a go with a small handgun. It was quite satisfying. Exhilarating in fact. Laura had a turn then we moved up to some rifles and finally the big, black Italian shotgun. BAM!

It thundered more loudly than the rest and I could still feel its kickback in my shoulder as we pedalled out of town. It was terrifying and fascinating, surreal and fun. I was unsure how to feel about it, but I thought that if I had to have a crash course in guns from anyone, I was glad that it came from a member of the United States Federal Government. Better to go shooting with a trained law enforcer rather than being driven out into the desert by some crazy gun nut.

'You think he was a trained law enforcer?' Laura asked, pulling up next to me. 'Did you see a badge or any ID? Did you see anything at all to suggest that he was actually a Federal Agent or did we just hear some tall stories and see a whole lot of guns?'

Laura shook her head and pedalled back out in front. With the hearing returning slowly to my ears, we set our sights on reaching our next state: Texas.

Guns were a recurring theme of our time in the South. Upon hearing that we were British, complete strangers would frequently ask us if the police in England have got guns yet. In the UK, we think it is mad that Americans have so many guns. In America, they think it is mad that we don't, particularly our police.

Some people that we met were real gun nuts, Sam being the prime example. He carried a gun at all times and said he would never move back to his home state of New York because of the state law limiting weapons to a maximum of eight bullets in a clip: 'It's illogical and totally unnecessary. I could never live there.' His entire home state was ruled out because he could not carry a gun with ten bullets in it. That guy really liked guns.

Not everyone that we met was like that. Jerry and Lainie, who took us in a few nights later, were originally from the north. No one had guns up there and that included them. They had never planned to move south, but they spent a year or two driving an RV around the country, travelling up as far as Alaska before eventually finding themselves settling at the other end of the map, down by the Mexican border. They still had their RV parked outside their house: a lovely wooden building on the top of a hill, a good few miles from the main road at the end of a gravel track. We slept in the RV and it was clear how much the vehicle meant to them. It had been their ticket to adventure and they hoped it would be again one day.

It had never occurred to them to buy a gun, just because they had moved to New Mexico.

'But everyone's got one,' said legal attorney and keen bird watcher, Lainie, 'and if they've all got guns and you don't, then you don't stand a chance. Jerry's away a lot so it's just me out here on my own. If word got out that I didn't have a gun then I would just be a sitting duck.'

A couple of months after settling in the South, even Lainie got herself a gun.

Jim and Stacey had a gun too. Stacey told us as much before we went to sleep when we stopped for the night at their house later that week.

'If you get up to have a pee in the night,' she said, 'call out your name first because Jim's got a gun and, y'know, we don't want any mix ups.'

'Stacey! What the hell? I'm not gonna *shoot* anyone!' cried Jim.

'I'm just saying!' she replied, with her hands up defensively.

They had been living in California until recently but felt they could not stay in the state any longer because it was getting too liberal.

'Too liberal?' Laura asked with a raised eyebrow.

'Not gay marriage if that's what you're thinking,' replied Stacey. 'That's great. But the plastic bag thing was the final straw.'

Earlier that year, the state banned single use carrier bags. It was aimed at reducing waste but was a step too far for some. Not for the last time, we heard the Golden State described as the Socialist Republic of California.

They had never owned a gun back in the Republic, but they bought one for protection once they got to New Mexico. In fact, of all the people that we met during our time in America whenever the issue of guns came up, it turned out that every single one owned a firearm. Some were embarrassed about it, some were proud and some clearly never gave it a second thought, but without fail, not a single person we stayed with was without a gun.

Chapter 40

'I have no idea what time, date or day it is. All I know is that I wake at sunrise, stop cycling at sunset and eat when my tummy rumbles.'
– Laura

'Proud to have achieved a full body wipe down with just 150ml of water and a flannel. Bet that's not in the SAS Desert Survival Guide.' – Tim

If Texas was a country, it would have been the third largest that we cycled across.

Texas is bigger than the UK. If you measured the surface area of England, Scotland, Wales and Northern Ireland, and all the many, many islands that form the United Kingdom then added up your totals, it would not even reach half the size of Texas. Or, using the standard measure, Texas is 33 times the size of Wales.

If you hopped into your car in El Paso (Texas), set your satnav for Houston (Texas) and put your cruise control on a steady 60 miles an hour, even if your only stopped was for fuel, you would still be driving twelve hours later, having never left the state.

We did some of our longest days of cycling in Texas, but it still took us three weeks to cross that one state. Three weeks! Cycling right the way across France, the entire coast of Croatia and the length of the Malaysian peninsula all took less time than that.

When we crossed the state line into Texas (next to a driver who took one look at his satnav then let out a heavy sigh) we were still in desert: baking hot and bone dry. We had not even made it halfway to Louisiana before we saw frost on the ground and found ourselves sheltering from the cold in cafes, shivering around a pot of coffee. Not long after that, a hurricane hit and we had to seek refuge in a motel while entire towns were flooded and blown away. Scorching desert, frozen mountains and flooded towns, all in this one state.

It is not just Texas itself that is big. It is everything in it. Texas Margaritas, for example, are like normal margaritas only they are served in a quarter gallon glass, the size of your head. The Texas steak we ate overlapped the already large dinner plate on which it was served. And it was in Texas that I came across the Heart Attack Burger: two half pound meat patties served in between two cheese toasted sandwiches. It made for an excellent afternoon snack.

And it is not just that Texas is big and that everything in it is big. It is also that the gaps between places are big. Texas is really empty. People often ask us what we did for food on our trip and where we got our water. Normally, the answer is boring: we just bought food from the nearest shop and filled our water bottles up from a tap at the end of the day. But not in Texas.

We had crossed Vietnam, Oman, Iran and Japan and never really had to plan ahead with food or water. We always just stumbled across a shop or someone's house. Those countries all sound terribly exotic and remote, but we were rarely more than a few hours or minutes away from civilisation.

But that did not work in Texas. Texas is really big. Did I mention that? There were times there when we would cycle all day and barely see a man-made structure or even a water source, let alone a shop. The closest to it that we had experienced anywhere else on our journey was the empty stretch of road leading to that Australian roadhouse with the Swedish girls, but that was a one-off. In Texas, it was a regular occurrence. It was the emptiest place we had ever cycled through, which meant thinking ahead to plan our food and water supplies carefully.

We entered Texas at El Paso, cycling beneath the big, open sky, a brilliant blue canopy above a vast expanse of grassy plains.

We rode through that for days, stopping at service stations to fill our water bottles and resting at the roadside for snacks in whatever shade we could find. The train line was always at our side, making every scene feel like one from an old Western movie. It was hot, dusty and desolate.

We rode through that for days until one evening we found ourselves a long way from civilisation with no water left in our bottles. The sun had been cooking us during the day, but after it set the twilight hours made for more pleasant riding conditions. Normally, when darkness came and we found ourselves without water and were unsure where we would sleep, I might feel a little anxious, but my overwhelming feeling that evening was of tranquillity. It was peaceful out there and, when I put the lack of water out of my mind, it felt as though I could have happily cycled in that state forever. The warm evening air was like a bath at just the right temperature, the road was smooth and the pedalling was effortless. The world had slipped away leaving behind no trace of its worries, only peace and quiet.

We rode through that for days until we came upon a house, the only one for miles around. We drew to a stop and approached the front door with caution.

We did camp outside a lot of the time, but despite being surrounded by vast swathes of empty land, camping spots were surprisingly rare. There was often just a tiny strip of ground between the road and fenced-off, private land. So, even when we had enough water, we sometimes struggled to find anywhere good for the tent. As such, we often knocked on doors for permission.

A side effect of having so much land available was that the houses tended to have very long driveways: a hundred yards or more. For the approaching cyclist, that meant there was a long time for the tension to build as bikes were wheeled towards the front door, unsure of what we would find on arrival. The night before, we had reached halfway down one such drive when a pack of dogs came hurtling towards us and we were forced to make a hasty retreat. Tonight's drive was no shorter, but there did not appear to be any dogs. We knew however, that whoever lived there would have at least one firearm. Being just a stone's throw from the Rio Grande and Mexico, we figured they might also have a twitchy trigger finger.

Shout from a distance and risk sounding aggressive? Or wait until we get closer and risk looking like we're sneaking up on them? We let indecision decide and snuck up by default. The front door opened to reveal the outline of a huge form behind mosquito mesh.

'Well now, how I can be of help to y'all? Sir? Ma'am?'

The deferential greeting burst the tension and we relaxed as the large man in the doorway led us round the back of his house to park our bikes.

Johnny had been the local deputy since first getting elected in 1995.

'Got more votes than anyone before,' his wife Georgia chipped in. 'All 92 of them,' she added with a laugh.

'93 actually. Not that I'm counting,' he shot back with a smile. It was a well-worked routine and all the more enjoyable for it.

Theirs was a modest wooden house surrounded by dust and rocks, set against the silhouette of distant hills in an otherwise flat expanse of land.

'Only 93 people? Seems like a small place to need its own deputy,' Laura asked. We were sitting in their front room sipping ice tea by this point.

'Well now, ma'am, my county stretches from the Mexican border to right up past Pine Springs and I-62 a hundred miles north of here. It covers an area of 4,500 square miles. It'd take me six days just to walk from one side to the other,' he replied. 'Not that I'd ever try.'

I looked out the front door at the miles of dusty rock then out the window at the same stuff in the opposite direction and asked:

'You get a lot of trouble round here?'

'Well now, sir, folks round here don't cause too much trouble at all. They're good people. But the folk coming over that river, well, they cause all sorts of problems.'

That river was the Rio Grande. It was as dry as a bone right now but usually flowed freely. It broadly marked the border between the USA and Mexico and was within spitting distance.

'We get Mexican folk swimming across that river all the time. They go straight to the phone box to make the call. Let whoever it is know that they're here. It's my job to pick them up and send them back home again.'

He continued: 'A few years back, a Mexican man came to our front door when I was out. He told Georgia here that I needed to stop sending them people back. Said there wouldn't be any trouble if I just stopped sending them back. Not too friendly like.'

Did he stop?

'No, sir. I just kept on picking them up and shipping them back. Coming to a man's home and threatening his wife just ain't right. But I got my gun and I ain't afraid of them.'

Georgia chuckled. She wasn't from Texas. She was from way up north where drug cartels were just the stuff of legends and guns less a part of everyday life.

'But I like it down here,' she said. 'It's quiet and there's no one around. Can't step out your front door and take a piss in the city. Least not twice, anyway!'

Johnny winced at his wife saying 'piss', but Georgia waved him off.

'I took him to New York once, but he was too scared to go on the subway.' Scared? Deputy Johnny, scourge of the cartels. Scared of public transport?

'No guns down there,' he added by way of explanation. 'I ain't going nowhere without my gun. No ma'am. Don't know *what* could happen.'

'People call us racist when they hear about Johnny sending back those Mexicans,' Georgia said, picking up the earlier thread with a clear sense of hurt. 'But that ain't right. We got plenty of Mexican friends here in town. We even sponsored a family to get their visas. But they've got to do it right. Can't just turn up here on the streets. There are laws.'

Georgia made us dinner and set us up in the spare room. They went to bed early and we stayed up watching a film in the dark. The following morning they were worried about us cycling in the heat.

'I don't even walk my dogs when it's this hot.'

They filled all our containers with water and foisted half a dozen plastic water bottles into our panniers.

We left with handshakes and hugs. 'You need some money?' Georgia said with sudden alarm. 'Let me get you some money.'

She got as far as rummaging through her purse before we stopped her, but we put up less resistance when she offered to make us some sandwiches.

We followed an old abandoned road up through dry, rocky foothills, away from the warm hospitality of Georgia and Johnny. Across the hillside, hardy shrubs fought against the harsh environment to make their steady progress upwards as we fought against gravity to do the same. The concrete beneath our wheels had been ripped up by roots, leaving a deteriorated surface punctuated with cracks and holes. I squinted against the bright sun from behind my sunglasses to focus on navigating the bumpy road and, from the corner of my eye, spotted the coiled form of a rattlesnake.

I veered immediately to the other side of the road where I continued pedalling until at a safe distance. My heart was pounding and I turned back to warn Laura. I made the gesture we had invented in jest some months earlier, mimicking a snake's venomous teeth with two curled fingers on one hand while using the other to point towards the deadly creature, lurking in the shadows. Laura dismounted and walked on the far side of the road, with her bike between her and the snake.

It was dark grey with a square head and the tell-tale tail of a rattlesnake. The poison of a rattlesnake can variously cause your flesh to decay, your internal organs to haemorrhage and your nervous system to paralyse. We had been told by many locals about how common rattlesnakes were and how dangerous they could be. It was hard to take the warnings seriously, when we had not seen any for ourselves, but now that we had I could understand the fear. I shivered despite the heat and re-mounted my bike.

A little further up the road, another cyclist came towards us. His bike was loaded with luggage and he had clearly been cycling for some time. His state of dishevelment was not as advanced as ours, but it was still a good few stages beyond what you might expect from a guy who was just cycling to the shops.

'So, have you actually *seen* any Mexicans yet?' he asked.

He was a reporter from up north who had come down to the border to investigate the many scary stories that he had heard.

'There's only so much you can do by email,' he explained, 'so I flew down. But staying in a hotel in a city, you're still pretty detached from it all. I figured if I got out here on my bicycle then I'd see it first hand and meet some more interesting people, but I've not had much luck so far.'

We told him about some of the people we had stayed with: the border guard who tracked the smugglers' footprints, Johnny picking up illegal immigrants and Georgia getting threatened by the cartel. I felt like spending all those evenings in people's homes afforded us a rare insight into their lives, thoughts and feelings.

'You believe all of those people? They say there are thousands of illegals getting in, but no one knows for sure. They're just guessing.'

He was clearly sceptical, a Northerner who had come down south to expose what he saw as mistruths, borne out of petty racism.

'I'm not saying that people don't occasionally try to sneak across the border and I'm sure some of them are carrying drugs. But if there's so many of them doing it,' he swept his arm in the general direction of Mexico, 'where are they? It's open country out there. How hard could it be to spot them?'

It was hard to know what to believe. We had heard plenty of tales but not seen anything for ourselves. Perhaps the stories get exaggerated and the numbers inflated, but when the cold hard facts involve cartel controlled drones and drug smuggling submarines, I am not sure how much scope for exaggeration remains. We were left to contemplate this as the liberal-minded journalist set off in search Mexicans.

'Oh, hey!' I shouted after him. 'There's a rattlesnake on the right hand side of the road in about half a mile. Stay on the left!'

Chapter 41

'Two big days under our belts. With so much empty country and big gaps between towns, no distractions from cycling.' – Laura

'I love the fact that, in Texas, those who ride bikes are known as "cyclers".' – Tim

Sheriff Johnny was not exaggerating about the sparseness of his constituency. We had to cycle for ages before finding a shop and, when we did, it was just a Dollar General.

A large chain of supermarkets-come-general-stores, Dollar Generals seemed to dominate the small towns of Texas. The ones that we visited were usually large and the shelves were always well stocked so, when we first encountered, it took us a while to work out what was missing. These shops had an excellent range of long-life products with use-by-dates many months and years in the future, but they never had so much as an onion's worth of fresh produce. No fruit, no vegetables and nothing that required a fridge. In other words, they were the exact opposite of what we needed.

With a country as vast as the United States, getting fresh food to all its farthest flung and least populated corners is a challenge. Whilst the importance of everyone having easy access to fruit and vegetables is hard to dispute, the economics of stocking far-flung shops to provide such a service do not always stack up. Shipping fresh produce across vast swathes of empty countryside to be sold in tiny quantities to a small community is not an easy business proposition.

This problem creates what are known as 'food deserts': large areas of America in which access to fresh food is limited. These food deserts tend to be associated with the poorer end of society and are particularly common in actual deserts, like the ones through which we travelled.

But whilst fresh food was hard to come by, fast food was not. On that same street with the Dollar General, in the far reaches of Deputy Johnny's constituency, there was a Taco Bell, a McDonald's and a Jack-In-The-Box chicken shop.

It is estimated that there are five fast food outlets for every supermarket in America. So perhaps we should not have been surprised that, in the wilds of Texas, it was far easier for us to find potato fries than potatoes. Although we got a bit sick of eating so much junk, it is not the end of the world if a cycle tourist eats lots of cheap, calorific food. Unfortunately, most people do not get eight hours of exercise every day to burn off the calories they have eaten and use the sugar as soon as it hits their system. They get fat and ill instead.

For the next couple of weeks, it was Dollar Generals or nothing and we had to learn to live without fresh food. The dusty plains gave way to rolling, grassy hills as we travelled across the state, and the weather transitioned from bone dry to very wet. We sheltered in a motel during the worst of the heavy rain and, after another few days of riding, we found ourselves dealing with low temperatures again. Unlike the chilly ride across Australia and New Zealand, we at least had proper shoes this time, but the speed of transition from hot desert to icy hill country still came as something of a shock.

Cresting a hill on a cool afternoon, we reached a tiny, frontier-like settlement of wooden buildings. We wheeled our bikes towards an old, dark building with swinging saloon-style doors, which appeared to be the village store. We entered in the hope of finding an apple or some carrots and exited with a tin of spam and an overwhelming sense of disappointment. Sitting outside on the shop's veranda, a pickup truck pulled up in front of us. The door opened and a cacophony of barking dogs erupted.

'Shut up! Shut the hell up in there!' the driver shouted back through his open door.

He wore blue jeans, a check shirt, cowboy boots and a cowboy hat. This genuinely is the standard attire for a lot of people in Texas. As he walked past, he paused to stare at us and I noticed that his arms were covered in blood. He entered the shop and emerged two minutes later with a sack of potatoes, which he slung onto the back of his truck. He strode back towards us and stopped at the edge of the wooden deck to loom over us.

'Where you come from?' he said.

'We're from the UK…'

'Police there got guns yet?'

'Er, no, not yet.' I finished my answer to his original question: 'But we've cycled here from California.'

'Socialist Republic of. Good thing you got outta there. No good hippies.' An awkward silence fell.

'So,' I said eventually, 'what do you do?'

'Kill people.' He stared at me, waiting for a response. 'I kill people for a living. Unconventional warfare. I was in Iraq the first time around, Desert Storm. If they had given me the order, I'd have blown 15 million people away.'

He spat on the floor before detailing how he worked for a specialist unit during the Gulf War which, in his telling, had covered the entire of Baghdad with explosives. If things had 'gone wrong' with the American assault then his team were to blow up the whole city.

'Oh, that's interesting,' I said politely for want of anything more appropriate and tried to change the subject. 'Are you from around here?'

'Yup. Texas born and bred. Ain't never gonna leave neither. Government can't interfere with us out here. See, the United States is a Federation. There's no national government. Feds have jurisdiction at checkpoints and inside a ten mile radius in Washington DC, but they ain't got jurisdiction here.'

Right up until the middle of the 19th century, Texas was an independent republic. Its motto – 'The Lone Star State' – is in homage to this. But although it became an American state back in 1844, many of its residents are still fiercely proud of its historical independence and some of them, it appeared, wish it wasn't just historical.

Apparently, this man's view was that there was no constitutional basis for the national government. As such, members of federal law enforcement only had power in tiny slithers of land, like checkpoints between states and in the capital, Washington DC. As such, he believed, he was well within his rights to treat a visiting Federal Agent as he would any other trespasser.

'I see any Feds coming onto my land, I'll make them an appointment with God.'

During this speech he had fixed us with a stare and spoken with some intensity. I did not believe for a minute that his interpretation of the law was accurate, but he did seem sufficiently psychopathic to kill a civil servant trying to deliver a census form.

It felt like he was daring us to challenge him, knowing that he could beat us down with a well-rehearsed argument and the violence of his convictions. I don't know much about the American constitution, but I knew he must be talking rubbish. I also knew that there was no way in hell I was about to share that with him. I just avoided eye contact and nodded meekly until his diatribe was over.

A lot of the people we met in Texas had strong views. Thankfully though, he was the only one with views like that. Interestingly, however, Laura has since commented that America was the only country in which she actually felt scared. This came from a combination of the driving (which was genuinely scary), the guns (which we knew were everywhere) and characters like this.

He was not the only disturbing person we met over there. A few nights earlier, a lady had let us sleep in her front garden. When a neighbour drove past and saw us pitching our tent however, he angrily accused us of tricking the lady into letting us stay so that we could steal from her. When we denied it, he turned bright red and drove off in a fit of rage, leaving us terrified that he was going to return with a gun. It was one of the very few times on our entire trip that we felt threatened. Before leaving home, I think we probably worried most about the more exotic and less developed countries, like India, Iran or Cambodia, but it was the land of the free that brought the most fear.

The scary people in America were nevertheless vastly outnumbered by the nice ones. Night after night after night, we were treated to the finest of American hospitality. We stopped with a disabled former-cycle tourer who took us to an all-you-can-eat buffet, we stayed at a beautiful wooden eco-home hidden in the woods and we enjoyed barbecued ribs while staying with a doctor in Austin. As if that was not enough, we also had a wonderful dinner prepared by a couple who home-schooled their kids for religious reasons, we were given the keys to a roadside RV in remote Texas hill country and we got free dried meat from the wonderfully American-sounding: 'Dwayne's Fresh Jerky.'

The sky darkened as we rode away from the village store with spam in our stomachs and an uneasy feeling. We reached a town later that evening and were halfway across an overpass when a car pulled onto the shoulder in front of us, blocking our path. We knew that we probably should not have been cycling on an overpass, but it was a quiet road with a big shoulder and we did not think that anyone would mind. We continued pedalling and made to go round the vehicle but the driver had got out.

'Hey!' she shouted. 'Hey!'

274

In hindsight, the tone was probably friendly, but on the side of a dual carriageway, fifty feet off the ground with cars whizzing past at high speed, it seemed confrontational. Besides, the last person we had spoken to had told us that he killed people for a living, so we were a little nervous about the sanity of Texans at this point. We pulled our brakes, stopped next to the driver and prepared to be lectured on road safety.

'I passed you guys on my way into Austin this morning and I passed you again on my way back.'

I was not sure where this was going and how it related to our traffic violation.

'And I said to myself: if I see them again, I've gotta stop. So...' she paused with inadvertent dramatic effect. 'Do y'all have a place to stay?'

She did not have to ask twice.

It was hospitality like this that left a big impression on us. Not only did it impact directly on the journey itself by providing places for us to stay and giving us the opportunity to meet people, see inside their lives and understand their countries better. It also affected the way that we viewed the world and the people in it. We saw unthinking kindness everywhere that we went, time and time again, in country after country, all around the world, and that sense of humanity has stayed with me ever since.

People sometimes ask if it was those with the least who showed the most hospitality. When they do, I think of Lucy, who stopped us on that overpass. We followed her car as she led us into a large gated community, with pristine lawns and sparkling lakes, to a house that might best be described as a mansion. She showed us to our en-suite room in a separate wing of the house, instructed us on how to use the hot tub then left us with two large glasses of red wine whilst she set about preparing steak for dinner. Her husband, Hal, was an environmental lawyer and she was a housewife. They lived in a beautiful home and shared it with us in a blink of an eye.

In short, we found no such correlation between poverty and generosity. We stayed with families in Turkey who were clearly very poor and who treated us like hallowed guests. We also stayed with people in a dozen different countries who were very well off and treated us just the same. We found neither the country, nor the religion, nor the richness or the poorness of the people determined the level of hospitality we received. Lucy not only had one of the fanciest houses that we visited, she was also the only host to hand out song sheets.

'What's going on?' Laura whispered, as Lucy disappeared with her wine and left us holding the words to a John Denver song. She and Hal reappeared with two guitars.

'Neither of you two play, do you?'

'I do, actually,' I blurted out.

'Great!'

An hour earlier we had been surrounded by concrete, riding our bikes on an overpass beneath a menacing sky, traumatised from a brief encounter with a madman, and worrying where we would end up that night. Now, we were freshly showered, a little light headed from wine on an empty stomach and joining in a four-person chorus of Take Me Home, Country Road. It was surreal but delightful. A metaphor for our whole trip. Like our time on the road however, Texas was coming to an end. We only had a few more days' riding ahead before we left the state.

Chapter 42

'Footsteps, grunting and digging noises outside the tent: curious wild hogs of Texas.' – Laura

'What could make a day of cycling into a headwind worse...? Distinctly recalling a forecast for tail winds.' – Tim

After the heat, the cold and the rain, the final climatic condition that Texas threw at us was wind. And, as all good cyclists know, the only kind of wind is a headwind.

For days we battled against it, riding wheel to wheel, sheltering one behind the other. We bowed our heads in a vain attempt at obtaining an aerodynamic profile on our bulky bikes, but still we could not get our speedos to clock double digits, even on the flat. In contrast to pedalling uphill where it feels like your efforts are rewarded by a sense of achievement at having conquered a climb, fighting a headwind feels utterly futile. The only effect of extra effort is extra tiredness. When you stop to look back at what you have achieved, there is no vista, only disappointment.

On a particularly long stretch of perfectly straight road with a surface of rough, broken concrete, Laura shouted over her shoulder: 'Has my tyre got enough air in?'

It had. A puncture was not the explanation for our slow progress.

'Can we stop at that junction? I need to get some sugar in,' I asked, but half a packet of biscuits later, I was no faster than before.

'Let's get some coffee at that petrol station,' Laura suggested, imagining that caffeine might be the answer. It was not. There was no solution. Just several hours of backbreaking work with little to show for it.

Passing a large Walmart store, we took the opportunity to stock up on supplies and escape the headwind. It was much the same as a supermarket back home except for one thing: it sold guns. Many take the ability to buy a rifle in Walmart as an indictment of America's gun controls. They may have a point, but in a strange way, it actually made me a little more sympathetic to gun ownership. The weapons on sale were squarely aimed at hunters (they were all hunting rifles and sold alongside binoculars, hides and camouflage clothing) and, for many in the South, hunting was just a part of life.

Although intrigued by the idea of buying a gun in a supermarket, we made do with a pie. It was pumpkin season so we picked up a family-sized pumpkin pie and headed back out into the wind.

Later that afternoon we approached a nice looking cafe. It was cold and we were tired so we agreed to pull over for a rest. We wanted to go inside to shelter from the wind and get warm, but we were also hungry. The problem was that while our daily budget could accommodate stopping for a coffee, it could not accommodate buying a proper sit-down meal.

Earlier in the trip, my inexperienced self would have just gone into the cafe and sipped my drink for an hour while I warmed up. I would have neglected to eat anything then set off hungry and regretted it: Getting grumpy and having to stop again for food half an hour later. Over time, however, I had developed a tactic for dealing with the issue: I ate before I went inside. Of course, the whole point of attending the cafe was to find somewhere warm and sheltered. Sitting outside to eat lunch would have defeated the point. The solution, I realised, was to eat a large quantity of calories very quickly.

When we arrived at the cafe after a long afternoon of battling against a headwind, we were ravenous so I followed my normal tactic.

'I might just have a bit of that pumpkin pie we bought,' I said, before rummaging through my panniers to find it. I tore the packaging open by the cafe's front door, balanced the pie on the back of my bike and began to eat. Our sporks were not easily accessible so

I just dug in with my hands. Laura's sense of decorum initially gave her pause, but within seconds, she too got her paws straight in and started shovelling pie into her face.

Given that it was quite cold and we were both wearing shorts, we huddled together with our backs to the wind and our bodies hunched over the pie. It was a bit tricky to pull out proper chunks of it so we held our faces as close to the tray as possible, scooping mouthfuls directly into our jaws.

This crude, pig-like, troughing performance was carried out in full view of the cafe's more civilised customers. They had come out for a quiet coffee on a Sunday afternoon and, instead, been treated to the kind of animalistic act that would normally be accompanied by a breathless voiceover from David Attenborough.

'Touring cyclists are known for their ability to consume vast quantities of food, at astonishing speeds. But while their appetites may be something to be admired, their manners are not.'

When we eventually came up for air, it was apparent that we had eaten the entire pie. A pie designed to feed a family had disappeared as a pre-lunch snack. Slightly ashamed but not feeling as sick as I deserved, I pushed the packaging into a nearby bin and composed myself to re-join civilised society. I shook the crumbs from my shirt and brushed them from my beard.

'How do I look?' I asked Laura.

'Awful.'

They still let us inside. We enjoyed our coffees and left an hour later, feeling warm and sated with enough money left for dinner. The wind had died down, allowing us to exit Texas with a little less effort. By the time the sun set that evening, we had crossed the mighty Lone Star state, our third largest 'country'.

Chapter 43

'Entering alligator territory: spending large parts of each day planning defence strategies if one attacks as we cycle past.' – Laura

'Walked into the gas station cafe, 20 pairs of eyes swivelled to look at us. All men, all wearing hunting gear. Just a *little* intimidating.' – Laura

We were welcomed into Louisiana by the Martin Luther King Junior Bridge. It carried us over the Sabine-Neches ship canal that separates Louisiana from Texas and launched us into the fifth state of our journey across America.

From there, we picked up Louisiana Highway 82, which runs from the Texan border all the way along the Gulf of Mexico coastline. It is a quiet, sleepy stretch of the United States with a distinct character like nowhere else we had been. The road extended to the horizon in each direction and we pedalled in a straight line for hours, barely having to adjust our steering (except to dodge the two-metre long snake that appeared in the road). Houses were few and far between and the only traffic was the occasional pickup truck driven with untypically good manners, at a slow speed, allowing us plenty of space. We followed Highway 82 past sandy beaches, through coastal marshland and over the state's many, many waterways.

After the feeling of exposure in the vast expanses of Texas, the banks of vegetation flanking us in Louisiana were like an embrace and the reflective still waters running parallel to our route only added to the serenity. It felt like a peaceful place, but there were still clues to the violence that had so recently visited it.

Lost in Louisana's calm, I barely registered the pickup truck that had pulled up next to us. The window came down and an arm leaned out. From behind some sunglasses came the words: 'Where are you guys staying tonight?'

'We're hoping to get to Abbeville,' Laura replied.

'You should stop at my place. I'll bake a cake,' the driver shouted back.

Juanita introduced herself and explained that she lived about an hour's ride up the road. It was a kind offer, but it was only lunchtime and we had planned to get a bit further than that before stopping for the night. We were tired and needed a break, but as absurd as it may sound to turn down the offer of hospitality, sometimes providing company for a host was more tiring than cycling.

'OK, we'll see how we get on.'

It seemed ungrateful to turn down such a kind offer, but since vowing never to do so back in Switzerland a year earlier, we had come to realise something: being hosted can be hard work. Although the privilege of being let inside the homes and lives of people across the globe was, without doubt, the single greatest thing from our sixteen months on the road, it did not stop it being tiring. Being thrown into a stranger's home is difficult. As well as the effort involved in spending an entire evening with someone you have just met, there are all sorts of practical and social considerations.

Should we insist on camping outside and risk seeming weird and ungrateful, or are mum and dad just offering us their bed out of politeness? Should we keep out of the way and entertain ourselves, at the risk of appearing like we are using them as a hotel, or are we getting in their way and stopping them from getting on with their evening? Is there a reason they have not shown us where the toilet or shower is? Should we be sorting out our own food?

Of course, it must have been just as hard for those that hosted us, but knowing that did not make it any less draining. So, when Juanita pulled over and offered to take us in for the night when we were desperately in need of a rest, the decision was not as easy as calculating whether a bed would beat our tent. It came down to whether it would be more restful to quietly eat a bowl of pasta at the roadside, read our books and go to sleep at 8pm, or spend the whole evening making conversation with a stranger.

We mulled this over while pedalling along the empty Highway 82. There was no doubt that staying at Juanita's house that evening would be less restful than camping in the wild, but we had the rest of our lives to eat dinner on our own and it is not every day that a Louisiana local invites you into her house for tea, cake and conversation. We would have been foolish to turn it down. We would keep riding until we reached her house and, if the offer was still open, we would accept.

As we continued our way along Highway 82, we were surprised by how new all of the houses were. It did not seem like a rich area, but there was no doubt that most of the buildings we passed were not long out of their wrapping. The explanation was not riches however, it was Rita.

Hurricane Katrina was the one that hit the news, not Rita. When it struck in August 2005, the footage of the aftermath was beamed around the world, giving a tiny glimpse into the devastation wrought upon New Orleans, where 80% of the city was flooded and over a thousand people were killed. But for the particular stretch of Louisiana along which we travelled, it was the unwelcome arrival of Hurricane Rita, a few weeks later, which changed everything. Katrina was the strongest hurricane ever recorded when it struck the Gulf of Mexico, but within a month, Rita arrived with even more force.

Think about that for a moment: the two most powerful hurricanes ever to hit the area, did so within 24 days of each other. 24 days after a city was laid to waste, thousands of homes destroyed and miles of dry land buried under water, another Category 5 hurricane came straight back at them.

When the coastal residents of Louisiana and its neighbour, Texas, saw the warnings for this second hurricane, they did not hesitate. They had seen the devastation Katrina had caused and an estimated three million people evacuated their homes. Three million!

We later discovered that Juanita was one of those people. She had lived just up the road on Pecan Island all her life. It is a tiny community of only a few hundred people. Although not technically an island, the area is completely surrounded by waterways: to the north lies White Lake and the wetlands, to the south lies marshes then the sea. When Hurricane Rita struck within weeks of Hurricane Katrina, little Pecan Island did not stand a chance. After the storms passed, evacuees returned to the community in which they had spent their whole lives and found nothing left: nearly every single structure in the village had disappeared. Their homes and memories had been dragged into the Gulf of Mexico.

Although Pecan Island was hit particularly badly, the story was much the same right the way along that stretch of coast. The land was low and the buildings fragile. Rita swept most of them away.

Nearly a decade had passed by the time we arrived and much of the infrastructure had been repaired or rebuilt. Reconstruction in different areas seemed to have taken one of two approaches: the first was to build houses on huge concrete stilts with front doors two storeys off the ground. Such homes tended to be quite fancy and had clearly been built to withstand the next hurricane and survive the next flood.

The other type of post-Rita erections were simple, single storey wooden houses built firmly on the ground, exactly like the ones that had been washed away a few years before. Undoubtedly, these were built because the big houses on stilts were not affordable for everyone, not least those who had just lost their livelihoods in a storm. They were built low of necessity, not choice, but a part of me respected the chutzpah nonetheless. The gall to rebuild – in response to having their home destroyed by one of the most intense hurricanes in history, at a location just a stone's throw from the ocean and surrounded on all side by waterways – the exact same, tiny building in the exact same spot. As if to say, 'Knock me down and I get right back up again.'

We were yet to discover all of that, however. At the time, we were just concentrating on getting to Juanita's house.

By the middle of the afternoon, we reached the address we had been given and pulled up alongside the huge tree at the front of Juanita's home, which was very much of the small, wooden, two-fingers to Rita design.

'Hi!' I shouted in the vague direction of her front door. A loud commotion of scrabbling and shouting could be heard before Juanita's foot appeared through a gap in the door.

'Stay, Trash. I said *stay*!'

A ragged, little white dog shot out the door, ran towards me and jumped at my waist.

'Trash, get down!' Juanita cried. 'He gets excited easily but he's harmless.' Trash ran around our bikes in circles, yapping loudly. 'See? He's alright. It's Roadkill you wanna watch out for. He's still pretty nervy,' she added, dragging a larger, wild-eyed dog by the collar.

We brought our bags in through the front door and received introductions to each of the seven dogs in her care. 'This here's Bullet; the big guy over there is Wire and, well, you already met Trash and Roadkill.'

'Lovely to meet you all,' I said, although I could think of few things worse than a house filled with dogs. 'That's an interesting selection of names you have for them.'

'Yeah, they've all been rescued. Trash was put in a trash bag and beaten half to death by his owner. Bullet got shot and left at the side of the road. And I found Wire hanging from a barbed wire fence.'

284

I did not ask about Roadkill.

Juanita had a modest wooden bungalow, dark inside with a long galley kitchen. We sat around a wooden table at one end of the kitchen while she poured some tea and served the cake she had promised to bake for us. She made her living cleaning nearby hunting camps. People came from miles around to hunt in the area and spent big money in the process. She was not a hunter herself, but cleaning their lodges paid her bills and paid to rebuild her house after Hurricane Rita had knocked it down. Rebuilding was not her only option, however. There were alternatives.

'They offered me a lot of money to buy this land.'

The area may be poor but, apparently, the land is worth a lot.

'One and a half million dollars,' she said matter of factly. It seemed an extraordinary sum for a small patch of land with nothing on it, but it was a prime plot for holiday homes.

'Wow. You must have been tempted?'

'Nope,' she replied without hesitation. 'Where'd I go without my dirt? This is where I'm from. Pecan Island is home. Them people up north just use this place for holidays. They ain't from here.'

'What counts as 'up north'?' I asked, imagining New York or Boston, up the top end of the country.

'Pretty much anything past I-10.'

'I-10' is Interstate 10, a highway that runs east-west across Louisiana. It is about 30 miles from the southern coast. Beyond it, the United States stretches for a further 1,200 miles through another half-dozen states. 98% of the country is north of that road and the minute fraction of land to its south is not exactly densely populated. It is mostly swamp. But by Juanita's definition, it was those select inhabitants that counted as the true Southerners. Anyone not within that tiny strip of land between the interstate and the sea was a Northerner, an out-of-towner. I loved how defined and localised her sense of identity was.

'Down south, that's proper Louisiana. It's all French and Spanish and Canadian and Vietnamese. Up there,' she continued, in reference to those far flung lands some 40-minutes' drive away, 'it's all cowboys and prospectors. They just got smeared across from the East like butter. But here, in the real Louisiana, the influences come from Europe and Asia.'

While she told us this and we helped ourselves to another slice of her almond cake, she busied herself around the kitchen making dinner. It involved homemade pesto and some fresh crayfish that she had caught herself, earlier that afternoon. We wondered how she had managed to do a full day's work cleaning lodges, while looking after an army of stray dogs, and still found time to catch crayfish and make her own pesto.

'I find I've got a lot of time on my hands since going sober,' she explained.

Juanita had been an alcoholic. I do not know when or why, and I did not ask, but you could forgive someone for turning to drink after going through an experience like Hurricane Rita.

It must have been an utterly horrible time after Rita washed away everything that Juanita had grown up with. The school was destroyed. The library was destroyed. Homes were lifted from their foundations, spun around and ripped apart. Residents who returned after the storm described getting lost in their own backyards because everything had been turned upside down. And those are the ones who came back. Many did not – children, in particular. One estimate puts the number of school-aged kids on Pecan Island before the hurricane at 200, and the number after at just seven.

Photos after the event show the roofs of buildings poking out from the water line and entire houses being carried downstream. Once the water had started to retreat, roads were strewn with fallen trees, fallen pylons, upturned cars and roaming cows, like a scene from a post-apocalyptic movie.

Juanita was sober by the time we met her and, judging by the number of other travellers for whom she told us she had baked cakes, she had been for a while. And with hindsight, she even managed to find a silver lining amidst all the chaos:

'It's not all bad,' she quipped as she served her latest guests a bowl of steaming hot Louisiana fare. 'Ever since Rita, I can catch crawfish in my backyard!'

We pulled our sleeping bags out after dinner and slept on the spare bed. The dogs came to say hello at 5am so we got up to make ourselves breakfast from the food we had in our panniers. Juanita appeared fresh as a daisy at 6am and started shaking her head as soon as she saw us.

'You are the first guests I've ever had that had to make themselves breakfast.'

Our early start had inadvertently thwarted her natural instinct for hospitality. After we shared a morning coffee with her, she did her best to compensate for her perceived lapse by packing our panniers with food and bags of exotic loose-leaf tea. She gave us so much tea, in fact, that I still have enough to brew a pot in her honour as I write these words. The tea was something to remember her by; Juanita passed away the year after our visit.

Chapter 44

'After 2,000 miles in six weeks with just four rest days, very glad to have a weekend off in New Orleans.' – Laura

'6 days without washing our clothes. Even at this late stage of our journey we are still *setting records.'* – Tim

We wobbled away from Pecan Island, our panniers bulging with food, and set our sights on the next destination: New Orleans.

Sadly, as well as leaving Juanita, that meant leaving the calm of Highway 82 and exchanging it for bigger, busier roads. Instead of locals popping to the shops, we shared the roads with sugar cane trucks travelling interstate. We entered proper swamp territory too: dense tree-filled bayou surrounded us. There was a constant stream of bridges and raised highways to make it possible to traverse the swamps. One of the causeways stretched for a full ten miles; the best part of an hour's cycling on a single bridge.

The roads were not just busy, they were full of potholes too, a common occurrence in America. I was surprised by how poor the road surfaces often were, right the way across the world's largest economy, particularly given its well documented love of cars. Those long Louisiana bridges were also lined with huge cat's eyes that were big enough to derail a careless cyclist. Between the potholes and the cat's eyes, we really had to concentrate on the concrete beneath our tyres rather than looking out across the swamp or watching out for speeding cars.

Compared to Highway 82's considerate drivers, the ones on those larger roads seemed especially aggressive. Cars flew past within touching distance, swerved around us at the last minute and routinely pounded their horns in protest at our presence on the road. On a long, open stretch, a lady in a pickup truck drove right out in front us from a side road without even pretending to stop. When Laura slammed on her own brakes to avoid getting killed, the driver gave her the filthiest of looks then screeched off shaking her head.

We stopped for the night beneath a house on stilts (with the blessing of the owner), pitching our tent in a warm breeze, the temperature mercifully having picked up since Texas. We had been working hard to ensure we stayed on track for our flight out of Florida in a few weeks' time. Combined with the wind, the potholes and the dangerous driving had made for a tiring day. As we cooked our dinner on the camping stove, Laura and I were at the point where conversation was out of the question and communication was purely perfunctory.

A college student in a baseball cap and hoodie walked past the house under which we were camped. He saw our bikes and came up to us to say hello and ask what we were doing. We told him that we were cycling across America on our way around the world.

'Woah, nice! What made you want to do that?' he asked.

'Oh, I don't know,' I replied wearily. 'See the world I guess. Meet people. Try new food.'

He paused, looked at our pan simmering away on the burner, and then looked back at me.

'You guys don't get instant noodles in the UK?'

Perhaps that was not the best time to name culinary exploration as our motivation for travelling the world. He disappeared up the street, chuckling to himself at his little joke, even if we had been too hungry to see the funny side. Half an hour later, the same guy appeared and handed us two cans of beer: 'You looked like you could use these.'

We leaned back, soaked by Louisiana's humidity, our bellies full of noodles, and enjoyed the refreshment of a cold beer.

We had to wake early the next morning to catch a ferry and we skipped breakfast as a result. Dumped on a beach road with nothing around for miles but water and a headwind, we cycled onward with empty stomachs.

Laura was in a bit of a low sugar funk and set off in search of food at a terrific pace, focussed on nothing but sating her hunger. It was an hour before we reached somewhere selling food and Laura did not turn her head once during that ride. I imagined having to stop for a flat tyre and looking up to see just a tiny dot on the horizon, wondering whether she would turn back when she realised I was gone or would press on for breakfast first. When we arrived at the cafe, we stared at the menu in a hunger-induced haze.

'What can I get y'all?'

'Grits,' Laura declared, zombie-like. 'We want grits.'

Grits are a Louisiana staple. They are made from corn and mushed up into a sort of paste. The result is like semolina, but they are typically served with a fried breakfast, as they were on that hungry morning in the cafe. Grits are a common breakfast constituent across the South, along with 'biscuits and gravy', which we happily embraced once we realised the dish involved neither biscuits nor gravy (it is more like savoury scones in sauce). Other foods we tried were more peculiar to Louisiana, like the thick, flavoursome 'gumbo' stew; Cajun 'boudin' sausages; the tasty 'po boy' baguettes (named after the sandwiches carried by striking workers in the 1920s: 'poor boys') and jambalaya. They were all fine fare for hungry cyclists.

Rejuvenated by grits and fried breakfast, we continued on our way. Unusually for the approach to a city, the traffic actually got quieter as we neared New Orleans. We wound our way through smaller side roads until we reached the mighty Mississippi river, which we crossed on a giant bridge, high above the city. Rolling through the suburbs, we pulled into a roadside fast food joint and picked up a large box of another local delicacy: Southern fried chicken.

We sat on the curb outside, basking in the sunshine and eating the greasy chicken with our hands. A homeless man sat next to us, doing the same. We introduced ourselves and told him it was our first time in New Orleans.

'New Orleans!?' he hooted in his best English accent. 'Ain't nobody here calls it *New Orleans,'* continued Bodie. 'It's *Nor*-lins, man. *Nor*-lins.'

Although not the capital, New Orleans – *Nor*-lins – is Louisiana's best known and biggest city. 'The Big Easy' is known for many things: its colonial history, French architecture and multicultural make-up; its laid back air and readiness to party; its Creole and Cajun cuisine; and its annual Mardi Gras festival, among other things. It is also known, however, for being utterly devastated by Hurricane Katrina.

This came up when our lunch mate, Bodie, asked about our route into the city. We described it, pausing occasionally to lick chicken fat from our fingers: over the big bridges, through the suburbs then along the road on which we were sitting. Bodie shook his head.

'You wouldn't have made it a mile up that road before Katrina. It was all projects.'

'Projects' are a bit like council estates in the UK, except with higher crime rates and worse reputations.

'You'd have been shot,' he added.

He was right. Well, I could not vouch for the claim that we would actually have taken a bullet had we tried to cycle along that particular stretch of road, but the area had certainly changed. Before the rains came, it was a rough neighbourhood. That area of New Orleans was full of projects and may not have been the safest place to hang around. In the aftermath of Katrina however, the whole place had been given a face-lift.

'It's all white folks and big houses now,' Bodie said as he polished off the last off his chicken.

Perversely, some saw the washing away of the projects and other homes of New Orleans's poorer residents as an opportunity. An area like that, so close to the elegant centre of one of America's most visited cities, was prime real estate. But it could never have been developed while there were lots of people living there. Katrina soon saw to that.

'We finally cleaned up public housing in New Orleans,' a local congressman declared in the wake of the hurricane. 'We couldn't do it ourselves, but God did.'

Katrina wiped the slate clean. Rather than rebuild social housing to which the previous tenants could return, developers moved in, replacing the old tower blocks with large, modern town houses that were nicer to look at. They were also far too expensive for the former residents. People and buildings alike were gentrified, and the poor were left with nowhere to live.

Some saw this as a direct assault on the poor: a deliberate strategy to rid the area of the poor and unsavoury, and replace them with the better behaved middle classes. This led to Bodie's theory: 'They broke them levees on purpose, man. They won't never admit it but they did.'

The city was supposed to have been protected by flood barriers: levees. We saw the new ones as we cycled through town. They were huge. But when Katrina struck, the levees failed and thousands of homes were ruined.

'The government blew those levees with fifty tonnes of dynamite. You could hear the explosions.'

The theory was that the government had deliberately burst the levees to save the wealthy white areas from flooding at the expense of poorer black areas. It might sound far-fetched but it would not actually have been unprecedented. The Louisiana government had indeed used dynamite in the past to do that very thing: to flood a poorer suburb to keep the centre of New Orleans dry. It later turned out to have been completely unnecessary as the floods never came, but they did not find that out until several thousand people had their houses washed away as part of government policy. The victims were given $20 in compensation – about $280 in today's money – which might have been enough to buy a front door but certainly not a house.

That all happened in 1927. That is almost eighty years before Katrina arrived and I like to think that the world has moved on since then. It is hard to imagine something like that happening in 21st century America and the consensus seems to be that, while the government did a poor job of helping, they did not blow anything up. As for the sounds of explosions that were widely reported, they have been attributed to the noise of the levees themselves cracking. But whether or not explosives were involved was probably not the first thing on the minds of those whose communities were flooded and houses demolished.

'Some folk got straight out of town when they heard it was coming,' Bodie continued. 'They did alright. Said it was like scout camp. Camaraderie and all that.'

He described friends who had evacuated as soon as they received the warnings. They left before the chaos hit and were able to escape easily. They went to friends and family out of town or just set up camp on high ground, away from the flood plains. It did not stop their homes getting flooded, but it made those first few days and weeks a lot easier. Everyone was working together and looking after each other, away from all the looting that later took place in the city centre.

Bodie paused for breath and pointed at our half-drunk bottle of Coke with raised eyebrows. Laura nodded and he helped himself.

'Some of us stayed behind though. Thought the government would look after us. Dumb,' he added with a grimace. 'Dumb, dumb, dumb.'

Bodie went to the Superdome, the city's main sports stadium. He was one of at least 15,000 people to do so. It was used as a refuge after the storm, as it had been following two previous hurricanes, but the stadium was not prepared for the volume of people or the duration of their stay. There was no power, no sanitation and no drinking water. Bodie and his townsfolk endured a week of hell. Inside, there were throngs of people sweating in the Louisiana heat, with the stench of faeces and a pervasive distrust as belongings were stolen and traded for cigarettes. Outside, even if you got over the fence and passed the armed National Guard, the flood waters were rising.

'We waited and waited for help. But it never came,' he said, shaking his head before adding: 'You done with that?'

He was pointing at our leftover chips. 'Sure, help yourself,' Laura replied.

'Thanks. I gotta shoot now. You folks have a nice day now,' he said, and walked off around the corner.

We wiped our hands clean on some serviettes and hopped back onto our bikes. We carried on cycling towards the centre of town, along the road that had been flooded nine years earlier. Along the road upon which we may or may not have been shot before it was re-developed. Along the road on which Bodie may or may not have lived on before the projects were demolished.

But despite all of the stories, it was still hard to imagine the destruction that had descended on the city just a few years earlier and it was all too easy to forget all about it. Shortly after we arrived in town, our friend Jon flew in to meet us. We had last seen him in Istanbul where he had also come out to visit us. During the day, we wandered around the historic French Quarter, admiring the architecture and sampling the local cuisine, which included attending an entire festival dedicated to 'po'boy' sandwiches. In the evenings, we watched jazz bands play in smoke-filled bars and drank more 'Hurricane' cocktails than was sensible. On our last night together, I left Jon and Laura outside a bar at 3am, still going strong and enjoying New Orleans' infamous party scene.

While cycling across Louisiana, we learned a lot about the havoc caused and the inequalities exposed by the hurricanes and floods that had hit New Orleans and the rest of the state. It was fascinating and depressing in equal measure, but these are not the principal memories and impressions that remain with me. Instead, I remember Louisiana for its tranquil Highway 82 and the houses rebuilt after Katrina: on stilts or in defiance; for the lady who flagged us down, invited us to her house, baked us a cake and sent us packing with bags full of food; and for the fact that New Orleans appeared to be carrying on as it always had done: in style.

Chapter 45

'I am thankful for Southern hospitality and the American (hard) shoulder. Both very welcome to the cyclist. Happy Thanksgiving y'all!' – Tim

'There are four main food groups in this part of the USA: carbohydrate, protein, fat and batter.' – Laura

Finding ourselves in darkened suburbs the night after leaving New Orleans, we turned down a side street in search of somewhere to put up a tent. We were still struggling to find anywhere suitable when we spotted someone having a barbecue in their back garden so we rang their door bell.

The man who opened the front door must have been six foot six, but he was quietly spoken and invited us straight in to join his barbecue. We wheeled our bikes around the back of his house and threw on some warm jackets to huddle around the barbecue while he flipped burgers.

Ryan was a Navy Seal, part of the American Navy's number one crack unit. Three years before we had arrived at Ryan's front door, a dozen of his colleagues had jumped out of a helicopter into a high-walled compound in northern Pakistan and, in a few swift minutes, ended the hunt for the world's most notorious terrorist.

Three weeks before we had arrived at Ryan's front door, one of those colleagues publicly claimed to have been the man who fired the fatal shot; the man who killed Osama Bin Laden. We mentioned the story to Ryan.

'We saw it on the news,' I said.

'Well, you've got to be careful which news channel you watch over here. There are a lot of biased, partisan channels that you just can't trust,' he replied. 'That's why I watch Fox News.'

Fox News is usually the butt of jokes about flagrant impartiality and low-brow reporting. In a cafe earlier that day, it was running a feature on the dangers of car travel, which was interspersed with adverts from airbag manufacturers. The channel epitomised everything that I thought news should not be, but here was a thoughtful, intelligent man who had considered his options and decided that it was the best.

'What did you think about that guy coming out and saying he was the one who shot Osama?' I asked, guessing that it might have been a controversial move.

'I do not advertise the nature of my work, nor seek recognition for my actions' he quoted, from the Navy Seal's rule book, with a grim look. 'It's a fraternity and he broke the code.'

Ryan seemed genuinely affronted by this breach of his team's ethos. He was not involved in Operation Neptune Spear – although he *would* say that – but it was clear that claiming credit for teamwork and seeking adulation were not, in his view, what the Seals were about.

'I'd like to see him dead,' he added. 'Anyway, where have you guys cycled from today?' he said, changing the subject.

'We came east out of New Orleans, through the ninth district and along Chef Mansour Highway,' I replied.

'You did what?' Ryan asked, looking us up and down as he did so, as if to check he had not missed something.

'We left our motel in the ninth district and followed Chef Mansour out of town,' I repeated.

'Chef Mansour Highway?' he shook his head as he spoke. 'I wouldn't drive through there no matter how many guns I had.'

Apparently, New Orleans had the fourth highest murder rate in the country, behind only New Jersey, where the Sopranos is set, and a couple of places in Michigan. That at least explained why our motel the previous night had an eight-foot chain link fence, razor wire and security intercom at the entrance. Our Navy Seal host said he would not go to the 9th District, no matter his arsenal, yet we had just cycled through it, oblivious to any danger. Was that luck on our part or unnecessary fear on his? We will never know. But I do know that Ryan made a good burger; he tried to give us two each but one was more than enough.

'You'll never leave a Southern home hungry,' he said. And he was right.

We crossed into Mississippi next, where we were invited into a family home for Thanksgiving. We put our tent up in their garden then joined four generations of family around the dinner table. The kids had some wonderfully unusual names, including Thumbelina, Jaybird and Stink.

Stomachs filled from another Southern home, we rolled out of Mississippi and into the tiny finger of Alabama that reaches down and touches the coast. After witnessing three car accidents on a single stretch of dual carriageway, we spent the morning riding on the pavement for safekeeping. Finding ourselves in a quiet village when night fell, we headed straight for the Baptist church. Religious buildings had served us well the world over and, in America, the Baptists in particular had been good to us. It was probably just due to their prevalence in the South, but as my parents are Baptists it felt like a happy coincidence.

The church was surrounded by the graves of soldiers from the American Civil War, one of which was draped with the Confederate flag. Originally used during the war as a symbol of the secessionist Confederacy, the Confederate flag's use in modern life is controversial. Some see it as a symbol of pride in Southern culture, or even just historic commemoration, but it is also used to show opposition to African American civil rights.

We were not sure what to make of seeing the flag on display but continued pushing our bikes towards the church nonetheless. As we did so, a large man carrying a rake approached us and introduced himself:

'Hi there. My name's Flash. How are y'all doing?' he asked, speaking exactly like Forrest Gump.

We gave him our usual spiel and his eyes widened. Having become so accustomed to the idea of 'cycling around the world', I had forgotten that some people were impressed by it.

'Wow! I guess you must have had one of those things,' he said, trying to remember the word.

'Things?' Laura asked.

'Yeah, them things. Those document things. From the government.' Laura and I exchanged a glance.

'Do you mean a passport?'

'That's it! A pass-port. Did you get one of them?'

'We certainly did,' Laura said. Flash had rarely travelled outside of Alabama and the idea of visiting another country was totally alien to him. We met several other Americans who had never been overseas and, having cycled across a tiny slither of the country, we were starting to understand why. The United States is such a vast country with the most varied landscapes that you could forgive its citizens for feeling like they had enough exploring to do in their own backyards. We showed him the various stamps we had collected in our passports, much to his delight.

'I don't suppose there's anywhere we could put a tent for the night?' Laura asked.

Flash said that we should sleep inside the church hall and led us over there. As we approached the front door, it opened and a stream of old women poured out.

'Well, hello now! You just missed our tea and cake evening. Lucky for you, there's plenty left!'

Lucky indeed. We ate heartily from the home-baked delights then spent the night on the wooden floor of the church hall.

We left Alabama after breakfasting in the church and were welcomed into Florida by sunshine. It was our last state and signalled that the end of our trip was near. We enjoyed a pleasantly warm few days riding through woodland, where we also enjoyed the cheery signage on the signs we passed, like: 'God comes without a manual... tech support on Sundays' and 'Find God here on Sunday mornings... also, find us on Facebook!' We even passed a drive-through church.

Before it got dark one evening, we stopped in a petrol station to ask about filling up our water bottles and the attendant directed us towards a drinks dispenser. We wanted water for cooking dinner that evening as well as for tea and breakfast in the morning, plus enough left over to fill our bike bottles for the following day's ride. As such, I spent several minutes filling our huge water bladder from the drinks machine.

'I don't suppose you'd mind us putting our tent up in the parking lot back there, would you?' I asked, carrying my giant water container back past the check-out. There was a big empty car park, hidden from the road by bushes, behind the petrol station.

We wheeled round onto the concrete, pitched our tent and got the stove going. However, when I went to fill a pan from our bladder, I discovered that I had not spent five minutes filling it with water but instead spent five minutes filling it with lemonade. Instead of availing myself of the shop's free tap water, I had disabused it of 10-litres of fizzy drink. There would be no pasta tonight, just cheese sandwiches and lemonade.

We went back into the shop the following morning to get some actual water and buy a few things that we did not need, out of guilt for stealing their drink.

'You guys survived the bears then?' the attendant asked.

'Bears?' Laura replied, looking outside. There was nothing but shops, houses and concrete. It hardly seemed like bear country.

'Oh yeah, we get them here all the time. They usually go for that dumpster,' he said, pointing out of the window to the exact spot where we had pitched our tent.

We spent the next few days riding with our eyes peeled for bears. At night, they were a scary concept, but during daylight hours on our bikes, they would have been the ultimate sighting.

As the sun fell ahead of our last night on the road, we attempted to put up our tent, but fittingly we were thwarted by hospitality and invited to sleep inside a church.

Chapter 46

'Alligators, snakes, bison and a baby snapping turtle. An excellent morning of Floridian wildlife. Eyes desperately peeled for bears.' – Tim

'Three miles from the Atlantic Ocean. So close now.' – Laura

We awoke with a sense of urgency. Today we would reach the east coast. There were several days before we actually needed to board our flight home, but the finish line was within reach and we wanted to cross it.

Although saddened by the idea of our trip coming to an end, I think we were also both ready for it. We had always known it would not last forever and it was some months ago that we booked our flights home and fixed the end date. As such, we had time to prepare ourselves and to begin mentally winding down. We had been liaising with family about plans for Christmas and Laura had already lined up job interviews for the New Year.

Knowing that the end was imminent, we started allowing ourselves to think about normal life, instead of this life of constant wandering. We talked about sleeping in the same bed every night instead of constantly waking somewhere different. We imagined having ready access to fresh fruit and vegetables, instead of being [...] to the biscuits and pasta we relied upon on the road. And we pictured a life in which we did not have to pack away all of our belongings every morning. We even dared to dream of not having to ride our bikes every single day of the week.

Going home also meant seeing all of the friends and family that we had left behind over a year ago. We had deliberately timed our return for the Christmas period, knowing that it would be the perfect time of year for catching up with people at the inevitable festive gatherings.

But for all of our talk about the excitement of coming home, we knew that it would not be long before we looked back on these days with longing. The time when our lives were simple and our needs basic. When every day brought a new adventure.

We were getting ahead of ourselves however, as the ride was not yet over. We still had to reach the coast. For the final time, we performed the familiar ritual of packing our sleeping bags, camping mats and stove into the same panniers we always packed them into; and cleaned our teeth together, as we always did, since Laura had carried both our toothbrushes since leaving home.

The day passed like any other. We rode our bikes in the Florida sunshine until we got hungry and stopped at a petrol station to refill our water bottles and eat whatever snacks were left in our panniers. Some drivers honked their horns at us, some waved and smiled. As we grew closer to the sea, the area became more built up, requiring regular stops to check the map. We were both itching to reach the ocean and found the interruptions for map reading a frustration. We followed long, straight two-lane roads through block after block of suburbs before stopping at a traffic light on red.

'There it is!' Laura shouted, and I buried the map back in my handlebar bag. The lights turned green and we pedalled towards the beach. Laura was in front so I could not see her face, but I have no doubt that she wore a grin as big as mine. We crossed the final road, hopped onto the pavement and rolled down a concrete ramp onto the sand. Without stopping, we dismounted and strode across the beach, wheeling our bikes through the sand. We whipped our shoes and socks off, threw them into a pile and continued into the ocean, one hand on our handlebars, the other raised in the air.

Chapter 47

'Made it across America with 13,044 miles on the clock. We are D.O.N.E.! See you all on Sunday.' – Tim

'Not checked the weather in London but I presume it's pretty much the same as it is here in Florida?' – Tim

Our journey around the world was far from being an unbroken, overland cycling route, but it somehow still seemed imperative that we arrived home on our bikes. To be picked up at the airport and arrive at a 'welcome home' party by car would have been a little unconvincing. It would be hard to claim you have cycled around the world when everyone has just seen you pull up in a Volvo.

Technically, it is not possible to leave Heathrow airport on a bicycle, because the exit tunnel is designated for vehicles only. However, we were not sure what else we were supposed to do so, once we had reassembled our bikes, we ignored the signs and rode through the tunnel. No one batted an eyelid.

Our route back to Hampton Court took us through Bushy Park and it felt odd to be cycling somewhere so familiar. In most respects, it was just another day of our trip: we rode the same bikes and we carried the same panniers. But at the same time, it was entirely different because we were doing those things somewhere that I knew. We were riding around the world but we were doing it through the town in which I had grown up. That meant that our holiday was coming to an end, our break from life was about to be interrupted by it.

Somewhere before Diana's fountain, we stopped to savour the moment and brace ourselves for the end. Ahead of us, by the Lion Gate at Hampton Court Palace, were the friends and family who had waved us off sixteen months and a thousand years earlier. I recalled the last time we had seen them all, outside those same gates: me clean shaven and both of us in new clothes and on shiny bicycles. Then I looked at the two people who had returned, long haired and scruffy, wild eyed and happy.

I remembered the double rainbow that had marked our departure and the campsite barbecue we shared with family and friends on our first night out. I pictured my grandpa waving us off from his wheelchair at the side of the road and treating us to dinner on his cruise ship. I imagined my parents, last seen in Dubai, and Laura's, last seen in San Francisco.

I also thought back to the state I had been in before we left home: scared to go outside, unable to exercise and constantly on the verge of tears. I remembered how close we had come to giving up on the idea when I could not bring myself to crawl out from behind my bed, let alone contemplate cycling around the world. That felt like a long time ago and I felt like a different person.

Above all, I thought of all the people we had met on our way around the world. The dozens of strangers who invited us into their homes; entertained and educated us; made us laugh and cry. A network of helping hands had shepherded us across the globe and we were grateful for every single one. Those acts of kindness had permanently changed the way I see the world. It would be impossible to see so much warmth and hospitality, and not conclude that people are fundamentally good.

There were only a few hundred yards left of our journey. Just a few moments' cycling before we passed through the gates and all of this came to an end.

Evidently, these were facts of which Laura was acutely aware. As I stood at the roadside contemplating the changes to our lives that lay ahead of us through those gates, she stood up on her pedals and charged into the distance shouting: 'I'm going to beat you!'

Epilogue

At the start of this book, I described the concern we had about whether we would be able to cycle across the Alps. That was a good metaphor for the journey as a whole: it was something that we worried about beforehand, but once we had started on our way, things turned out just fine. Having now done it, I can safely say that cycling around the world is not nearly as hard as we worried it might be.

As you may have gathered, when we left home we had not even worked out how to get to the south coast of England, let alone mapped out what roads we would take across Italy, Albania or Vietnam. Once we got going, we just looked at what country we were aiming for next and planned a few days ahead. Similarly, we did not arrange a single visa before leaving home. In fact, of the 26 countries we visited, only two required visas to be arranged in advance.

Part of this could be attributed to our laissez-faire approach to life, preferring to take things as they come rather than map them out in detail. But mostly it is a testament to the ease and simplicity of cycle touring. You carry everything you need to be self-sufficient so it does not really matter where you end up at the end of a day.

You could plot an entire route around the world on a GPS if you really wanted, but we just set off with enough maps to get us across Europe, and then picked up free ones from tourist information offices as we went. Everywhere has road signs and people can usually point you in the right direction if the worst comes to it. Besides, navigating is rarely as hard as it is in the UK, with its dense network of intertwining roads. In lots of countries, we would follow one road for several days without making a single turn. Whenever we struggled in big cities, we used Google Maps on our phones. Cycling around the world is not complicated.

As with the practical preparations for the trip, very little physical preparation was required. We didn't do any training. We cycled around London a lot, but never went out of our way to get fit for the trip; we just got fit as we went. There are those who set off around the world at record speeds, pushing their bodies as hard as they can, but it was not like that for us. Sometimes it was hard work, but we would often cruise all day and simply enjoy the scenery. Cycling around the world need not be a gruelling experience.

The trip did not cost a lot of money either. We were away for almost a year and a half, and during that time our total expenditure was £6,500 each. That is still a reasonable sum of money, but I know people who have spent more on a two week holiday. Averaged out, we each spent £406 a month, which is far less than the monthly rent we had been paying on our London flat. That amount includes all of the food we bought from supermarkets, cafes and restaurants. It includes every visa fee we paid, multiple repairs to our bikes, campsite fees, hotel bills, several international flights, a few bits of medical attention, travel insurance for America, replacement clothes, local SIM cards, cups of tea, cups of coffee, toothpaste, toothbrushes, soap and more. Every penny that left our bank accounts while we were away is included in that sum of £406 per month. It was the cheapest we have ever lived, and probably ever will. Cycling is cheap.

We were very lucky to be given some top quality touring bicycles for our trip by Ridgeback. Having previously only ridden bikes that were either second-hand or very cheap (or both), it was a real luxury to have good quality bikes that ran smoothly and reliably. However, a fancy bike is not a prerequisite for doing a big trip. All of my previous touring was done on a £180 bike from Decathlon, and hundreds of people have ridden across the globe on old mountain bikes. Others have used Brompton folding bikes, penny farthings and even unicycles. Ann Wilson, a friend who cycled around the world aged 59, only got as far as Bulgaria before her custom-built touring bike was stolen. Undeterred, she bought a cheap replacement from the local bike shop and carried on regardless. Another friend, Tom Allen, cycled from Lands End to John O'Groats using a bicycle he found at the local tip. You can cycle around the world without a fancy bike.

Although Laura and I had expedition and travel experience before we rode around the world, we had never undertaken an adventure on this scale before. We were reassured however, by knowing that experience is not a prerequisite for such a trip. Loads of people set off into the unknown on two wheels, without any cycling pedigree. Veteran adventurer Sarah Outen bumped into a guy in China who asked if he could come with her. He had never cycled beyond his hometown before, and did not own a bike, but he joined her anyway and cycled across China. The only experience Ann Wilson had when she decided to take early retirement and head east was riding her bike from Carlisle to Ipswich. There are even round-the-world cycling veterans who still do not know how to change a tyre. You do not need a lot of experience to cycle the world.

In short, our trip did not take much planning, require any training or cost a lot of money. It could have been done without a flash bike and it did not require any experience. Cycling around the world is not as hard as you think.

In fact, although our adventure was remarkable to us in so many wonderful ways, going on a big bike trip is not remarkable in itself. Anyone can do it and thousands have. Students fresh out of college have done it, as have those in their 50s, 60s and 70s. Men go on their own, as do women. Dervla Murphy cycled solo to India in the 1960s. Families do it too. Nancy Sathre-Vogel, for example, completed a 27,000 mile trip with her eight-year-old twins in tow. Even serious disabilities need not necessarily rule it out: Karen Darke crossed the mountains of Central Asia on a bike, and she is paralysed from the waist down; and, despite being legally blind, Christi Bruchok and Tauru Chaw pedalled from Alaska to Ushuaia.

Anyone can cycle around the world.

You can cycle around the world.

I did not know that when I set off, but I know it now. And, now that you have read this book, I hope you believe it too.

*****

Laura and Tim now live in hilly Yorkshire where they cycle to work every day. Laura is expecting her fourth bike any week now.

Acknowledgements

Hosts

My first and warmest thanks must go to all of the wonderful people that we met on our way around the world: the hundreds of strangers who gave us food and drink, and invited us into their homes at the drop of a hat.

In practical terms, you kept us warm, dry, well fed and headed in the right direction, but your hospitality was worth so much more than that. You made our trip infinitely more interesting and our lives are all the richer for it. It would be no exaggeration to say that you renewed our faith in humanity.

You also gave me a book's worth of tales and more. To those whose stories appear in the preceding chapters, I apologise for the inevitable liberties I have taken. To the many more whose stories are not covered, you have not been forgotten.

Sponsors

We paid for the trip ourselves, but received some generous equipment sponsors. We would like to thank the following companies for their support:

- Ridgeback – for our superb 'World Panorama' touring bikes. They are still going strong.
- Lyon Equipment – for the Ortlieb panniers, Tubus racks, Exped camping mats, Petzl head-torches and more.
- Berghaus – for our waterproofs and other clothing.
- Adventures Insurance – for our comprehensive travel insurance policy (which I'm glad we didn't have to use).

We would also like to thank Keen for the shoes; Brooks for the saddles; Buffalo for the jacket; Sealskinz for the gloves and socks;

Rab for the sleeping and bivvy bags; and Whitby & Co for the ultraviolet Steripen.

Editors

My editor-in-chief was Laura, who has spent more than a year turning my terrible drafts into the book that you have just read.

Thank you to all of those who gave me feedback on the final draft: Isla, Jo, Mum, Nancy, Sarah, and, in particular, Aubrey.

Thank you to all of my proof-readers: Alan, Alice, Anna, Annabelle, Dad, Dave P, Dave V, Karen, Jayne, Jon, Jon B, Jon M, Mum, Paul, Robin, Roland, Sam, Sharon and Suzanne.

Friends, family and followers

Thank you to everyone who followed our journey, sent us supportive messages, commented on our blog, replied to our Facebook posts and tweeted to us. Knowing that you were out there added an extra element to our trip and really helped us in the tough times.

Thank you to all of our friends and family who supported our decision to quit our perfectly good jobs to go and ride bikes instead. I think it all worked out OK in the end.

A particularly special thank you needs to go to Eddie Copeland. Every Sunday night for the last two years, Eddie rang me up to ask how many hours I had spent writing my book that week. It was that weekly call, more than anything else, which kept me focussed. Without your support, this book would never have been written. Thank you.

Finally, I would like to thank Laura. For all the hours you stayed up late, reading my sketchy drafts and dealing with my arsiness when you dared to suggest changes. For all of the bad moods over the last two years, when I have been stressed by my self-imposed targets.

And for helping write a book that is infinitely better than anything which I could have produced on my own.

Most importantly, thank you for looking after me during those dark, dark days when there was no light at the end of the tunnel. When I couldn't get on a train or walk round a supermarket without having a breakdown, it was you that got me through. Now look how far we have come!

And thank you for joining me on the adventure of a lifetime. I told you I was serious.

Trip statistics

- Duration: 483 days (1 year, 4 months)
- Countries visited: 26
- Continents visited: 4

- Total distance cycled: 13,023 miles (20,959km)
- Average daily distance: 29 miles (46km)
- Average daily distance (excluding rest days): 44 miles (71km)

- Fastest country: USA, 55 miles (88km) per day
- Furthest cycled in one country: 2,914 miles (4,690km), USA
- Longest day: 81 miles (130km), Malaysia

- Number of nights on which we were hosted: 224
- Number of nights on our own: 223
- Punctures: 17 (between the two of us)
- Crashes: 5 (of which Tim: 4, of which involving vehicles: 0)

- Best drivers: France
- Worst drivers: Switzerland and America
- Craziest roads: India
- Best cycle lanes: South Korea
- Cheapest countries: India, Vietnam and Cambodia
- Most expensive countries: Switzerland and Greece
- Hilliest country: Armenia
- Best food: Turkey, Iran, Japan and America

About the cyclists

Tim Moss

Tim spent five years working in the expedition industry, as a freelancer and for 'British Exploring', supporting expeditions on all seven continents. His own expeditions include scaling unclimbed mountains in Kyrgyzstan, Bolivia and Russia; travelling around the world using eighty different methods of transport; and setting the Guinness World Record for the longest distance cycled in a rickshaw (1,000 miles).

Tim now works as an accountant. In his spare time, he runs 'The Next Challenge' website, where he encourages others to undertake their own adventures, regardless of what time, money or expertise they have, and offers grants to help them do so.

His first book, 'How to Get to the North Pole and Other Iconic Adventures' was published in 2010.

www.thenextchallenge.org

Laura Moss

Laura is always on the look-out for a new bicycle, and she funds her habit by working as a solicitor for charities and social enterprises.

Her adventures include swimming across the Hellespont from Europe to Asia, walking across frozen Lake Baikal in Siberia, crossing the Wahiba Sands desert on foot and running the length of every London Underground Tube line.

Inspired by her experiences cycling around the world, she founded the 'Cycle Touring Festival', which takes place in Lancashire every May and is the UK's only event dedicated to bicycle touring.

Laura is also a director of 'The Adventure Syndicate', an organisation that encourages and enables women and girls to undertake adventures by bicycle, in order to challenge what they think they are capable of.

www.cycletouringfestival.co.uk
www.theadventuresyndicate.com

About the bikes

We rode Ridgeback 'World Panorama' bicycles on our trip. They are traditional, steel-framed touring bikes with drop handlebars, 700c wheels, rim brakes, 27 gears and three bottle cages.

We both opted for shorter handlebar stems, and Laura bought a gadget to raise hers by two inches, so that she had a more upright riding position.

We set off with the 32mm Continental Contact road tyres that came with the bikes then replaced them in Turkey with 35mm Schwalbe Extreme Marathon Plus tyres. They were still going strong when we finished our trip, 10,000 miles later. If I did another big tour, I would get wider tyres for comfort.

Before we went on the trip, we were advised to use 26-inch wheels because these would be easier to replace in remote areas than 700c versions. That may have been true 20 years ago but we never had a problem finding replacements. Even if we had, many bike shops will ship parts internationally these days.

Besides punctures, the only mechanical problems we experienced were cracked rear rims (mine in Turkey, Laura's in Vietnam). This was undoubtedly caused by our heavy loads and the poor road surfaces. Wider tyres may have helped with this. We replaced our chains twice and rear cassettes once.

Our Brooks B17 saddles were excellent. The only time we really got saddle sore was in the humidity of Southeast Asia, but I don't think any saddle could have avoided that.

We used Tubus racks to carry our Ortlieb and Brooks panniers, had Ortlieb handlebar bags and, in winter, strapped Ortlieb 'rack packs' to our rear racks. All of them performed really well.

About our kit

Clothing

We each took one set of clothes for cycling in and another set for the evenings. We cycled in zip-off trekking trousers and long sleeved cotton shirts. The outfits made for comfortable riding, gave us sun protection and, unlike tight-fitting sports gear, were modest enough for everywhere apart from Iran and did not smell as bad. Evening wear was a second pair of trekking trousers and a bamboo base-layer. We also carried a pair of shorts and a t-shirt to sleep in when we were guests, and to wear while washing our other clothes.

Laura took two bras and five sets of underwear, while I took two (I never wore underwear while cycling). We each took two pairs of socks, one thin and one thick. For cold or wet weather, we also each had a pair of Sealskinz socks.

We cycled in Keen SPD shoes through Europe and the United States; fleece-lined winter boots from Costco during the winter month; and Keen sandals the rest of the time.

We carried waterproof jackets, trousers, over-mitts and over-shoes.

We each had a fleece and an insulated 'Primaloft' jacket (a synthetic version of down) for warmth. In winter, we added bamboo/merino leggings, thick pile 'Buffalo' smocks and down jackets, as well as myriad hats and gloves.

Sleeping

We carried a two-person MSR 'Hubba Hubba HP' tent. It is free-standing, which means we could pitch it without pegs in car parks and garages. It could be pitched with just the inner tent during warm weather, or with just the outer tent, like a tarpaulin. It has two separate entrances with porches, which is an excellent feature for maintaining marital harmony. It also has a high ceiling, even at the ends, so you can comfortably sit up straight. In addition to that, we carried ultralight bivvy bags (Rab 'Survival Zone Lite', 200-grams) for the occasional night under the stars.

We slept on Exped 'SynMat UL Basic' inflatable camping mats. They were embarrassingly comfortable and very warm. I would pay extra for the non-basic version next time, as they delaminated twice during the trip (they were swiftly replaced by Exped at no cost). We also carried very thin foam camping mats (3mm), which gave us something robust to sit on outside and could be put beneath the fragile inflatable mats for protection.

We started off with down sleeping bags that were rated to -2°C (Rab 'Neutrino 300'). In winter, we added cheaper synthetic sleeping bags (Berghaus 'Flare 1100') over the top and were never cold. Despite being heavier and less warm, we kept hold of the synthetic bags when winter ended and sent the down bags home. We liked not having to worry about the precious down filling and being able to put them through a washing machine once in a while. We also used sleeping bag liners (silk for Laura, polycotton for me).

Cooking

We carried a Primus 'OmniLite Ti' multi-fuel stove that could operate on petrol as well as gas canisters. We never once needed to use petrol however, or any other liquid fuel, because we found gas canisters the world over. This was made easier by carrying special adaptors that allowed us to use the three main types of gas canister available (see my website for details).

We cooked on two Primus 'Eta' cooking pots, which have heat exchangers to make cooking quicker and more efficient (at the cost of being bigger and heavier). We carried a thin plastic chopping board, a small wooden spoon, an Opinel folding knife and a vegetable peeler, which we used to chop vegetables finely so they would cook quickly. Small plastic bottles were used to carry washing up liquid and oil. We ate with titanium sporks.

We carried two 10-litre Ortlieb water bladders, which we filled up before camping each night or before long dry stretches in Australia and Texas. We took a Katadyn water filter pump but never needed it so sent it home. The smaller, lighter ultraviolet 'Steripen' was used in India and on a handful of other occasions, but on the vast majority of occasions we simply used clean tap water.

Personal hygiene

We carried a large Ortlieb folding bowl, which was used for washing dishes, bikes and ourselves. A small flannel each was vital for strip washes when showers were not available (which was most of the time), along with travel towels that squashed down to fist-size.

We carried a small first aid kit, the usual personal toiletries and Laura carried a Mooncup.

Electronics

I made several references in the book to using our phones for navigation and Google Translate. We were actually using tablet computers (7-inch Google Nexus) but they are much the same as a smartphone. Our actual phone, for emergencies only, was a cheap, non-smart, quad-band Chinese import with dual SIM (one international, one local).

We read books on Amazon Kindles and carried tiny MP3 players. Laura took photos on a Canon digital SLR camera and Tim filmed on a GoPro Hero. We had two head-torches each, which doubled as bike lights when required.

All of our charging was done through plug sockets. We did not have, or need, dynamo hubs or solar panels.

Miscellaneous

Laura took her knitting and Tim carried a ukulele for much of the journey. A friend gave us a pack of cards before we left, which had photos of friends and family on. These were all great for communicating where there was a language barrier.

We carried basic bike repair equipment: puncture repair kit, spare tubes, bike pump, chain tool, spoke adjuster, spare spokes, various llen keys and a J.A. Stein mini cassette-removal tool.

r a full item-by-item list and reviews of much of the equipment, it: www.thenextchallenge.org/resources/kit

About our charity

ıring our ride, we were supporting the charity JDRF. JDRF funds arch to cure, treat and prevent type 1 diabetes. They are the rld's leading charitable funder of type 1 diabetes research.

You can find out more about JDRF, and make a donation, at: www.jdrf.org.uk

Resources

If you are interested in going on a bike trip, be that around-the-world or to the next town, below are some resources that might help.

The Cycle Touring Festival – www.cycletouringfestival.co.uk
Laura runs an annual event in Lancashire, England, with stories and practical sessions on all things cycle touring. It is the perfect place to come while planning a bike trip or after getting back from one.

The Next Challenge – www.thenextchallenge.org
I have spent ten years building a collection of expedition resources on my website, The Next Challenge. As well as practical advice and adventure stories, I also offer an annual expedition grant, funded by advertising on my website and donations from the public.

The Adventure Syndicate – www.theadventuresyndicate.com
A collective of female endurance athletes that aim to encourage and enable more women and girls to get into adventuring by bike.

Other websites
The Travelling Two have an impressive array of cycle tour resources at www.travellingtwo.com, as does Tom Allen www.tomsbiketrip.com.

Books
How to Cycle Around the World by Tim Moss
A very short e-book answering basic questions about long distance bike trips. Available from www.thenextchallenge.org.

Adventure Cycle Touring Handbook by Neil and Harriet Pike
The definitive guide for big bike trips, recently updated by our
friends, the 'Pikes on Bikes'.

*The TomsBikeTrip.com Guide to Adventure Cycle Touring by Tom
Allen*
An excellent e-book recently published by our friend Tom Allen.

Warm Showers – www.warmshowers.org
This fantastic network of cyclists gave us beds and hot meals right
the way around the world. Sign up to find hosts or to be one yourself.
The Couch Surfing website (www.couchsurfing.com) offers a similar
service but not exclusively for cyclists.

The Database of Long Distance Cycle Journeys –
www.longdistance.bike
While cycling around the world, Laura and I collected data from over
100 other long distance cyclists to create a huge database of cycling
statistics, including daily distances, monthly costs, routes and more.

hope that some of the above will be of use, but don't get too bogged
wn with all of the 'expert' advice. If you know how to ride a bike
n you already know enough to get started.
That said, if you still have any questions about cycle touring then
l me an email: tim@thenextchallenge.org. I would be delighted
ar from you.

The people we met while cycling the world

Index of photos:

1. The 'Road to Malta' cyclists going over the Alps.
2. The Croatian bar-owner and his twin brother.
3. Uncle Niko, who handed us fresh figs at the roadside.
4. My grandpa, John, and his partner, Pat, on the Saga Ruby.
5. Our Albanian family, who said yes when they meant no.
6. Father Paeseus, the Greek monk.
7. Panos, 'known throughout all of Greece for his hospitality'.
8. Hakan, the Istanbul protester who made a mean kebab.
9. Ali, the Turkish farmer.
10. Berna, Ali's neighbour, who made us breakfast.
11. The Georgian policeman and family (granny is out of shot)
12. The man on the left called me 'Infidel!' in Qom's shrine.
13. The Iranian brothers from Bostanabad.
14. The garage attendant from Natanz, Iran.
15. The Omani family that eventually saved me from hunger
16. Thieving monkeys in India.
17. Two of the men from the Indian village who took us in.
18. The family of our host in Seoul, South Korea.
19. The flower seller and his wife, near Fukuoka, Japan.
20. The English-teacher from Long Tho, Vietnam.
21. Rob, the Brit who loved his adopted country of Cambo(
22. The police who flagged us down in Thailand.
23. The Buddhist monk who gave us the temple wifi code.
24. The Malaysian border guard who tried to give *us* money.
25. The Malaysian bike-shop owner and conspiracy theorist.
26. Stink, whose family fed us on Thanksgiving.

27. Sheriff Johnny and Georgia.
28. Dwayne of Dwayne's Jerky.
29. Stacey and Jim (who didn't shoot us).
30. Juanita.